Edited by Warren Neidich

# The Psychopathologies of Cognitive Capitalism: Part Two

ESSAYS BY
INA BLOM
ARNE DE BOEVER
PASCAL GIELEN
SANFORD KWINTER
MAURIZIO LAZZARATO
KARL LYDÉN
YANN MOULIER BOUTANG
WARREN NEIDICH
MATTEO PASQUINELLI
ALEXEI PENZIN
PATRICIA REED
JOHN ROBERTS
LISS C. WERNER
CHARLES T. WOLFE

ARCHIVE BOOKS

This book collects together extended papers that were presented at *The Psychopathologies of Cognitive Capitalism: Part Two* at ICI Berlin in March 2013. This volume is the second in a series of book that aims attempts to broaden the definition of cognitive capitalism in terms of the scope of its material relations, especially as it relates to the conditions of mind and brain in our new world of advanced telecommunication, data mining and social relations. It is our hope to first improve awareness of its most repressive characteristics and secondly to produce an arsenal of discursive practices with which to combat it.

Edited by
Warren Neidich

Coordinating editor
Nicola Guy

Proofreading by
Theo Barry-Born

Designed by
Archive Appendix, Berlin

Printed by
Erredi, Genova

Published by
Archive Books
Dieffenbachstraße 31
10967 Berlin
www.archivebooks.org

ISBN 978-3-943620-16-0

# CONTENTS

# CONTENTS

SECTION 3

# The Cognitive Turn in Cognitive Capitalism

# Introduction:
# The Early and Late Stages
# of Cognitive Capitalism

*The Psychopathologies of Cognitive Capitalism* is an ongoing event structure composed of symposiums, workshops and publications initiated by Chiara Figone of Archive Books and myself through my art project the Office of Aesthetic Occupation. Our intention is to raise consciousness by disseminating information about cognitive capitalism in general and its associated discourses. This volume emanated from a conference held at the Institute of Contemporary Inquiry in Berlin in the spring of 2013. This was preceded by our initial event, co-sponsored with California Institute of the Arts and Art Center School of Design, in collaboration with my colleagues Arne De Boever and Jason Smith in the fall of 2012. *The Psychopathologies of Cognitive Capitalism: Part Two* is being launched, on the occasion of our third happening at Goldsmiths College, University of London in cooperation with Mark Fisher and the Department of Visual Cultures.

The idea of specifically focusing on the psychopathologies of cognitive capitalism was inspired by reading the books of a number of authors originally connected with Italian political movements such as Operaismo and Autonomism and included the writers Paolo Virno, Franco "Bifo" Berardi,

and Christian Marazzi, amongst others. I was especially
inspired by Bifo's *Soul at Work*, which I read sitting on my
porch in Venice, California, formally a quiet hippie haven
on the edge of Los Angeles, where incidentally Google has
moved its southern headquarters. (That emigration initiated
a mass migration of other high tech corporations producing
what is now known as Silicon Beach.) Of course earlier
readings of Deleuze and Guattari, especially the *Anti-Oedipus*
and *Chaosmosis*, provided the idea with extra layers of
complexity. I met Bifo when I attended one of his lectures
in Berlin and it was there I realized that many of my own
ideas registered with some of his core intuitions. Cognitive
capitalism, like other forms of capitalism that preceded it,
is a contingent formation that subsumes the social, political,
economic, psychological and technical relations in which
it operates. My interest in materialist ontologies as they
related to cultural plasticity and neural plasticity might
provide bridging concepts with which to frame anew his
Autonomist and Operaist arguments.

## What is Cognitive Capitalism and Three Disclaimers?

Cognitive capitalism heralds a mutation of post-Fordist
capitalist accumulation with its emphasis on flexploitation
of labor processes and flexible specialization, just-in-time
production and consumption, rapid acceleration in the
pace of product innovation, faster product turnover times,
computer and robotic interventions and an increase in the
complexity of supply chains.
Pascal Gielen in his essay included here entitled, "A Chronotopy of Post-Fordist Labor," adds two more conditions of
post-Fordism that are relevant in its transition to cognitive
capitalism. First what he refers to as de-verticalization.
In his model, space and time have lost their vertical dimension and are characterized by superficiality and horizontality resulting in hegemony of a global chronotopy.

This condition leads to specialized symptomologies manifesting themselves as lethargy, stress, depression, tunnel vision and burn out. The globally "organized free market economy" manifests itself "as instant bottomlessness or bottomless instantaneity." (p. 198)

John Roberts, in his essay "The Psychopathologies of the Bourgeoisie," focuses on the implications of the social and economic hegemony of neoliberalism from the angle of artistic production and distribution. After elucidating the conditions through which the left has maintained their grip on the discursive practices surrounding art theory, he explains how the 'nuts and bolts' operations by which art is produced and funded have been taken over by the right. Of the many results of this new condition, the entrepreneurialization of the cultural worker is the most invidious. (p. 60) But he also writes of the positive effect in which simultaneously a dispersionary force of cultural producers operate in defiance of the market. Together these two authors create the platform upon which to construct the next formation: that of cognitive capitalism itself.

Cognitive capitalism is defined by an early phase and a later phase, in which we are presently living. Three disclaimers need to be announced before moving on. Firstly, the actual date(s) of the transition are not clear although some have suggested, for example by Yann Moulier Boutang, that 1975 marked the first pure elaboration of its conditions (Boutang 2008, 9). (Note: Maurizio Lazzarato in his contribution assigns Enzo Rullani as the inventor of the term.) But can one really designate a moment for the emergence of the characteristics of cognitive capitalism with its emphasis on the predominance of knowledge as a commodity, the new nature of conflictual tendencies between capital and labor and the overriding technicity of new forms of computational machinery as it is insinuated directly into society and the workplace? (Vercellone 2007, 13-16)

Could not one instead argue that the so called machinic intelligence of the 19th century factory assembly line, in which the machine itself designates, organizes and informs the intelligence(s) needed to perform specific tasks and that the notion of abstract labor in its various forms of scarcity could be seen as the real roots of cognitive capitalism? Secondly, this designation does not claim that the conditions of the early phase, whenever and wherever they may be designated, have been subsumed by those of the later phase. In fact those contingencies of the initial phase still predominate much of the laboring landscape. Certainly this is true of the way that valorization creates artificial needs and desire leading to over-consumption and debt. What has been referred to as the asymmetry of debt and credit (Lazzarato 2011, 20). Thirdly, in opposition to those theorists whose use of the word cognitive is not meant to denote the brain but rather to refer to information and knowledge and who refuse any appeals to science as positivist I would embrace the position of Sylvère Lotringer who writes, "It would, by the way, be utopian to think one is able to situate oneself outside of these machines of meaning, these machines of science. [...] It all depends on what you want to do with them in a perverse way, catching them off guard, quickly snatching them up in order to plug them into something else, onto the *socius*, or the *cosmos*." (Lotringer 2005, 47) As such this project refuses to elevate cognitive neuroscience above cultural studies and the theory of cultural history in the production of the knowledge commons. Rather it understands that the two forms of knowledge creation can be co-determinant and coextensive as well as territorializing and deterritorializing. If we are to understand and deterritorialize the normalizing conditions of the cynical dispositions of cognitive capitalism as it is instituted through the networks of its own faith/truth structure, then we must understand the logics of its terms, mechanism and *dispositifs*.

Importantly, we must understand what challenges we face today so we can collectively cultivate and facilitate the proper response. For instance by using, producing and implementing a transverse armament of resistant social/cultural/political/psychological *dispositifs* to counter its overwhelming dispositions; especially when it is linked to the hypercomplex objects of neoliberalism for which it does its bidding. Hopefully this collection is a step in that direction.

Cultural plasticity is a term that denotes the degree to which any particular culture can adapt to objects, things and ideas erupting from outside the logics of its own historically developed institutional regimes and practices. As such its flexibility is tested when its, to use Quentin Meillassoux's words, extro-scientific potentialities are made explicit, or it utilizes strategies of post-aesthetic poetics as Peter Osborne has intuited or it redistributes sensibility in order to engage forms of materialism that modulate some of its effects. *Metanoia* as elaborated by Armen Avanessian and Anke Hennig and discussed in this volume by Patricia Reed is another example. (p. 84) One of the underlying themes of this collection is that these mutations of the cultural landscape, for instance built space, has ramifications for analogous and sometimes complimentary changes in the brain.

The development of new possibilities for the elaboration of autobiography which resulted from the invention of the Portapak video tape analogue recording system as developed in Ina Blom's essay "Video and Autobiography vs. the Autobiography of Video" is a case in point. She delineates how the changing conditions for the production of autobiographies of selfhood in the early stages of new media, for instance in the works of Joan Jonas and Keith Sonnier, simultaneously produced an analogous transformation of the autobiography of video. Her delineation of the autobiography of video and its complimentary effect on the process of subjectivization present a looking glass through which we might observe and understand the technologies of the late 20th century, such as the Internet, CAD software or After Affects, that have followed and have produced transformational effects on the laboring subject.

Karl Lydén delineates the heroic act of *parrhēsia* in which one speaks the truth freely even it might mean risking ones life as an antidote to the chatter of communicative capitalism and the overwhelming subsumption of image culture. In the transition between the semiotic turn of the late seventies and early eighties and its transition to communicative capitalism in the nineties and now to the cognitive turn in the early 21st century, knowledge, in its many forms, is the prime force for the processes of subjectivization. As such *parrhēsia* and truth as truth building for collective reinscription becomes a new form of therapy. Importantly for us here is "The care of the self as expressed in a set of truth acts, and even shaping of the formal conditions for such acts, has to transform into the collective shaping of a communist set of practices." (p. 129) In the last section of the book a number of authors will use theories of epigenesis, in which the brain's neuroplastic capacity is sculpted by culture, to understand the importance of such practices like *parrhēsia* as a therapeutic regimen for the psychopathologies of cognitive capitalism.

This book is divided into three parts; 1. Cognitive Capitalism – The Early Phase; 2. The Psychopathologies of Cognitive Capitalism and its Responses; 3. The Cognitive Turn.

# Section 1:
# Cognitive Capitalism – The Early Phase

The early phase of cognitive capitalism is delineated by the following traits. It is constituted by precarious labor in which part-time employment is performed in isolation. The precarious worker is a freelancer and always on call, anxiously awaiting their next assignment, working in multiple time zones simultaneously with clients sometimes halfway around the globe. This is related to its second characteristic that is what Jonathan Crary and others have called the "24/7 work-day," in which the formal subsumption has given way to real subsumption (Crary 2013, 33). Thirdly, value has been replaced by valorization in which the cost of a product to a consumer depends to a great extent upon the quality of its lived or imagined experience. Valorization is one of the strong links between cognitive capitalism and post-Fordism through its connection to attention which is captured by quick-changing styles and marketing. Behavioral economics and herd behavior join valorization as forces that effect investing practices and market "labile affect." Immaterial labor in the knowledge economies concerns a form of creativity and virtuosity. Poesis and Praxis become entangled as both do not leave a trace. Artistic labor becomes a key model for labor in general and in cognitive capitalism, which is also called creative capitalism. We will understand as this book unfolds that immaterial labor is not so immaterial as it plays an important role in reconstituting the memory circuits and attention networks of the material brain. Cognitive capitalism has redefined the definition of the consumer from someone who simply shops to someone who produces data as a result of unpaid labor. These activities of the shopper produce data profiles that are bought and sold by data barons. Data barons are the 21st century analogue of the Robber Barons of the industrial revolution.

Financialization of capital describes the process whereby worker compensation funds are invested in the market and hedge funds thus tying their future incomes to the success or failure of the companies they work for. This has repercussions on their ability to resist unfair labor practices as any demonstration created to put pressure on the company's profits may also affect their own profits.

Maurizio Lazzarato in his essay "Does Cognitive Capitalism Exist?" questions the very notion of the cognitive in cognitive capitalism because of its entangled relation to science and cognitivist paradigms. He argues against this approach because "A new subjectivity cannot come from a mere treatment of flows (linguistic, cognitive, economic, etc.), nor can any new knowledge or innovation." (p. 111) Accordingly cognitive explanations do not have the capacity to reach down to the substructures of inarticulate and undifferentiated understanding. As a result the concept of the cognitive threatens to shield off the possibility of change and rupture. The semiotic, cognitive and discursive systems form a system of extensive crystalized relations, modular systems are extensive while networked systems are intensive, and as such are linked in a chain of narrative linkages. As a remedy to this condition Lazzarato introduces an idea from Guattari called the existential function "which will function as the creative motor of enunciation and subjectivation while being perfectly *non-discursive*." (p. 97) He later links this existential function to the 'aesthetic paradigm' or the topical art of cartographies. Cartographies are like diagrams and as Gilles Deleuze states in Francis Bacon: The Logic of Sensation, "The diagram is indeed a chaos, a catastrophe but it is also a germ of order or rhythm" [...] "The diagram or abstract machine is the map of relations between forces, a map of destiny, or intensity, which proceeds by primary non-localizable relation and at every moment passes through every point, or rather in every relation from one point to another." (Deleuze et al. 2002, 102 and Deleuze et al. 1998, 36)

This art of cartographies has the potential to jumpstart the production of a new form of subjectivity in order to combat the stasis that has set in. For as we will argue shortly the productions of this aesthetic paradigm not only mutates the conditions of the sensible, changing it from an extensive to an intensive existential assemblage but its underbelly as well. As such aesthetics through reconfiguring surface representations affects the sub-structural and tectonic relations releasing new emergent patterns that redefine the explicit cultural landscape and subjectivity as well. This volume suggests that another component to conditions of evolving subjectivity needs to be considered. The evolving map of political-social-psychological-economic and spiritual relations produces a cultural landscape, for instance the designed urban space, that has implications for the brain as well and calls out through a process of interpellation the indeterminate and living variability of its neural plasticity sculpting it anew. (See discussion of Pasquinelli and Kwinter)

Patricia Reed in her contribution describes what Marx called "fictional capital" and realizes that it is imbedded in a network of other machinic fictive phylum that together create the hyperobjects of our virtual world which has implications for the image of thought that attempts to cognitively map it. Is Reed calling attention to a new form of alienation in which human beings are alienated from their own condition of alienation? That in this totally subsumed fictive condition a new form of sublime alienation arises. Alienation in the past was first the result of a fear of nature, which then mutated to a condition of alienation from the incomplete productions of ones own laboring in industrial capital which were abstract and incomplete. In cognitive capitalism what Reed is alluding to and what Arne De Boever later on will further unpack is an "extro- machinic intelligence" created outside humanities episteme.

Machinic intelligence today concerns creating laboring platforms for other machinic intelligences, like robots, rather then human beings and is formed by superordinate algorithms and super complex parametric equations. Machinic intelligence today and in the future, think here of ubiquitous computing, is precisely that, referring only to itself, no longer linked to human reason yet stimulating, probing, affecting various contingencies as a puppeteer would influence the actions of his or her puppet. Reed asks if poetics can 'deregulate' the conditions of this all-consuming fiction rendering its seamlessness inoperable to expose new surfaces and "uncalcify common sense."

# Section 2:
# The Psychopathologies of Cognitive Capitalism and its responses

Cognitive capitalism is also characterized by a number of distinct psychopathologies such as attention deficit disorder, panic attacks, depression and autism. The specificities of the psychopathologies of cognitive capitalism is a bridging concept between its early and late phases. First they are produced by living in the moment of cognitive capitalism; the anxieties and constant stress produced by the continual need to adapt to the accelerated pace of the new, its loneliness, its precarity and uncertainty, its linkage to surveillance and paranoia. On the other hand they are the product of neurobiological alienation in which the accelerated pace of cultural change, or cultural plasticity, outstrips the ability of the brains neural plasticity to adapt thus creating a lack of adequate perceptual and cognitive processing. In this form of what is called opaque alienation individuals experiences a real psychological syndrome with material sequelae registered as inconsistencies and aberrations in the neurobiological architecture of the brain, which create adaptation difficulties.

They are aware of the deficits and usually search out assistance. Full-blown attention deficit disorder and autism represent this opaque form of neurobiological alienation. I would like to suggest that, like sleep, transparent and opaque forms of neurobiological alienation especially the psychopathologies in their milder forms could be sites of creativity and experience beyond the reach of capitalist intervention. *That they are in fact the sites of a recurring freedom!* (Neidich 2014, forthcoming) The notion of an alternative way with which to regard the role of psychopathology reminds us of similar ideas of the famous Berlin Neurologists Kurt Goldstein's in which illness, as Matteo Pasquinelli reminds us, is a normative process that creates other possibilities for creativity and understanding, conditions that may have consequences for the image of thought. We will return to the implications of his work in the last section of this book.

The authors of this collection give new life to the concept of psychopathologies. This kind of freedom, erupting as it does from the bowels of power's grip, undermines it, tethers many of these essays together. For Yann Moulier Boutang a pattern emerges in history in which melancholia follows the defeat of the hope for radical transformation. He asks whether this sort of B-phase of depression follows the manic phase that greeted the information and computer age. This kind of regret and longing for modernism erupted from a realization that the utopian aspirations of a new connected world were now being supervised by a new form of beekeeper who was monitoring our moves and selling it to the highest bidder. But this is where Boutang's pessimism ends. Far from the ashes of a new world of technological promise a phoenix appeared. With it emerged a business model that required more freedoms and creative impulses to keep it going. Instead of melancholia one is faced with the burnout. Finally, "Primitive accumulation of cognitive capitalism however is a much more complicated task.

Subjection of the forces of invention needs to compete with an unavoidable condition; that of extracting value from the living. A much higher degree of liberty and socialization is required if you want to capture innovation and collective intelligence, which is by far the most valuable and hegemonic part of value today." (p. 157)

For Arne De Boever, psychopathologies—and specifically panic, an overlooked psychopathology of cognitive capitalism—needs an extro-scientific apparatus to create forms of therapeutic fiction to deal with the pseudo-surrealistic conditions of the new economy and the machinic algorithms that control it and that constitute (in De Boever's reading) a version of what Quentin Meillassoux calls the "great outdoors." What is criticized in De Boever's article is the ways in which human beings, born from inside an overwhelming nature, create a second nature as a form of protection from their fear of being overwhelmed. In this way, they at least still have linkages to nature through their self-actualization (which is, all the same, a kind of immunization against over-whelming nature). However, with the alienation of nature resulting from our present contemporary and algorithmic condition, a machinic intelligence develops outside what human beings can imagine with the common-sense tools they have at hand. This is the situation, delineated in De Boever's article through a reading of Robert Harris' novel *The Fear Index*, of the computer virus gone wild. Under this sublime condition, which in the 21st century has become the order of the day, fear is pointless; panic, and the corre-lationism it springs from, only adds oil to the fire. Could this hark back to what Ina Blom means when she states that "human seeming quasi-subjects taking on specifically human temporalities and forms of cognition also alert us to the tenuous nature of all such identifications"? What can be literature's role in this kind of situation, in particular in view of the criticism that all narrative is correlationist?

Two kinds of pathology are endemic, according to Pascal Gielen, of cognitive capitalism. First as we mentioned is this chronotopy of bottomless instantaneity. The distinction between past and future is consumed by a bottomless present. Trauma is no longer something that needs to be uncovered from the unconscious as it can be recovered from the endless streams of omniscient data. Every trauma is recorded and continually circulating in the endless nomadic dance that is the Internet. There are no any longer any defenses with which to hide the past: everyone is exposed 24/7. "Our digital lives are evolving as a public portfolio." (p. 199) We need what he calls a "techno-mental" ecology to deal with these new conditions. (p. 199) In this way he reconfirms Ina Blom's above statement about the repercussions of new media on the autobiographical self. Gielen's second psychopathology is related to a kind of hyper precariousness of exchangeability. Thus in a hyperconnected world in which one is always on call 24/7, a hyperconnected hysteria emerges. Hysteria in its 19th century guise was constituted through, according to the logics of psychoanalysis a relation between the contents of the symbolic unconscious and its outward manifestation as an improbable paralysis of a limb or blindness. In its 21st century form it is rather substituted for with a kind of hysterical fear of an impending precarious loss of ones connection to the web itself. The interior chambers of Charcot's Salpêtrière Hospital demonstration chamber has now gone global and with it the fear of not being on call, not being wanted by the collective, being totally disconnected.

In his essay "The Only Place to Hide? The Art and Politics of Sleep in Cognitive Capitalism" Alexei Penzin once more confirms what Jonathan Crary in his book *24/7* suggests that sleep is the only natural barrier to an insistent non-stop laboring. But for him the philosopher must be a night watchman guarding the contents of sleep. Importantly, what was a model of sleep disruption in post-Fordism, so called insomnia, is substituted for by the much more dangerous sleep apnea in which respiratory and cardiovascular disruptions can endanger life itself.

# Section 3:
# The Cognitive Turn in
# Cognitive Capitalism

The later phase of cognitive capitalism is delineated by its 'cognitive turn' in which labor itself is predominately mental in nature and is located in the 'factory of the brain.' In a world in which the predominate forms of labor are intellectual and service oriented, the machinery of the brain takes on added importance as a locus of capitalistic adventurism and speculation. As such various interdisciplinary approaches have been engaged to understand its logics.

Matteo Pasquinelli's essay, "The Power of Abstraction and Its Antagonism: On Some Problems Common to Contemporary Neuroscience and Theory of Cognitive Capitalism," brings forward many important issues that deal with what is meant by the cognitive turn. Like the basic conception of this book he traces the relation of the mind and body and world back to the German notion of the '*Lebensphilosophie*,' in which the living was rarely detached from the dimension of cognition or abstraction. Following the model of Kurt Goldstein it becomes his central condition for understanding both biopower and abstraction. "Going deeper in this genealogy, the *power of abstraction* will be disclosed at the original core that inspired the paradigm of biopower. It is not an exaggeration to affirm that neuroplasticity (as understood by Goldstein) was the original inspiration of the notion of biopower."

Crucial to our understanding of the relation between biopower and neuropower is presented in a quote by Elizabeth Grosz with which Pasquinelli begins his essay, "Life cleaves to matter, elaborating and contracting matter, bringing to life the virtualities within the material in unknown directions." (p. 275)

But as Catherine Malabou has noted plasticity's native land is the field of art. Plasticity characterizes the art of modeling and in the first instance, the art of sculpture. The plastic arts are those whose central aim is the articulation and development of forms; among these are counted architecture, drawing, and painting (Malabou 2005, 8). Key for us here are the notions of bringing to life the virtualities locked deep within the materiality in unknown directions and the idea of the plastic arts whose central aim is the articulation and development of forms. The plastic arts when they are delinked from commercial enterprise create a multiplicity of forms and variation. This variation is coupled to an inherent variation in the brain. As Olaf Sporns states, "The indeterminancy of the information content of world objects and events is matched by the structural variability of animal nervous systems, at many levels of organization." (Sporns 1994, 5)

This variation of the brain is also a key component for what the neuroscientist Gerald Edelman calls the primary repertoire. This primary repertoire is the brain one is born with at birth. It is the result of a contribution of each of the biological parent's genetic contribution to the child genetic make up and the events incurred upon the brain during pregnancy, such as, the effect of starvation, drug addiction, illness and the events of the birth event itself. As these events are particular to each individual each brain at birth is very different from each one another. Through its relational coupling, not correlation, with the unspecified world of objects its variability is sculpted by those consistent relations or features characteristic and essential for the animals survival. This is the key in which to understand Grosz last part of the statement, "Life emerges as a becoming thought or-as a consciousness, a becoming-brain." Importantly it is a political becoming. For this becoming is the site of modern day capitalisms interventionist tactics. For how that matter is sculpted details the ontogeny of the *neural zoe* as it becomes the *neural bios*.

Pasquinelli's understands that "abstraction is intended also as the power of differentiation with respect to neural matter, the power to produce further bifurcation of information and perception perceptual flows" is key to this ongoing ontogeny. (p. 277)

Sanford Kwinter elaborates upon this further as it relates to architecture in his text "Neuroecology: Notes Toward a Synthesis." Following the work of Bruce Wexler, incidentally a speaker from our first conference in Los Angeles, he reiterates the role of epigenesis in sculpting the brain in the infant and then proceeds to elaborate the second phase in the process occurring in the adult phase, "the focus shifts toward reversing the action of the sculptural knife, so that the shaping now of the external world becomes the main priority, in order to bring about, or simply extend, what I call the dynamic sympathetic mutuality with reality." (p. 328) In other words adults modify the world to coincide with the in relation to the new contingencies of their neurobiologically modeled self-image. Or do they? For importantly each successive generations neural architecture is sculpted anew. The inherent variability and difference that is the function of the brains' primary repertoire samples the pluripotential cultural plasticity according to different generational logics entangled and deranged as they are by the social, political, economic, psychic, and technological that delineate it. This leads Kwinter to make the concluding statement, "For every maturing organism notes, almost without delay, the unavoidable non-match between its internal (rearing) environment and the persistent elements of those of the previous (parental) generation's, and hence seek almost immediately to impose upon it images, shapes, relationships whose effects will better correspond to, and generate, the desired internal states that have become existentially necessary to their intuitions of freedom and well-being. This is a profoundly creative as well as destructive and aggressive act." (p. 329)

Liss C. Werner's text "Towards A*cognitive Architecture: A Cybernetic Note Beyond – or the Self-informing Machinery" takes this idea one step further and proposes what she refers to as a 'A*cognitivist architecture,' "Architecture in a cyber-biological framework embedding its construct within the mind/body phenomenon immanent in social environments." (p. 296) The world we live in is no longer defined by static Euclidean geometries and rather the result of multiplexed, distributed and form finding algorithms that have mutated the conditions of built space as a site defined by calculus. Think here of Otto Frei's German Pavillon, Montreal World's Fair, 1967. The crux of *A*cognitivist Architecture*, a product of digitisation and the Internet, lies in the intensity and amount of cognitive capital highly dependent upon it in perpetuating collective brainpower that is all but reduced to aesthetics only. It is about understanding the logic of becoming form, breeding forms, and understanding form as a result of communication processes and the ability to decode within a system, rather than form for forms sake. Cognition is extended: the world and the inhabiting organism constitute a single system. Their differences are fuzzy and nondescript. What this means for the brain is that in a world of non-linear, distributed intensive systems the brain is also a non-linear and distributed network system.

Charles T. Wolfe adds another dimension to this problem of how this environment might become interiorized as Lev Vygotsky states in his *Mind and Society*, "What takes place is what we have called internalization: the external sign that school children require has been transformed into a an internal sign ... produced by the adult as a means of remembering." (Vygotsky 1930) As Wolfe surmised this process is another key to unlock the mechanisms by which the environment can sculpt not only the individual but also the group. To do this he utilizes Balwinian Evolution or the Baldwin Effect.

Because of the importance of these claims in understanding the "cognitive turn" in cognitive capitalism I want to look at this idea more closely. As I show in my essay "Computational Architecture and the Statisticon" although neural plasticity is an important component of how culture might sculpt the brain it sometimes it is not enough. An interesting example is what is referred to as the "neuronal recycling hypothesis" (Dehaene 2004, 141-142). I explain this construct in detail in my own text so there is no reason to do so here except to say that reading popped into the cultural repertoire about 6000 years ago with the Sumerian Tablets and most evolutionary biologist believe that there has been too little time for genetic evolutionary factors to have played a role in the explanation of how we now have areas of the brain that light up during reading when we are being scanned in an MRI machine. (Dahaene 2004, 141-142.) Two complimentary theories could explain this. First is that this area called the Visual Word Form Area, located in the posterior brain, is the product of neuroplastic modulation from the pressures of the symbolic environment upon it as suggested by Terrence Deacon. In this case a given afferent message will cause long term stabilization of the neurophysiology of a given set of synapses that regulate each other forming a maximally intergrated and efficient network while others will regress." (Changeux et al. 1993, 376) A second explanation would be that certain predispositions predetermined in the anatomy of that area make it the likely place for reading to be processed as suggested by Stanislas Dehaene. He points out that there is an area in macaques called the Inferior Temporal Area that does very similar things. That it is related to the Visual Form Area and is most likely its analogue. That in fact over generations the Inferior Temporal Area evolved to become the Visual Word Form Area through a series of small steps in which the primary area sculpted reading in accordance with its proclivities so that it would fit its already elaborated neurobiological architecture. Over time language would adapt itself.

This is a parsimonious explanation Together they create the dance that is so much apart of this volume between genetic and epigenetic factors. But there is one more key to this and that is what Wolfe alerts us to. That is to say Baldwinian Evolution (Deacon 2003). As we saw previously the brains of humans are highly variable. First, during human development as a result of different genetic contributions from the mother and father but also because of events occurring during pregnancy and subsequently as a result of very different events occurring during their lives especially early on during what are referred to as critical periods. This variability gives certain members of a population different adaptive capacities for the wide variety of changes that they *might encounter* in the environment: reading in this case being one. Some members of the population could adapt better and take advantage of what reading provided in a broader cultural context. This is where reading comes in and Wolfe quotes Peter Godfrey-Smith. Importantly, "The population will then have the chance to reproduce mutations that cause organisms to exhibit the new optimal behavioral profile *without* the need for learning. Selection will favor these mutants, and in time the behaviors which once had to be learned will be innate." (p. 252) Could architecture and art provide the abstract contingencies? He then goes on to say, that is significant for us here that the Baldwin effect is very close, in fact, to the promise of the social brain, namely that "the human cerebral cortex [is] an organ of civilization in which are hidden boundless possibilities." (p. 252)

This volume embarks upon a journey that is now in its beginning stages. To confront a cynical materialism in which research on the complexities of the brain are being used by neoliberal and capitalism formations to produce a normalized citizen consumer. It is my hope that the knowledge developed in these various events will begin a search for new methods with which to confront this trend or at least to slow it down. We need to produce an emancipatory materialism in the world and in the brain too!

Changeux, J.P. and Dehaene, S., 1993. "Neuronal Models of Cognitive Function." in *Brain Development and Cognition: A Reader,* M.H. Johnson (ed.). Oxford: Blackwell, p. 376.

Crary, Jonathan, 2013. *24/7: Late Capitalism and the Ends of Sleep.* London: Verso, p. 33.

Deacon, Terrence, 2003. "Multilevel Selection and Language Evolution" in *Evolution and Learning, The Baldwin Effect Reconsidered*, B. Weber, D.J. Depew (eds.). Cambridge: MIT Press, p. 100.

Deheane, Stanislas, 2004. "Evolution of human cortical circuits for reading and arithmetic. The 'neuronal recycling hypothesis'" in S. Dehaene, J. R. Duhamel, M. Hauser & G. Rizzolatti (Eds.), *From monkey brain to human brain*. Cambridge: MIT Press.

Deleuze, Gilles, 2003. *Francis Bacon: The Logic of Sensation.* New York: Continuum.

Lazzarato, Maurizio, 2011. *The Making of the Indebted Man.* Los Angeles: Semiotext(e).

Malabou, Catherine, 2005. *The Future of Hegel: Plasticity, Temporality and Dialectic.* London and New York: Routledge, p. 8.

Moulier Boutang, Yann, 2011. *Cognitive Capitalism*. Malden: Polity Press, p. 9.

Neidich, Warren, 2014 (forthcoming). *Resistance is Fertile*. Berlin: Merve Verlag.

Sporns, Olaf and Tononi, Giulio, 1994. "Selectionism and Instructionist Ideas in Neuroscience." in *Selectionsism and the Brain*, Review of Neurobiology, Volume 37. San Diego: Academic Press, p. 5.

Vercellone, Carlo, 2007. "From Formal Subsumption to General Intellect: Elements for a Marxist Reading of the Thesis of Cognitive Capitalism." in *Historical Materialism,* 15, p. 13-16.

Vygotsky, L.S., 1978. *Mind and Society*. Cambridge: Harvard University Press, p. 33.

# Cognitive Capitalism
# The Early Phase

# Video and Autobiography vs. the Autobiography of Video. An Historical View of the Ambiguities of Self-monitoring Technologies

I

Video and autobiography. The coupling of the two terms seems self-evident, a cliché even. In an age of ubiquitous camera functions, video seems to present itself as an autobiographical medium par excellence, a technology at the service of subjects continuously tracking their existence on digital devices big and small, cheap and expensive, stationary and mobile. But the coupling in fact goes back to the early days of analog video. The 18 lb. Sony AV-3400 Porta Pak camera that came on the market in 1969 was also considered an intimate appendage to the human body—a harbinger of today's self-monitoring technologies. In distinction to the floor-bound cameras of official television, the Porta Pak was understood to be 'handheld,' like a pen, and like a pen made seemingly limitless tracings in real time. Not only did a 1969 tape reel allow an entire 30 minutes of continuous recording (as opposed to the 3 or 11 minute runs of Super 8 or 16mm film rolls), you could also connect the camera directly to a monitor, eschewing the temporal limitations of tape. From this moment onwards, video emerged as a signal-based corollary to the first person narratives of the modern novel—a literary form that not only veered towards the self-exposure of actual living persons, but that had its historical roots in the handwritten private letter.

For the crux of the epistolary genre was ultimately that of asserting the evolving existence of a writing subject, however banal. This subject was at once self-observed and presented for observation. Ray Johnson, an American artist best known for shaping his entire artistic activity as a postal network of private letter writers, was dead on target when—in a 1978 mimeographed document—he presented this network as "Ray Johnson's History of Video Art." (Blom, 2003, p.60) It was a joke, of course, but, on that offered a sudden flash of insight into actual connections. Analog video at the hands of private individuals was just the latest and most efficient technological framework for the production and exposition of the self-monitoring being, otherwise known as the modern subject. Clearly video was to become a key technology of the so-called culture of the self-alternatively defined as the open-ended production of subjectivity characteristic of cognitive capitalism and its real-time media environments.

To review the close association between video and autobiography is, inevitably, to revisit a key question in the debates on the recent transformations of capitalism: the relation between media technologies and processes of subjectivation. Real-time technologies are here seen as apparatuses that capture and exploit the forces of intellectual and spiritual labor. Since such technologies produce rather than represent time, they establish relations of proximity and collaboration with the production of time that takes place in the human brain and that is a key feature of mental operations. Hence, real-time technologies do not just control and augment the *consumption* of intellectual and aesthetic materials but, more importantly, access the creative processes of memory and self-relation that are an inevitable part of any affective and cognitive activity. It is in this precise sense that video technologies may be called the machineries of subjectivity-production (Lazzarato 2007, 93-122).

For an art historian interested in the introduction of real-time technologies in the sphere of art production, these perspectives are suggestive insofar as they also resonate in the discourses of early video art. More precisely, they resonate in the specific forms of social imagination that emerge in a practice in which the close interaction between human and technical forms of memory have been exposed and explored. Yet if early video art tended to produce a close association between video technology and the memory-genre named autobiography, this autobiographical tendency was at the same time marked by dilemmas and conflicts, bifurcations and divergences. And these divergences touch on the question of who or what actually count as memorizing agents in the theories of recent subjectivity-production: how they are to be defined, from what elements they are constituted and how they interact in the production of the social. Ultimately, this question concerns the very functioning of the social machines of post-industrial capital: it emerged as a critical site of investigation the moment video technologies were 'released' for use beyond the confines of state or corporate broadcasting.

The most readily evident feature of video in this context seems to be its intimate association with the very *question* of subjectivity. When it comes to video, technology tends to be more or less equated with subjectivity, to the extent that, conversely, subjectivity also emerges *as* a technical medium. There are obviously multiple dimensions to this mediatic-autobiographical conundrum, which spans from the formatting of identity in the name of control and domination to the exploration of subjectivation as open-ended 'dividuation'—processes that pass above or below the frameworks of individual identity. What marks this field of activity is, however, a tendency towards a naturalization of the human/machine link—to the extent that this link almost comes across *as* a distinct identity.

One symptom of such naturalization is a curious lack of interest in the video technologies themselves. In relation to the richness of human autobiography and subject-formation, video here often appears in a reductivist guise, i.e., as a limited set of standardized operations that seems to corroborate and support the dynamic flow of human life-time.

However, the same artistic context also opens toward a parallel form of autobiographical existence—a related, yet very different phenomenon. To study early video art is notably also to be confronted with a marked investment in the pluralization and individuation of the various affordances of real time technologies, to the extent that video *itself* may come to appear as an electronic subject exploring its own capacities for cognition and memory. Video, in other words, appears as an autobiographical agent. And with this point of view comes the realization that those capacities might not necessarily converge with human perception and memory. In the context of early video art, the widespread intuition that video may operate as a human-seeming quasi-subject, taking on specifically human temporalities and forms of cognition, *also* alerts us to the tenuous nature of all such identifications: Instances of apparent identity are often precisely those sites where all-important differences emerge. In early video art, such differences may involve competing takes on the place of technology in its relation to human subjects, attesting to competing social ontologies. Tracing the autobiography *of* video may therefore be a process in which the coupling between video *and* autobiography is at once asserted and opened up, its logic reconsidered, perhaps even reconstructed.

At stake here, obviously, is a politics of memory—a key feature in a form of media capitalism closely aligned with the modern effort to govern the very forces of life. Here 'life' is not just a question of the survival and reproduction of the population—it is more closely aligned with the definition of life as memory introduced by molecular biology, as the physical preservation of the past in the present. The life forces modulated by real-time technologies are then approached in terms a capacity for memory shared with all living entities, including a number of technical machineries (Lazzarato 2006, 183-4). Such a biopolitics of memory must necessarily affect the concept of social memory, which may now be explored in terms of the future-oriented concerns of living matter at the molecular and microtemporal level, rather than as a process of 'storage' of a collective past. Yet, in the disciplines of cultural history, the question of who or what are counted as the social agents of this volatile memory/life remains. This question opens up the new horizons of control, exploitation and regulation as well as the new margins of freedom.

The early association between autobiography and analog video appears as a site where this question is raised to a principle—explored, excavated, and turned into a crisis point. And this is no doubt due to the duplicitous effects of video's 'living' signal-based materiality. Such effects were perhaps more keenly felt in a pre-digital age where the material reality of the electronic substrate was closer to human media users, in the sense that the modulation of voltages were not supporting the abstractions of binary processing and today's plethora of user-friendly, blackboxed applications. Nam June Paik's (1963) manipulation of televisual scanning patterns made him intensely aware of the existence of flows of signals that he could (at this point) neither hold on to nor control. The dynamic feedback patterns that emerged in the interaction with such signal flows alerted him to powers of becoming that were on the one hand understood as entirely asubjective, part of the 'constantly changing nature' celebrated by John Cage, and on the other hand as instances of the new modes of human flexibility and self-extension that characterize a media age of instant information transfer, learning and networking (see Paik 1973).

The generative signal flow may have asserted the dynamic reflexivity of emergent life forms—a general autobiographical principle that has expanded to become the emblematic cultural form of today's information society. And yet, the work of Paik and a number of other early video experimenters show that the allocation of a self-memorizing agency within a general (and expanding) memory culture could in no way be taken for granted.

## II

If the coupling between video and autobiography comes across as one of several automatisms delivered by video, this is in no small part thanks to the critical literature on what is often referred to as the 'autobiographical impulse' in video art and related forms. The notion that there is some impulse at work here obviously indicates the presence of something automatic, not fully willed or consciously thought out. Interestingly enough, the authors for the most part takes this as their cue to remain strangely passive or uninterested when it comes to the question of the more specific features or functions of the technologies that would produce such an impulse. Video here is even at times unquestioningly paired with film, as if the assignment of autobiographical affordances to two technologies as different as film and video might not in fact complicate the concept of 'autobiography' as a modern media genre.

The reason for this technological disinterest may stem from the fact that focus here is invariably on the *subject* of autobiography—notably the human subject and the way in which its auto-representation through signaletic media seem to open for a destabilization of specific ideas about subjectivity and identity. The drama surrounding such questions of subjectivity all but cancels out more detailed perspectives on the material substratum of the autobiographical technologies. But, even more pertinently, it seems to be rooted in a mode of thinking in which the individual subject is *already* understood as a medium, with the result that the technical apparatuses at its disposal are easily conflated with this medium-subject.

From one perspective it could be seen as another story of technological servitude. Video, it appears, is fundamentally, ontologically, tied to the first person perspective of an individual subject at once reified and dynamized, asserted and displaced. (It is of some interest to note that the term *video*—the first person present tense conjugation of the Latin verb *videre*—literally means 'I see,' not 'you see' (*videt*) or 'we see' (*vidémus*)). To see the very open—in fact limitless—terms of this servitude it is enough to recall literary historian James Olney's brilliant exposition of the ontology of autobiography:

> I suggest that one could understand the life around which autobiography forms itself in a number of other ways beside the perfectly legitimate one of "individual history and narrative." We can understand it as the vital impulse—the impulse of life—that is transformed by being lived through the unique medium of the individual and the individual's special psychic configuration, we can understand it as consciousness pure and simple, consciousness referring to no objects outside itself, to no events and to no other lives, we can understand it as participation in an absolute existence far transcending the shifting, changing unrealities of mundane life, we can understand it as the moral tenor of the individual's being. Life in all these latter senses does not stretch back across time, but extends down to the roots of the individual being, it is atemporal, committed to a vertical thrust from consciousness down into the unconscious rather than to a horizontal thrust from the present into the past. (Olney 1980, 239)

It is worth noting that autobiography is here not tied to the
representation of history and the recording of the past. It is
simply a vital impulse that asserts itself through what Olney
calls the *medium* of the individual. It is a pure consciousness
and an existential force that finds in the individual its technology of inscription, self-relation or expression. Its atemporal
mode is that of the eternal present, the now-time of a constantly unfolding memory that instantiates itself in a living
organism in action. Olney's topic may have been literature
and more specifically the writings of Paul Valéry, but word
for word his analysis evokes the intuitions and terminologies
through which a real-time medium named Video emerged as
a cultural force to be reckoned with. Video *is* the medium
of the individual, seeing/being processed through the first
person present tense. In fact it is almost as if the medium
of the individual only reaches full cultural autonomy, a full
realization of its forces and potentials through *this* specific
technology. Paper and pen was fine, but only live signals
could imbue the still-shaky historical construction of the
individual subject with the indisputable presence, authority
and contingency of a distinct life force. As a medium, the
individual subject was quite simply in need of a bit of dis-
creet technological updating.

This conflation of video and autobiography in the name of
existential forces and real-time presence makes sense in
light of the fact that video autobiographies are, for the most
part, narratives of subjectivities at risk, on the margins, in
process or up for radical questioning. The general autobiographical emphasis on becoming subjectivity and the attendant
concepts of continuous modulation and flexibility are, in other
words, instantiated with respect to subjects that find themselves
in the position of being particularly exposed to problems of
adaptation or demands for self-transformation. Topics such
as AIDS, feminist politics, gender identity, race, migration
and youth inform almost every single one of these accounts.

Evidently, autobiographical video is not the form through which white adult masculine middle class heterosexual culture expresses itself. To the extent that this particular subject position was at once hegemonic, naturalized and normative, it seems to have had little need for the self-explorations of 'the subject in history' that Michael Renov, for one, sees as the key ambitions of autobiography in film video and film. Video autobiographies, in his view, pursue the 'documentary' impulse of Michel de Montaigne's essay format, in which a subject's 'gaze upon the world' is paired with a 'forceful reflex of self-interrogation' that displaces any stable boundaries between subject and object.

It is interesting to note, of course, that such reflexivity provides no shelter against the spectre of commoditized subjectivity or reified identity-positions that haunt this complex media landscape. This is in many ways the critical drama in relation to which autobiographical video is understood to be at once the symptom and the cure. Hence, as Roger Hallas informs us, confession is for instance not a critically valid option in autobiographical AIDS video. For confession simply plays into the hands of a media economy where first person accounts are already a key commodity, as well as an effect of a neoliberal tendency to privatize of the political. The self-memorizing of any AIDS patient is by necessity haunted by the ever-present reality of death, whose unrepresentable horror cannot be contained by the neatly formatted product known as the 'intimate disclosure.' However, creative use of the real-time immediacy of video—a technical corollary to consciousness itself—might provide a sense of the precariously live and present that underscores the reality of death precisely by *not* representing it (Hallas 2009).

In an analogous move, Julia Lesage asserts that since women's consciousness is *already* fragmented—an effect of women's social devaluation, labor in the domestic sphere and the ideological control of representations of gender and sex—its only adequate means of self-memorizing is the fragmentary, temporally flexible and non-representational visual/verbal realm of media production facilitated by video (Lesage 1999). Chris Straayer (1985) sees the distributed perception of video's camera/monitor set up as a discursive 'performance' of the subject, where the subject that says 'I' is brought out for inspection rather than concealed, as is typically the case in third person narratives. In his text on the autobiographical video art of Lynn Hershman, David James (1995) essentially sums up this tendency to search for points of *identification* between televisual technologies and appropriate modes of autobiography in the media age: 'Only in the multiple, dispersed yet interconnected practices that constitute television can be an adequately extensive, flexible, and nuanced metaphor for the self now be found,' he writes. Video autobiography may function as a technology-driven archaeology of the very question of the individual subject and its material production, but it is also, paradoxically, a technical corollary to the economic and political investment in individual subjectivity at its most 'flexible' and 'open.' The individualizing properties of this medium seems to resonate with more general attempts to move beyond purely formalist definitions of 'medium specificity'—most notably Stanley Cavell's description of the medium of the modern work of art as an automatism, a specific and 'individual' machinery generating its own specific instances. (Cavell 1979, 105-108)

The paradigmatic example for a number of critics is the early 1990s work of Sadie Benning—a precocious teenage artist who, armed with a Fisher Price PXL2000 PixlVision children's video camera, mixed bedroom confessions with a blend of audio-visual materials from the realms of television and pop music—much of it harking back to the mythical media age of the 60s and 70s. Here, it seems that the very simplicity of the toy camera—video reduced to a few rudimentary, handheld 'essentials'— provides a sort of technical validation of the precarious intimacy that is now seen as the hallmark of video autobiography.

Its lack of sophisticated production values and allegorizes the non-self-mastery of the autobiographer: Benning's radically anti-cinematic camera never seems to take in entire scenes, but slides impulsively between close-ups of body parts, notebook writings, TV images and various teenage room stuff, interspersed by voiced confessions. Here, the autobiographical subject comes forth as a fragmentary production that not only mediates the connection between an outer world and an inner self, but that from the outset eschews any attempts at 'imaging' the self as a consistent entity.

From this perspective it is interesting to note that the threat of reified or preformatted subjectivity presents itself with particular urgency the moment autobiographers start exploiting one of the camera functions that is specific to video and that film cannot simply replicate: specifically the act of turning the camera to yourself, while simultaneously following your own on-camera action on a monitor in real time. For some critics this particular strategy seems to evoke the psychological structure of narcissism. Performers resorting to this technical set-up are routinely accused of locking themselves up within a self-repeating matrix that excludes an evolving engagement with an outer world and its historical and material specificity. This type of analysis proceeds from the ambiguities of Marshall McLuhan's view of media technologies as prostheses. The 'prosthetic' metaphor not only indicates an augmentation of connectivity and a view of the human body as an infinite system of 'additions,' but also inevitably invites you to imagine an amputation of the human organs and their powers of sensual connection. Seeing the subject as a medium in this case indicates the possibility of being locked up in a feedback loop in which you will, ultimately, lose your ability to 'connect.' This is the ambivalent discursive terrain emerging out of the first attempts to associate human subjectivation with the specificity of video camera affordances.

The medium of the subject, on the one hand understood as a open-ended existential real-time force, is, on the other hand, haunted by a technophobia that seemingly cannot help situate the individual subject as an unalienable fact prior to its eventual (self)production. Symptomatically, self-monitoring video artists like Lynda Benglis and Joan Jonas are denounced by Micki McGee for having allowed themselves to be bracketed by the technology, turned in on themselves, trapped between themselves and the image of themselves like all narcissists. In contrast, Martha Rosler's use of the same camera technique in *Vital Statistics of a Citizen* is deemed acceptable, since what is brought forth in this work is not really an individual body or subject, but a sample from the realm of statistical anybodys—the ideal referent of standard sociology and hence a certified point of connection with the 'world out there.' (McGee 1981).

## III

When subjects are, in all seriousness, said to have been 'bracketed by technology,' it is actually technology itself that is bracketed, rendered ineffective and immaterial, pulled out of historical time and the contingencies of technical connectivity. But this seems to be the price for what is essentially, if ambivalently, a representational model of the relation between technology and subjectivity. Depending on how its specific temporalizing features are deployed, video is here basically understood as an instance that 'mimes' a more or less reified, more or less dynamic and more or less contingent version of the autobiographical human subject and the durations of existential time.

In view of this hypostatized version of the humanity of video (a form of reductionism that is also a key ideological figure of current politics…the individualizing machine as *me*, *my* body, *my* memory), it is worth recalling Dominique Janicaud's point that there is no such thing as 'time itself' that is subsequently captured and processed by technologies.

Time only comes to exist through the myriad of technical apparatuses and functions that generate its fundamental heterogeneity. This position resonates in the realm of digital technologies where we are constantly made aware of the importance of all the different microtemporalities, the processes and operations that have no correlate in human perception. But similar confrontations with microtemporalities took place in the encounter with video and television technologies as well: the merest attention to the realm of frequencies and wave phenomena (and all the technical syntheses that are based on the exploitation of these phenomena) exposed the limits of human perception. Bergson inadvertently gave a compelling example of this when he mentioned (in *Matter and Memory*) the 400 trillion vibrations per second that produces the colour red. This simple fact does not just give us an inkling of the mathematical basis of the frequency modulations underlying the constitution of any electronic image, but also their dependence on a realm of speeds alien to human perception and memory. Confrontations with the technical basis of video should then put us on the guard against too rapid identification between human autobiographical memory and video technology—at least to the extent that is is based on the idea of a similarity between Bergson's description of the 'pure duration' of consciousness and a general view of video's flexible processing of past materials within a real-time now rife with the virtualities of constant modulation. This is not because duration is at odds with measure and numerical abstraction. Janicaud is, if anything, critical of Bergson's opposition between measured time and pure duration, and one of the key points of his argument is that any 'sense' of duration or temporal qualification depends on *some* instance of rhythm, division or measure. The interesting thing is precisely the *differences* between the various measuring instances and the specific temporalities they produce.

To the extent that all forms of measure instantiate what Janicaud calls 'asubjective retention'—the minimal difference between a before and an after that is the general condition of all types of time production—we may rather choose to see the constant association between autobiography and video as a technical/political site exposing us to the complex and not-self-evident intersections of human and nonhuman forms of cognition.

This obviously does not mean that the much-discussed association between video time and Bergsonian duration supports the reified conceptions of individual memory and subjectivity that is symptomatic of today's media economy. Bergson's concept of duration is notably part of an ontology where memory is a general feature of matter itself, and where individual brains are just interfaces within the general flow of memory/matter. In Lazzarato's account, the production of video signals out of pure streams of light is simply seen as structurally similar to the brain's creation of signifying patterns out of the asignifying streams of stimulations or impressions. Yet in the context of an economy that capitalizes on the open-ended production of 'lifetime,' it is well worth emphasizing the extent to which video technologies are also *not* correlates of human forms of perception, memory and affect, and exhibit forms of cognition that do *not* support human forms of knowing and being. Various types of temporalizing operations performed by so-called memory technologies reveal different qualifications of the matter of memory and the forms of 'subjectivity' it produces, and these complicate our understanding of technical access to the ever more 'intimately' human. We cannot talk of a contemporary politics of memory without also considering the limits of such intimacy, represented by the manifold potentials and directionalities of the so-called apparatuses of capture.

From an art historical point of view, it is therefore interesting to observe that right alongside the prominent discourse of video as a medium of human autobiography, an alternative video-discourse emerged., one that we may perhaps call 'the autobiography of video.' Early video art, a privileged site of identification between human and technical "'subjects,' then also presents itself as the site of a marked des-identification or differentiation between human and technical forms of cognition. Autobiographical strategies—the reflexive tracing of memory operations—remained. But it is no longer certain whose autobiography it was. It might for instance seem as if the electronic subject, or subjects, named 'video' used the con-text of experimental art practices in order to appropriate this genre of human memory—to overtake it so as to open other avenues of thinking social memory. At the same time as the temporally oriented technicity of autobiography supported the production of human subjectivity, this same technicity seemed to generate questions regarding the various 'individualities' of time technologies themselves. If autobiographical investigations showed human subjectivity to be multiple, contingent, open and variable, video as a technological subject was no less so.

This is a mode of thinking that can be observed once you return to the technologically oriented sources of early video art—or, more precisely, to those sites where the range of technical features available under the term 'video' seem engaged in various forms exploration of their own memory capacities. Video technologies here present themselves as distinct forms of agency, with the powers to forge new alliances whose relations to existing social institutions (media, art practice, capital) remain an open question. (First encounters with such agency typically emerge in the artistic efforts to control or stabilize video images and in the quest for technologies that allow for more control but that in fact lead to new and unexpected inventions.)

On a technical level, the autobiography *of* video finds articulation through analog videotape works or closed-circuit camera and monitor set-ups that may or may not include frequency modulation by means of video synthesizers and other types of TV studio equipment. A key example is the early work of Keith Sonnier, where you come face to face with an inverted world in which attentive humans, ostensibly at the controls of the various televisual machineries, now emerge as the latter's accessories, parts of their working components. In these tapes, humans are sometimes heard but rarely seen. No longer faces or figures, they are essentially voices emerging from the depths of the studio situation, where they seem submerged in a sort of protracted operational dialogue with a number of technical personae—relays, wipes and switches, mat keys and machine clocks, 'Scanimate' and 'Kodalith' effects, to mention but a few. These are, for all intents and purposes, the real protagonists of these tapes. Presented as the key functions in the milieu of the television studio, they are also the operative forces of these technomorphic tapes. Only the most stubborn anthropocentrism would elevate the somewhat distant human presences in these works into sovereign or dynamic subjects, makers and users of technology. In fact, by accessing humans as voices rather than figures, video not only captures a particular mode of everyday intimacy and intensity in man-machine interactions that could not be further away from the awkward and alienated robot bodies that were (at the time) usually brought on to demonstrate such exchange. As voices, humans are here in fact defined *as* frequencies and in this sense quietly appropriated as parts of the electromagnetic spectrum that is video's particular sphere of operation. Video translates human action to signaletic phenomena and—even more pertinently—to the intensities of physical events whose temporalizing modes radically exceed the normal frameworks of human perception and memory.

What is taking place in these works is a technical recontextualization of human capacities that seem to open onto what might perhaps be called a videomatic inscription of social and political thought itself. Emerging here is a self-conscious collectivity moving to the beat of the experimental temporalities that result from the difficult encounter between temporal synchronization and heterogeneity. But videomatic thought may also be traced at the level of textual reflection—for instance where technical experts are compelled to think alongside the set of features that allow machines to respond to their environments within a time frame that is—in human terms—often perceived as 'immediate.' A key example is a 1968 text by the personnel researcher Hal Sackman of System Development Corporation of Santa Monica—a Rand Corporation spin-off that was charged with developing the systems software for the SAGE air defence project in the 1950s and early 60s. The text is entitled *A Public Philosophy for Real Time Information Systems* and reflects the macro concerns of an employee in a company said to have 'trained the (computer) industry,' i.e. a concern for the way in which interaction with real-time systems changes the object and impact of knowledge itself. In fact, the text establishes an ethical/political stance that depends precisely on a new form of *recognition* of technological agency. Sackman's intimate familiarity with the speed and immediacy of real-time technologies translates to worry about the lag between the speed of technical events and the much slower human cognition of change. But (in contrast to the more dystopic descriptions of thinkers like Paul Virilio) machinic speed is here at once the problem and the solution: the lag can be handled if human perception, memory and thinking is made to collaborate with real-time systems.

A real-time information system is here primarily defined as a set-up that allows you to *monitor* events in a specified environment with the intention of controlling the outcome of those events in a desired direction: it is at once an early-warning system and a system for corrective regulations.

The salient political/ethical point derives from the technical integration of knowledge and action. Older media technologies (books and films, traditional archives, and even new mass-distribution media like radio and, to some extent, television) are based on a model that separates storage and retrieval of knowledge from the passage into action. With real-time systems, the technical collection, organization and storage of information leads directly to action. Such systems are not just passive spectators of their own events but *active agents* that mould a partially plastic environment in accordance with a preconceived image. In other words, technology no longer figures as an instrument; for Sackman, it is explicitly presented as a form of agency. And it is only by properly acknowledging technological agency and its specific and autonomous forces that humans will remain political players in a world that is no longer their own. Politics is here defined in terms of a certain type of democratic *effectiveness*: notably the power for social change as self-change (as opposed to change imposed from without). Significantly, this videomatic inscription of political thought is retroactively identified with the one philosophical tradition that consistently links knowledge with action - the pragmatism of Charles Sanders Peirce, John Dewey and William James (Sackman 1968).

Recognizing the technological agency of real-time systems (as Sackman concludes) enables *social experimentation* on a scale not seen before and in 'a bewildering variety of forms.' Real time collection, reduction and analysis of social data introduce a new temporal dimension to social reflexivity, to the extent that it would seem as if social ontology had been reconfigured in terms of the duplicitous temporality of events. As it happens, video technologies enforced almost exactly the same type of inscription of social/political thought within the Raindance video collective (founded in 1969), an organization that saw itself as the radical or underground mirror of the Rand corporation, and their publication *Radical Software*.

In the multifarious writings of this collective and their many affiliates, generally seen as one of the theoretical and organizational cradles of video art, you see, over and over again, the forging of associations between technical time and social reflection. In a 1970 text by philosopher and family therapist Victor Gioscia, video is defined in terms of what Gioscia calls 'chronetics' and discussed from the perspective of A. N. Whitehead's critique of the fallacy of key memory-related concepts such as 'place' and 'location.' 'There is no universe anywhere, 'at' any instant, for there are no instants. '*There* isn't,' Gioscia asserts, before claiming that he wants to understand 'the chronetic laws of that accelerating process of which electronic software is the current mode.' The accelerating process referred to here is, again, the impact of time technologies on the notion of human centrality, since exposure to the pure temporalities that we call frequencies also alerts us to the fact that the human sense apparatus can only 'tune in' to an infinitely tiny spectre of universal frequencies. And once more, the emphasis on human limitation does not produce dystopic visions of loss, but alternative social ontologies—mainly through a critique of what Gioscia calls the sociology of expectation or prediction. The sociologist's desire to anticipate recurrence and periodicity so as to be able to generalize will have to be done away with if humans are going to politically mediate the event-like temporalities of frequencies that displace their self-proclaimed centrality in the social world. Hence, as Gioscia puts it, any software system that sets the outer limits of its responsibility as fostering the synchronicity of present human wavelengths could be guilty of a reactionary nostalgia (Gioscia 1970).

If video and real-time technologies are key machines in a form of capitalism that captures the creative forces of thinking and memory, the bifurcation of autobiographical modes of reflection in video art of the 1960s and 70s also demonstrates the way in which these technologies are implicated in the simultaneous development of *differing* conceptions of social memory.

Where video emerges as a technology representing human time and existence at its most dynamic and open-ended, it may support a questioning of the *construction and production* of subjectivity, but within a framework where the individual human subject is still *the* central figure, standing out against a background of technology, economics, politics and history. Where video technology becomes a cipher for modes of cognition and memory that may or may not correspond with those of the human sense apparatus, it is, in contrast, the very concept of a social/political *ground* that is opened up, dynamized and rethought in terms of the events of constant reflexive experimentation. It seems to me that this ontological 'conflict' within the autobiographical scenarios of early video art is indicative of some of the problems of political imagination that we are grappling with today (see Boutang 2011, 1-10). Once analyses move beyond a *generalized* focus on the virtual or event-oriented temporalities of these technologies, the default attentiveness to the existential and ethical-political conundrum of individual subjectivity is perhaps less easy to maintain. It is a truism that real-time technologies are regularities that support the emergence of new types of dispersed collectivities. However, our ability to think and act as if such collectives amount to more than simple interconnections of individuals will depend on our ability to appreciate the irregularities of such technologies, their constant invention and differentiation of temporal operations and modes of technical individuation.

As it happens, a more systematic unfolding of the non-formatted powers of video happened in the context of the nascent environmental politics of the 1960s and 70s—that is, in an atmosphere of risk, crisis, urgency and failure in which biological life itself could for the first time no longer just be taken for granted. Here, the biopolitical potentials of video actively reorient the televisual technologies of presence that have a special purchase on memory/life—primarily by producing new continuities between technical, biological and social forms of life.

In the environmentally oriented works of Frank Gillette and Paul Ryan, video instigated a form of surveillance of the natural world that might, on first impression, seem to illustrate Stanley Cavell's description of televisual perception: An anxious monitoring of a planet whose very survival seems to depend on our constant real-time attentiveness (Cavell 1986; see also Doane 1990). But here the familiar televisual reduction of the world to a precarious entity—the crisis version of McLuhan's global village—is counteracted by the contingencies of interaction between monitoring systems and 'living nature'[1]. The unfamiliar natural world, mediated through the various affordances of video technologies present a very different concept of life, as if engaging a set of uncategorizable forces that make us question normal gauges of mediation and measure: At exactly what distance will the objects of this world start to make sense to us? In what time frame? Related to which preconceived patterns, which memory systems? A biologist might have precise ideas about this and might choose a microscope or a satellite depending on the scientific argument at stake; if collaborating on a television nature documentary she would make sure the natural objects were clearly identified and inscribed in a coherent narrative. But a video surveillance system is not a biologist and may base its environmental engagement on technical properties that seem quite random compared with the established scientific, journalistic and artistic disciplines of nature representation.

---

[1] A key example here is Frank Gillette's six channel work *Symptomatic Syntax* (1981), in which a still camera surveys a biotope in a way that does not identify organisms and relationships and in which the technology itself comes across as a key component of the system under observation. A number of other works by Gillette revolved around similar issues concerning the complex interface between time technologies and biology.

What we encounter here is a natural world that is emphatically multifarious and expansive, even monstrous. To monitor such a world is to confront, head-on, the fact it is also invented by the specific velocities of video attentiveness. by microtemporalities and techniques of frequency modulation at odds with any human sense of time.

Such exercises gave a whole new twist to the idea environmental responsibility, creating a reflexive mode of involvement that was technical, material and pragmatic through and through. Paul Ryan used the term 'video perception' in order to underscore the intuition that whatever was produced by the video camera was not a representational image but a live memory of the world itself, shaped by the technical/perceptual apparatus—just as the human nervous system always already shapes the visions that seem to just 'hit' the eye (Lettvin et al. 1988). Nature was then neither an original 'condition' to which one should return, nor a separate entity whose need for protection could simply be proven with accurate scientific representation or by appeal to moral principles. According to video, both the imagination of crisis and the means to crisis management lay in constant perceptual and aesthetic involvement, a non-stop irritation or innervation of the senses that enforced, so to speak, a new type of feedback loop between the neuronal systems of protected, risk-averse, affluent, televisually connected humans and their larger technopolitical environment. The problem was how such innervations might be effectively shared—how, hopefully, thousands of individual nervous systems might be interlinked in such feedback loops. Where Gillette's monitoring of nature typically disclosed the perceptual production of new and disquieting biotopes, Ryan wanted something more systematic and also more distributed. The answer was the *Earthscore Notational System* (1971-) and its corollary, the *Ecochannel* design for a television project that would constantly broadcast nature from a number of locations.

Over time, this image stream would pick up behavioural patterns in the individual ecosystems, what biologist C. H. Waddington called *chreods* or 'necessary pathways.' Identifying such chreods might provide the basis for a notational system through which to interpret an emergent natural world. (Ryan 2001) *Earthscore* was then essentially a perceptual syntax: its whole point was to facilitate a veritable 'orchestration' of perceptions, so that a collective of TV-viewers would start to intuitively see and feel both regularities and critical changes in the environment. Knowledge about possibly damaging changes to the ecosystem would no longer be disembodied facts hurled at one by specialists and activists, but part of a shared sensorial apparatus.

The project was probably doomed to fail. Given the guerrilla habits of much of the 1970s counterculture—attacking institutions and corporations at the macro level, feeding off antagonisms—a form of activism built around the type of aesthetic attachment to the real-time apparatus that was also the driving force of capitalist media did not have much political leverage. Today, however, *Earthscore*'s mode of action and reflection (if not its technical solutions) may seem less quixotic. Today we know, for better and for worse, the technologies of tracking and coordinating the most microscopic sensibilities, and we are increasingly aware of how the technical agencies of specific programs and algorithms are key to the formation of differentiated collective forces. Under any circumstance, analog video produced intuitions about the political potential of attention to technical differentiation or individuation, in contrast to the analytic orthodoxies of technical/mediatic specificity. In the early 1970s, environmental monitoring emerged as one of video's key autobiographical modes: a mode of memory-action in which the technological capture of life forces also produced a rethinking of political dynamics from the ground up.

Blom, Ina, 2003. *The Name of the Game. Ray Johnson's Postal Performance*. Kassel: Stedelijk Museum Sittard.

Boutang, Yann Moulier, 2011. *Cognitive Capitalism*. Cambridge: Polity Press.

Cavell, Stanley, 1986. "The Fact of Television," in John G. Hanhardt (ed.) *Video Culture. A Critical Investigation*. New York: Visual Studies Workshop Press, pp. 192-218.

Doane, Mary Ann, 1990. "Information, Crisis, Catastrophe," in Patricia Mellencamp (ed.), *Logics of Television: Essays in Cultural Criticism*. Bloomington: Indiana University Press, pp. 222-239.

Gioscia, Victor (1970). "Frequency and Form," in *Radical Software* 1/2.

Hallas, Roger, 2009. "Related Bodies: Resisting Confession in Autobiographical AIDS Video," in *Reframing Bodies: AIDS, Bearing Witness, and the Queer Moving Image*. Durham: Duke University Press, pp. 113-149.

James, David E., 1995. "Lynn Hershman: The Subject of Autobiography," in Michael Renov and Erika Suderburg (eds.), *Resolutions: Contemporary Video Practices*. Minneapolis: The University of Minnesota Press, pp. 124-133.

Cavell, Stanley, 1979. *The World Viewed, Reflections on the Ontology of Film,* Cambridge: Harvard University Press.

Lazzarato, Maurizio, (2007). "Machines to Crystallize Time," in *Theory, Culture & Society* 24/6.

Lazzarato, Maurizio, 2006. "The Concepts of Life and Living in the Societies of Control," in Martin Fuglesang and Bent Meier Sørensen (eds.), *Deleuze and the Social*. Edinburgh: Edinburgh University Press, pp. 183-184.

Lesage, Julia, 1999. "Women's Fragmented Consciousness in Feminist Experimental Autobiographical Video," in Diane Waldman and Janet Walker (eds.), *Feminism and Documentary*. Minneapolis: The University of Minnesota Press, pp. 309-337.

McGee, Micki, 1981. "Narcissism, Feminism and Video Art: Some Solutions to a Problem in Representation," in *Heresies* 12, pp. 88-91.

Olney, James, 1980. "Some Version of Memory/Some Versions of Bios: The Ontology of Autobiography," in James Olney (ed.), *Autobiography. Essays Theoretical and Critical.* Princeton: Princeton University Press, pp. 236-267.

Paik, Nam June, 1963. *Exposition of Music – Electronic Television* (Printed invitation for exhibition, Galerie Parnass, Wuppertal, 1963).

Paik, Nam June, 1973. "Expanded Education for the Paper-Less Society" (grant report to Rockefeller Foundation in 1968), in Nam June Paik, *Videa 'n' Videology,* New York: Everson Museum of Art.

Sackman, Hal, 1968. "A Public Philosophy for Real Time Information Systems," in *Proceedings of the AFIPS 1968 Fall Joint Computer Conference* 33/II, pp. 1491-1498.

Straayer, Chris, 1985. "I Say I Am: Feminist Performance Video in the '70s," in *Afterimage 13/4*, pp. 8-12.

Lettvin, Jerome Y. et al., 1988. "What the Frog's Eye Tells the Frog's Brain," in Warren McCulloch (ed.), *Embodiments of Mind.* Cambridge: MIT Press, pp. 230-255.

Ryan, Paul, 2001. "The Earthscore Notation System for Orchestrating Perceptual Consensus about the Natural World." Available online: http://www.earthscore.org/themes.html [last accessed February 2014].

# The Psychopathologies
# of the Bourgeoisie

One thing that has irritated the conservative high bourgeoisie, despite the political defeat of the left and of Communism, is that *the left continues to dominate the debate in the arts and culture (in cinema, art, theatre and literature)*. And this has pretty much been the case since the 1930s and the rise of the Popular Front. This is why there are no influential right-wing cultural think-tanks devoted to ways and means of bringing to public prominence and approbation a reactionary aesthetic of hearth, home and nation. To do so would court ridicule, given modern culture's antipathy to patriarchal, nationalist and religious structures of observance over the last 100 years, and the broadly functionalist role liberalism plays in securing the 'creativity of the market'. Such conservatism would just not play in any practical sense. Moreover, it would take a strong and authoritarian state to implement this 'top down' view and as such would be utterly antipathetic to a free market ideology. Now, of course, the widespread acceptance of 'low culture' or religious conservatism on the right is admittedly something of a caricature; the modernist right's early influence on modernist culture (particularly literature) is extensive, and has contributed to the heteroticity of the novel form and poetry in the twentieth century (T.S. Eliot, Ezra Pound, Filippo Tommaso Marinetti, D. H. Lawrence, Wyndam Lewis, Ferdinand Celine, E. M. Cioran).

Divided between a largely anti-collectivist Nietzschean transgressivism and a high church respect for religious sublimity and pre-modern 'modernisms', this (heavily masculine) tradition has been particularly astute on the cultural costs of modernity, albeit within an utterly counter-revolutionary framework. Thus the trauma of modernity here may qualify the inter-war left's unexamined defence of industrial progress, but is invariably attached to a national-ist, racist and anti-semitic project. This is why conservative modernism appears particularly *retardataire* and exposed ideologically when posed against the post-colonial transcul-tural 'modernisms of resistance' in the second half of the twentieth century. Despite imperialism's draconian trading arrangements with the non-Western peripheries—preventing any realistic global and equitable process of moderniza-tion—globalization has produced an antipodal literary and film culture of immigrant and post-colonial narratives that has become a world historical cultural resource. Even if im-perial capital still holds most of the cards politically and cul-turally, this is a modernity of combined and uneven development in which centre and periphery are culturally in-terdependent. Thus conservatives now find it increasingly difficult to dismiss or denigrate this shift against the imag-ined 'quality' of the Western canon—even armed with a few of Harold Bloom's barbs.

Yet if religious conservatism and neoliberalism have withdrawn from direct confrontation with left-modernism and its post-colonial variants, the former are quite happy, of course, to fund social and economic think-tanks devoted to getting branches of the state to 'pay their way'. Thus neoliberal apparatchiks these days don't need to play the conservative culture war at all, when market cost accounting and the threat of the withdrawal of public funding can just as easily stop independent film, theatre, and post-conceptual art in its tracks, or block its cultural reception and influence.

Indeed, in those national cultures where neoliberalism is at its strongest, this is precisely what we have seen over the last 25 years. Rather than a rightist bourgeoisie confronting liberal and left modernism on the grounds of bad taste or misuse of public funds or loss of quality, it is now content to do its ideological work implicitly through the stringent effects of commercial accounting. This is the infamous 'privatization' of culture that has redrawn the boundaries of public funding and the horizons of a public radical culture since the early 1990s (Wu 2003). Three things have occurred as a consequence, in keeping with the monopolization tendencies of the stagnation or non-reproduction of post-1970s capitalism. Firstly, in the commercial sector—theatre, film and popular literature—thematic pre-formatting and the reworking of popular genres drive the need for immediate returns on financialization. For example, in London's West End, the majority of stage productions are now musicals (usually derived from familiar, popular cultural sources), producing a narrow 'bunching' of content, which of course, follows a similar and more successful model since the 1980s in Hollywood: the film franchise or extended sequelization. Indeed, stage shows are now commonly based on these franchises themselves. Financialization, then, is not so much geared to making quick and secure returns—backers have always wanted and expected this— but producing a flexible model that guarantees repeated returns *in the long run*. This is why 'pre-recognition' (ghost brands) is the great mantra of the neoliberalization of commercial theatre and commercial film. In turn, this has not only pushed out so-called serious bourgeois theatre from theatre's tenuous relationship to the public sphere, but also, the legacy of the avant-garde and its relationship to the idea of theatre space as 'political forum' and its possible interactive relationship to the other arts. The creation of a theatre of radical and partisan affects (Robert Wilson, Heiner Müller, Sarah Kane) and a theatre of discursivity and history (Tony Kushner), as moments in a wider engagement with the theatre's condition or telos, has been displaced from the main stage, to disappear or to return as a kind of 'whiny' little thing or niche interest from the margins. No neoliberal cultural representatives, of course, are saying in public that this theatre is unrewarding or pernicious, but the conditions of cultural production make it incredibly difficult to get a wider audience to open up *subjectively* to such works. And everything militates against this from within the capitalist sensorium. This has also had a huge knock-on effect on public arts funding. Again, 'neoliberal' accounting in the public funding of the arts rarely arrives with an explicit ideological and frontal attack on the leftist or radical influence on cultural debate. Rather, it lets fiscal probity (the shibboleth of 'value for money' in indebted times) and, in turn, the self-protectionist agendas of administrators, directors, curators and producers do this work for them. So, in this sense, the implementation of cuts tends to find the line of least resistance: 'in order to do our job under the given and restricted fiscal conditions we must find that which fits without constraint.' And finally, the third consequence is perhaps the most invidious, if the most naturalized, in the current period: the entrepreneurialization of the cultural producer.

The entrepreneuralization of the cultural producer, as a petty-bourgeois advocate of self-reliant and realist market values, brings cultural production into alignment with the 'indebted' logic of neoliberal ideology. As Maurizio Lazzarato (2012, 11) argues: 'The debt economy combines "work on the self" and labor, in its classical sense, such that "ethics" and economics function conjointly.' In turn, this reflects an 'asymmetry of forces, a power to prescribe and impose modes of future exploitation, domination and subjection' (Lazzarato 2012, 34-5). As a result, even in the post-conceptual radical sectors of the international artworld producers increasingly take account of how work will sit in relation to the demands of 'foot fall' and popular interaction.

But more significantly, art has also become a speculative field for art's post-conceptual transformation into abstract labor or waged-labor. With the unemployment or underemployment of artists in the light of the exponentially global increase in professional artists and occasional artists, and the increasing incorporation of artistic production into conceptual frameworks, neoliberalism is accustomizing the artist to working on 'social regeneration' and capital intensive projects in which artists' labor becomes a direct part of the accumulation process. In these terms, the artist-as-wage-laborer forfeits his or her (socialized) autonomy for a modicum of 'social engagement'. And this of course is deeply attractive to the artist under the prevailing precarious conditions of artistic production: he or she is guaranteed a living wage (for a short while) and is able to employ their skills in the creation of palpable use-values. However, if this provides a post-institutional solution of sorts to the deployment of unstable artistic skills, this move is nevertheless utterly assimilationist in its consequences, turning artists into conceptual/technical advisors or consultants and project employees within the cultural service industries. As such, neoliberalism increasingly lets the rationalization of accounting do its ideological work for it, turning everyone into market realists and service providers. Yet if this has produced a widespread centripetal pressure across practices and institutions to 'make things pay', it has also in the domain of art produced a countervailing centrifugal or dispersionary force, in which an increasing number of cultural producers, voluntarily or through sheer necessity, operate in defiance of the market and the socialized capital-intensive project. This is the rise of the second economy of art under neoliberalism, in which the expanded 'superfluous population' of artists, artist-activists, writer-artists, occasional artists and amateur artists have created a dissident or non-compliant realm of artistic production and exchange, invariably, but not always, attached to various political research projects (see Roberts 2011).

In many ways this excluded and underfunded domain has provided the social base for the socialized (participatory) anti-neoliberalism turn in art over the last fifteen years, and constitutes the unanticipated blowback to neoliberal entrepreneurial ideology. As a commercially un-assimiliable and un-exploitable mass of creativity under neoliberalism, these artists and producers represent the new forces of collectivity and post-professional productivity generated by the post-Fordist mode of network production (see Gielen 2009). In turn, this creates a pressure from below on the social division of labor and the wage form as artists, as the 'creative poor', engage in the production of non-market use-values that offer—despite the severe economic pressure on the artist to quit or fall in line with the market—other modes of working and being. The artworld is a highly ambivalent and contested domain, therefore. At its international high end, of mega-museums and auction houses, finance capital has never been stronger, in which the high bourgeoisie continues to give institutional support for, and gain huge financial returns from, blue chip investments. But culturally this is an increasingly dead-zone, given the increasing antagonism on the part of contemporary artists to producing for the market, opening up possible creative links between post-object and post-market artists, who show in museums and public art galleries, with the second economy. Indeed, this fraction of the high bourgeoisie is utterly disconnected from the production of contemporary practice, leading a ghost life as collectors of status modernist collectibles and contemporary flummery, and museum board members. Unlike the old liberal bourgeoisie, they have no productive role in the support of contemporary art, given that contemporary post-object and participatory practice provides no place for the collector and blocks off private patronage on strict political grounds. Even those collectors who know their way around digital culture—as network CEOs or managers of creative-industry start-ups—have little foothold in this new world of post-object production.

This tension between a 'collectors world'—linking overwhelmingly to the social rituals of finance capital—and un-mappable or un-biddable dispersed post-object and moving-image culture under neoliberalism is reflected in the ambivalent status of the biennale. On the one hand, the contemporary biennale is a familiarly prestigious realm of speculation in blue-chip dry goods and cultural state-building for national capitals, but it is also a forum for a vast array of second economy production, particularly digital video and digital film, that takes its critical point of departure from a renewed radical internationalism and global political contexts. The reasons for this are twofold. Firstly, the role of federal administrations or mayoralities allows biennales to become liberal forums for discussion and debate in recognition of the fact that the biennale has to be accountable to what artists of note are actually making and doing. This decision is, of course, tied to political majorities—and across national boundaries is subject to changing political realities and countervailing economic forces—but, nevertheless, biennales have been allowed to become 'clearing zones' that don't fall in line completely with the artistic dry goods market. Secondly, the distinctive way in which this constitutive openness of the biennale-form, in turn, is able to facilitate the low costs of art production itself, given the biennale-form's larger scale of operation. Overall, art institutions don't have to make the same draconian decisions about cost effectiveness as commercial cinema and theatre, and even literature, given, on the whole, the historically low level of capital costs for entry into artistic production and exhibition. Artists can produce and move their stuff about relatively cheaply, relative to film and theatre production (this is why artists have historically contributed to their own exploitation: work of quality can be produced, without support or patronage, out of the most restricted of circumstances).

Biennales in particular, therefore, (certainly an event like
Documenta in Kassel) can accommodate a huge amount
of low-cost, heterodox material that doesn't need careful
long-term financialization and management, as long as
the overall project or exhibition costs are met. This
lessens the pressure—certainly when biennales are committed in spirit to 'showing all of value'—to exclude or
censor on the grounds of political probity, or the commercial anxieties of sponsors. This is one of the reasons that
the international world of the biennale under neoliberalism has taken up the ideological slack in the culture. The
world of the biennale—and its links to various public galleries around the globe that see themselves as commis-
sioning 'research centres', rather than simply exhibition
spaces—has become one of the few large public arenas
still able to function as a space of open dialogue, in which
artists and intellectuals and the public can participate.
The rise of the philosopher-speaker and political activist
at such events since the 1990s is a case in point. Furthermore, this expanded cultural and intellectual space has
also colonized the realm of independent and radical film.

Over the last fifteen years we have been witness to an extraordinary incorporation of digital video and film production into the viewing circuits of the biennale and the public
gallery more generally, as independent and neo-avant-garde
film is increasingly excluded from cinemas and film festi-
vals, and sidelined into niche sites on the internet. Indeed,
this exclusion of the rich legacies of independent and avant-
garde film from public moving-image culture has been the
most corrupting of changes that have occurred since the
1990s. The neoliberal reification of the mass cultural image
in the new millennium as the site through which all value
must be measured—very different from the heteroclite
exchanges between popular culture and high culture in the
1980s—functions as a vast system of image 'enclosure',

in which the horizons of image production, drawn from an extraordinary narrow range of fantasy, entertainment and infotainment, are based on advertising, TV and popular film as interlocking 'content providers'. Finance capital is desperate to keep this loop in intact, in order to facilitate the smooth exchange of cultural commodities; there can be no content 'gaps' that might weaken the delivery of advertising to film, film to advertising, TV to advertising and film, and advertising and film to TV. In her book "The Wretched of the Screen" (2012), Hito Steyerl has talked strikingly about this neoliberal condition of the moving-image in terms of the rise of the excluded 'poor image'. This is a moving-image that in its non-compliant, heteroclite and ambivalent status is a hindrance and superfluous to these circuits of exchange, and thus finds itself pushed from out of public circuits of exchange into the 'boutique' consumption of the internet, where committed organizations and aficionados keep these independent traditions alive. But if the biennale has stepped in to relieve the downward pressure of these traditions—in particular documentary practice—and their exit onto the Internet, this new post-cinematic space of reception is confronted nevertheless by the centrifugal realities of the second economy. In a viewing situation such as the biennale where hundreds of films and videos are possibly shown, no one person is able to watch so much material and establish a critical overview. In this light, Steyerl talks sanguinely about the expanded conditions of reception in these art contexts as producing something akin to the 'collective spectator', and, as such, a possible source of liberation from criticism's reliance on the singular author and commentator. Yet, even if this is true, something significant is lost here that neoliberalism continues to benefit from politically: namely the loss of that space of cognitive mapping and critical legibility engendered by a stable and shared space of reception.

Now, neoliberalism has not in and of itself produced these conditions of compression, expulsion and monopolization in the production and reception of culture, as if these tendencies were not operative at some level in capitalism prior to the 1980s. In the early 1970s Alexander Kluge and Oskar Negt were offering a similar kind of (post-Adornian) cultural autopsy (Negt & Kluge 1993). This is why the attachment of the critique of neoliberalism to 'restorationist' capitalist logic is problematic, a position now increasingly favoured by those advocating a return to some new New Deal or socialized market capitalism, as if monopolization was an alien ideology imposed by neoliberalism on late capitalism. Monopolization is integral to the 'free market', as larger units of production swallow up smaller units, gravely weakening the 'free-market's' would-be dynamism. As Lenin was even saying in 1916, far from the rise of monopolization reflecting the power and productiveness of capitalism, it in fact represents its opposite: the long-term destruction of capitalism's own conditions of competitiveness (Lenin 1916). Yet, if neoliberalism has not itself created the new forms of monopolization, it has certainly accelerated them, inflating their pathological effects. This is why the psychopathologies of contemporary culture and the psychopathologies of the new bourgeoisie are indefatigably linked to a process of social and economic compression that derives its logic from the long-term realities of the capitalist system and not from the 'abnormal' particularities of neoliberalism itself. Thus the periodization of capitalism after the post-war boom, as a system that is in relative stagnation, is absolutely crucial in explaining the reality of these effects and the rise of neoliberal 'indebtedness' as a model of cultural and political accounting. As Robert Brenner has argued, along with many other 'stagnation' theorists in the new millennium: 'The long term weakening of capital accumulation and of aggregate demand has been rooted in a profound system-wide decline and failure to recover the rate of return of capital, resulting largely—through not only—from a persistent tendency to over-capacity, i.e. oversupply, in global manufacturing industries' (Brenner 2009, 2; see also Pröbsting 2008). In this respect capitalism is unable, as Brenner (2009, 3) puts it, to 'drive itself forward on its own steam.' The figures make startling reading (derived here from the 2006 "UN World Economic and Social Survey" and the 2007 "World Bank: Global Economic Prospect Report") and, therefore, are worth presenting in detail, in order to show how clear the arc of decline is since the early 1970s. Below, I list the figures for GDP growth, production growth rate (surplus value production), global savings and investment rates as a proportion of GDP, proportion of total investments in plant and machinery to GDP, net investment as a proportion of net domestic investment, net profit rates in the non-financial sector, wage share of GDP, and mortgage debt as a percentage of disposal income. These figures, in some instances, are admittedly only up to 2004 and 2007, but there is no indication, certainly since the crash of 2008, that the situation has changed, or looks likely to change, despite the opening up of new markets.

Since the 1960s there has been steady decline in per capita GDP growth (in the advanced economies from 3.5 in the late 1960s to 2.7 per cent in the 1970s, 2.0 per cent in the 1980s and 1.7 per cent in the 1990s; and in the developing economies from 3.7 in the late 1960s to 1.8 in the 1970s, followed by a slight rise to 2.0 in the 1980s and then back down to 1.7 in the 1990s). Global production growth rates were 3.0 per cent in 1980s, 2.4 per cent in the 1990s, and 1.4 per cent in the first half of the millennium (although the USA has been able to partially offset this decline). Global savings and investment rates as proportion of GDP during the period 1970-2004 are down from around 24 per cent of world gross product, to just over 21 per cent.

The proportion of total investments in plant and machinery to GDP is also down overall in the major industrial economies (in USA by under one per cent, in Japan by over 25 per cent, in the UK by around 15 per cent); the only countervailing tendencies to this drop in investment, as to be expected, are in China and India, the only major industrial countries to show an increase (around 60 per cent and 38 per cent respectively). Net investment as a proportion of net domestic investment is down between 1980-2006 in the advanced economies, from around 13 per cent to around 8 per cent, and net profit rates in the non-financial sector in the USA, Japan and Germany from 1948-2000 are dramatically down, around 30 per cent, around 40 per cent and over 60 per cent respectively. Wage share of GDP in the Eurozone has dropped (1991-2000) as an indication of the redistribution of wages to profits, from just under 62 per cent to just under 58 per cent, and in the USA from just under 64 per cent to 62 per cent. Mortgage debt as a percentage of disposal income has risen extensively across North America and the Eurozone (1992-2003)—around 36 per cent in the USA and an incredible 200 per cent in Spain.

These figures, then, are an extraordinary indictment of decline, pointing to how under neoliberalism capitalism has been unable to raise the standard of living for the mass of people, reducing the purchasing power of the working class, petty bourgeoisie and middle class alike. As even Larry Summers, former US Treasury Secretary and one of the architects of privatization in Russia, has admitted: 'for the first time since the Great Depression, focusing on redistribution makes more sense than focusing on growth' (quoted in Freeland 2012, xiii). These figures also explain why the system is driven to greater internationalization and global integration. The increased export of capital to the semi-colonies since the 1980s, for example, is the result of the declining rate of profit in home markets, as is the rise in financial speculation (between 1994 and 2000 speculative finance was responsible for three quarters of the entire increase in profits in the major industrial economies). Yet the bourgeoisie has been successful in raising the rate of exploitation despite the long-term decline of productive labor. Workers work longer for less, producing more. This suggests, therefore, something other than the threat of coercion is producing this new phase of labor-capital relations: there has been a massive material and ideological re-investment in the system (certainly for those who remain in work). This is partly as a result of the remaining social democratic illusions of the leadership of the left that continues to offer the hope of recovery—a capitalism shorn of its excesses, defended, in particular, by what remains of the Trade Union movement— but also the very real material entanglements of workers in the logic of indebtedness itself as a consequence of the long term fall in the rate of profit. Personal indebtedness admittedly is very uneven across classes and national boundaries, yet its global impact as a technique of governance and self-governance has been successful in shifting political perspectives and possibilities for action. This seems a sharper way of addressing the (conflicted) process of re-investment, than assuming that with the shift to new forms of affective and cognitive labor workers are more willing, as Franco Berardi (2007, 79) claims, to prolong the working day.

Stagnation and decline, then, do not presuppose collapse, or even ideological disinvestment (quite yet). Capitalism remains remarkably ideologically resilient precisely because of its continuing ability to link personal creativity to the overcoming of crisis. Because capitalism is a system that is materially and logically driven by its own crises, it is constantly able to link the possibility of recovery to a potent petty-bourgeois and individualist 'creative' overcoming of the present (so indebtedness is internalized as something to 'face down').

The left, in comparison, is yet to find a comparable set of subjective (collective) conditions that might contest the very meaning of crisis itself and its 'resolution'. For to do so, in any realistic fashion, it would be compelled to talk of the overcoming of crisis *beyond capital,* and this of course it is presently ill equipped and unprepared to do. Thus we have a peculiar aporia: reformism is dead, but it continues to have this attenuated afterlife as the imaginary reverser of decline. But the recessions are getting more frequent and deeper, transforming the very meaning and possibility of this creative overcoming of the system's recurring crises. In other words, the repeated creative overcoming of recession is not the harbinger of expansion, but the expression of a fundamental slow down. This is because the successive downturns since the 1970s have not been able to destroy enough capital value to revitalize the system overall; only a fundamental shake-up, as in the early 1930s, or a world war—which underwrote the post-war boom—is capable of achieving this. But the social costs of such a shake-up would be too great, and the possible radicalization of the working class too extensive, as in the 1930s. Policy makers and planners, therefore, have pursued fiscal and monetary policies that have avoided a full-scale destruction of capital value, which they know they may not be able to control politically. This is why downturns after the 1970s have not been as severe as the Great Depression, but also why the system is unable to re-expand (see Kliman 2012). In the major recession of the early 1980s, for example, the destruction of capital was only a fraction of what it was in the 1930s. Thus the bourgeoisie is always balancing the costs of capital expansion against the destruction of the social and metabolic conditions of reproduction that will enable such expansion.

Perhaps a more appropriate description of the current situation, then, would be 'rolling non-reproduction', rather than, expressly, stagnation. The former implies less a halting slow-down than a situation of narrowing options, within an attenuated process of continuation. It also recognizes how capitalist governance is producing a chronic loss of affect, even belief, in the efficacy of the system as whole, even amongst its staunch political advocates. This is reflected in the changing social role of the bourgeoisie under the logic of financialization and democracy-through-indebtedness (or austerity politics). The historical role of the bourgeoisie as a mediator between the cruel but necessary realities of capitalism and the consoling verities of humanism is discernibly weaker than it has ever been. There is little enthusiasm on the part of the high bourgeoisie to produce a 'universalizing' bourgeois discourse of progress and material well-being that captures the future collectively, for workers and the bourgeoisie itself. This is due to a crucial shift politically within the bourgeoisie under the new pressures of indebtedness and decline, to a primary commitment to state-as-capital, away from a tradition of 'political liberalization'. That is to say, the bourgeoisie's major concern under neoliberalism has not been the 'market' and its freedoms, so to speak, in opposition to the state, but on the contrary, securing the state for the market; markets free of state support can be exposed to all kind of vagaries and instabilities, markets operating under the protection of a strong state can flourish. This is why the attacks on civil liberties, the draconian anti-union legislation in the USA, Southern Asia and the Eurozone, and the increased global state surveillance, all point to a bourgeoisie increasingly preoccupied with the creation of a maximum state for capital-accumulation (particular in the imperialist zones), and a minimal social state for workers and everyone else. This shift though is easily misunderstood, as if the new bourgeoisie (CEOs, bankers, senior administrators, hedge fund managers, etc) were somehow betraying a long-standing liberal bourgeois project. The bourgeoisie today, certainly does not speak with the same degree of confidence as its forebears about fashioning a political programme that would incorporate the interests of the popular classes as part of a national consensual order.

But this is not a betrayal of any 'bourgeois liberal project' as such, as if the bourgeoisie today has abdicated its social responsibilities. On the contrary, there has never been a 'bourgeois liberal' project; bourgeois universalism and freedom was always constructed in the 'name' of the bourgeoisie from pressure below (or from within counter-factions within the bourgeoisie itself), and continues to shift its character. The bourgeois revolutions, therefore, were not classical liberal programmes in any strict sense. Indeed, all evidence points in the opposite direction. The bourgeoisie's commitment to political 'universalization' was always subject ultimately to the exclusion of the popular classes from the political process. What universalization largely meant, rather, was the inclusion of those elements of the ruling class into the political process that had previously been excluded, and not the inclusion and mobilization of the popular will (Chibber 2013, 75). All the subsequent democratic gains of the working class (from universal education, enfranchisement, trade unions) have been won from the bourgeoisie after lengthy struggle.

Today, however, faced with little pressure from below there is finally no *restraint* on the part of the bourgeoisie to express or defend its fictive 'universalizing' liberal role at all. Under the logic of indebtedness 'universalization' becomes the express credo of economic liberalization itself, in which personal freedom is identifiable with entrepreneurial self-valorization above all else—hence the widespread deference on the part of the new bourgeoisie to a post-class, 'human-capital' 'solution' to the labor-capital relation promulgated by the representatives of finance capital *and* productive capital. Everyone has the right to develop their own labor power as a source of creativity and well-being, *pace* Richard Florida's (2002) 'creatives' or Reid Hoffman's (2012) effervescent entrepreneurs.

One of the outcomes of this is that the traditional bourgeoisie's residual humanism is rarely brought to bear as a moral compass against the depredations of this ideology, and when it does appear it is invariably inconsequential against the demands of fiscal probity. This is clear from the weakened presence of the bourgeoisie in the public domain and public service, as it shifts its focus whole-scale into global charity work, or into what remains of high-cultural leverage in the art-world and classical music world. There is a kind of shiver of revulsion at participating in what remains (of their destruction) of the classical bourgeois sphere, for it means touching the edges of a world of collective provision that resists the language of accountability. In other words, what was once the industrial bourgeoisie's touchstone, humanism as a flag of convenience for 'shared values', produces a form of cognitive dissonance that sits at odds with the 'creative violence' of capital now. For in the dominant language of finance capital, the injuries and risks of capital are part of the constant flow and energy of the capitalist system that brooks no opposition. Thus no cultural institution, no set of practices and forms, are immune from the 'efficiency', 'creativity' and 'productivity' of the market. And this produces its own particular forms of psychopathology—virulent forms of disavowal, aphasia, victimization and persecution mania—that are very different in affect and aspect from the psychopathologies of Berardi's 'cognitive worker', with his or her extensive range of 'communicational disorders.' This is a world of 'rolling non-reproduction' in which the rich don't want to be described as rich—because this is just too divisive!—and who, in turn, believe that, 'what is happening at the top [isn't] class war it's arithmetic' (Freeland 2012, xiii).

Berardi, Franco "Bifo", 2007. *The Soul at Work: From Alienation to Autonomy*, Preface by Jason Smith, trans. Francesca Cadel and Giuseppina Mecchia, Los Angeles: Semiotext(e).

Brenner, Robert, 2009. "What is Good For Goldman Sachs is Good for America: The Origins of the Current Crisis," Prologue to the Spanish translation of Brenner's *Economics of Global Turbulence* (first published in a Special Issue of the *New Left Review* No. 229, May-June, 1998), Madrid: Akal.

Chibber, Vivek, 2013. *Postcolonial Theory and the Specter of Capital*, London and New York: Verso.

Florida, Richard, 2002. *The Rise of the Creative Class: And How It's Transforming Work, Leisure and Everyday Life*, New York: Basic Books.

Freeland, Chrystia, 2012. *Plutocrats: The Rise of the New Global Super-Rich*, London: Penguin.

Gielen, Pascal, 2009. *The Murmuring of the Artistic Multitude: Global Art, Memory and Post-Fordism*, Amsterdam: Antennae Valiz.

Hoffman, Reid and Casnocha, Ben, 2012. *The Start-Up of You: Adapt to the Future, Invest in Yourself, and Transform Your Career,* New York: Random House.

Kliman, Andrew, 2012. *The Failure of Capitalist Production: Underlying Causes of the Great Recession*, London and New York: Pluto Press.

Lazzarato, Maurizio, 2012. *The Making of the Indebted Man: An Essay on the Neoliberal Condition*, trans. Joshua David Jordan, Los Angeles: Semiotext(e).

Lenin, Vladimir Ilyich, 1916. "Imperialism and the Split in Socialism." Available online: http://www.marxists.org/archive/lenin/works/1916/oct/x01.htm [last accessed February 2014]

Negt, Oskar and Kluge, Alexander, 1993. *Public Sphere and Experience: Toward an Analysis of the Bourgeois and Proletarian Public Sphere*, trans. Peter Labanyi, Jamie Owen Daniel, and Assenka Oksiloff, Minneapolis: University of Minnesota Press.

Pröbsting, Michael, 2008. "Imperialism and the Decline of Capitalism," in Richard Brenner and Michael Pröbsting. *The Credit Crunch: A Marxist Analysis*, Special Issue of *Fifth International*, London: League for the Fifth International.

Roberts, John, 2011. "Art Beyond Art in the Expanded Field," in *That's the Way We Do It*, Bregenz: Kunsthaus.

Steyerl, Hito, 2012. *The Wretched of the Screen*, Berlin: Sternberg Press.

World Bank, 2007. "Global Economic Prospects." Available online: http://www-wds.worldbank.org/external/default/WDSContentServer/ IW3P/IB/2006/12/06/000112742_20061206155022/Rendered/PDF/ 381400GEP2007.pdf [last accessed February 2014]

Wu, Chin Tao, 2003. *Privatising Culture: Corporate Art Intervention since the 1980s,* New York and London: Verso.

# Logic and Fiction: Notes on Finance and the Power of Recursivity

> We have to create the real possibility of our
> fiction, certainly. Create the real possibility
> of our fiction which is a generic fiction in a
> new form, the new localisation is probably
> a question of a new political courage.
> (Badiou 2005a, 13)

With half a decade since the 2008 financial crisis, a far more distressing crisis has emerged among all the proposed reform strategies, austerity measures and jagged-edged line-graphs: a crisis of imagination. This is rather surprising seeing as how much creativity it took to get us into this plight. From the decoupling of the dollar with the gold standard in 1971, to a situation where even negative value (debt) generates profits in excess of our wildest dreams–to a layperson such as myself, this is an achievement of alchemist-like proportions. Just as currency was becoming an object of speculation (and not just a tool of equivalence), the first academic journal of finance economics emerged in 1974 (Mackenzie 2008,70), paving the socio-economic road we (rapidly) travel down today. That the ideas and spirit of the finance economics endemic to the neoliberal revolution were birthed in academia should give us pause against the many critics who suggest the university is an elitist tower at a gaping distance from 'lived' life. This is not to say that ideas floating about in specialist journals are the impetus of popular change, but that every novel transformation of our condition is rooted in thought, more crucially the experience of thought, and its incorporation into a localization or a 'doing' (Badiou 2005b, 46). Thought carries *real* potency.

Without resorting to utter discursive constructivism, when it comes to the contingency of socio-economic ordering (concepts driving the organization of peoples, exchange, technology, communication, logistics and goods), there are countless possibilities to be tested and presuppositions of the 'nature' of existence to be contested. The successful uptake of the financialization project testifies to the potency of enacted thought: ideas and ideals launched in a mountain village in Switzerland[1] and functionally modelled in Chicago have come to shape our everyday condition on a global scale. The self-fulfilling prophecy of financial models, evidenced by Donald MacKenzie's analysis of the incorporation of the Black-Scholes-Merton model of efficient pricing upon the development (and 'legitimacy') of the Futures Market[2],

---

[1] The Mont Pèlerin Society was inaugurated in Switzerland in 1947 with a group of 39 scholars (mainly economists) and continues to the present. Founding members include Friedrich Hayek, Karl Popper and Milton Friedman.

[2] In Donald MacKenzie's study of the financial turn in economics, he particularly highlights the incorporation of the futures market within the mainstream economy and the role of the self-fulfilling prophecy (positive feedback) of mathematical models upon reality. The first battle of the futures market was for it to be legal, making a distinction between delivering an asset (legal) and delivering in cash only (a wager, and therefore illegal). Through expensive and time-consuming lobbying and commissioned reports (for example, Milton Friedman's 'The Need for Future Markets in Currencies') the Chicago Board of Options Exchange (CBOE) was born—born of collective action paradoxically based on the economic ideology of a rational egoist. The thriving of the CBOE was due largely to the Black-Scholes-Merton model of efficient pricing (a Nobel prize winning model)—instantiating the market as wholly legitimate and not merely a site gambling. At first the correspondence between the model and actual prices was fairly inaccurate (the model did not reflect reality), yet as traders began to rely on the model—taking up its mathematical claims of legitimacy, directly using it's projections in their practice through the dissemination of purchased pricing charts—the model began to create reality, it became a tool of the trade, or what MacKenzie calls 'an engine, not a camera,' a (once inaccurate) model (now) driving reality.

points to the performative requirement (or positive feedback) underpinning the propagation of 'fictitious capital.' Marx's now infamously prophetic turn-of-phrase, fictitious capital refers to where value takes on properties beyond what can be realized in the commodity form (like credit, shares and debt), and is, in part, why those who write under the rubric of 'cognitive capitalism' often diagnose our situation as entirely linguistic, meaning that it, like language, refers to nothing other than itself (de Boever 2013, 104-5) in a logic of recursivity (Vishmidt 2013). It is the sort of potential embodied by the premise of recursivity that drives MacKenzie to pose the open question at the end of his book: 'What sort of world do we want to see performed?' (Mackenzie 2008, 275). It is also behind Arne de Boever's call for a 'reclaiming of fiction within financial culture' where 'sign-practices' are a primary site of action in a semio-capital world (de Boever 2013, 106) and the Accelerationists' call for the creation of an alter 'intellectual infrastructure' as a counter Mont-Pè-lerin Society in their manifesto (along with institutions and economic protocols) to cope with the cataclysmic socio-ecological condition that we are currently facing (Williams & Srnicek 2013, 03.16). Beyond the internal debates amongst these positions, which are plentiful, what becomes apparent is the urgent need for alternative modes of organisation, embracing a logic of and for a new world. These calls urge and provoke us towards the future (and not Futures!); they seek to affirm the creation of novel structures of cohabitation, rather than inhabiting a purely critical space (negation with no alternative); they seek more than an escapist tactic (solipsistic retreat); they do not aim merely to throw a wrench into the cogs of the machinery (sabotage); they demand much more. They ask of us not to rest on diagnostics alone concerning our contemporary plight, but propel us to speculate on what does not yet exist, to speculate on the inexistent—an imaginative force of the most rigorous and courageous sort.

# Hyperobjects and Apocalyptic Logic

Dominated by spectre of '*the* economy' (rather than 'economies' in the plural and diversified sense), the relations of production, distribution and consumption have been subsumed within a totalized and autonomous domain since the mid-twentieth century (Mitchell 1998). In more recent discourse, Nick Srnicek has extended the (non)picture of 'the economy' under neoliberal reign as a hyperobject, meaning that it has grown so complex and manifold that no one (including experts) can grasp its contours or scope, nor reduce its effects to individual, causal components (Srnicek 2012; see also Morton 2010). The autonomous hyperobject of 'the economy' that ideologically governs us today seems to obscure the possibility of a cognitive map, for there exists a vast gap between our localized experiences of the world and the real global conditions that produce it. As Srnicek suggests, fiction may be a tool for overcoming this gap, yet cognitively mapping our given condition does not alone propel us into the realm of a speculative future—it is but a humble (though daunting) first step. Hyperobjects (for example, climate change) display their properties only as traces of residual information, or after-effects of various component interactions, like carbon emissions depicted in multi-coloured, 3D, animated form. The fictions that loom today across popular media seem, at best, only able to evolve scenarios based on the extension of these informational residues evidenced by the obsessive treatment of the apocalyptic narrative of either war or climate induced catastrophe (the end-of-the-world before the end of capitalism position) (Fischer 2009, 1-11). The only other ready alternative is presented within the actual sphere of finance and the rather science-fiction scenario of increased algorithmic governance played out in the high-frequency trading arena—where the only limitations seem to be the laws of physics and geographical impediments that can be overcome 2013)[3]. The sphere of finance capital and the envisioning of our demise on a species-wide level seem to be at the reigns of our collective narrative—a world in which Ray Brassier proposes the image of the Phyllium, a leaf insect that mimics its own food and ends up cannibalising its others (Wilkins & Dragos 2013). These scenarios seize upon the diagnostic actuality of our situation and thrust it towards its existing logical telos, never, however, moving beyond diagnostic or 'known' thought. These fictions may appear to oppose or at least set off a warning siren as to our actual or 'logical' future, yet like the properties of hyperobjects themselves, they inhere and reinforce existing modes of operation without offering any alternatives (they merely dramatize and perpetuate the same logic). The possibilities of fiction and its potential role in cognitively mapping the experiential conflict between local existence and global paradigm, may serve as an initial step, yet it is worth to recall Oscar Wilde's (1891) romantic sentiment: 'A map of the world that does not include Utopia is not worth even glancing at, for it leaves out the one country at which Humanity is always landing.' A cognitive map of the future is always somewhat impossible. While we seem quite adept in the proliferation of dystopic fictions (a symptom of nihilism), we already inhabit a highly fictionalized world predicated on 'the economy.'

........................................................................................................

[3] In particular the proposal by MIT academics Alex Wissner-Cross and Cameron Freer to distribute 'optimal intermediate locations between trading centres, "leading to this science-fictional scenario of a terraforming inhuman distributed finance:" unmanned pods of densely packed microprocessors overseen by next-generation AI bots processing billions of orders streaming out of unmanned AI pods positioned optimally around the world, the silent beams of high-frequency orders shifting trillions across the earth's oceans at light speeds, all automated, beyond the scope of humans to remotely grasp the nature of the transactions.' (Toscano 2013, 77)

Even before credit swaps and options, the sublimation of everyday objects into a commodity form is wholly dependent on fiction—the fiction of value perception. As the supreme energy driven by capital-fictions steer reality towards pyramidal inequality (with a steeple) and socio-climactic devastation, we must seize upon the recursive power of fictions to repurpose their plastic force with an ethos of jujitsu-like acceleration.

## Fiction and Recursivity

The Accelerationist critique of dominant leftist strategies with respect to simplification, slowness, localness and '68 era protest techniques is most welcome, a position embodied more collo-quially in Jodi Dean's (2011) quip that 'Goldman Sachs doesn't care if you raise chickens.' Although admirably tackling questions of Promethean scale, they neglect the politico-economical force of fiction in their purview. Neglecting the role of fiction in the anticipation of an alternative future forecloses the necessity of belief and commitment to said belief, crucial to any political project of ideological and operational restructuring. What we need are not only novel forms of activism and tangible intervention played out on the algorithmic/technological/organisational plane (amounting to more than mere sabotages of current systemic weaknesses such as false rumour hacks of twitter-feeds leading to brief market crashes and public relations disasters[4]), but more

---

[4] The Syrian Electronic Army's attack on Barack Obama's Twitter feed where a shortened URL directed users to a 24 minute video of terror attacks committed by US supported rebels, along with their hacking of the Associated Press Twitter account citing a fictitious attack on the White House that caused US Stock Markets to sporadically loose 200 billion US in value. Src: http://blogs.wsj.com/digits/2013/08/27/new-york-times-website-down-again/

importantly, new logical fictions where an imagined 'we' can incline towards an 'uncancelled' future, foretasting the incorporation of novel thought as a recursively alternative political practice.

The pairing between logic and fiction may at first appear to be odd, as some sort of basic fact vs. untruth dichotomy. Let us step back for a moment to erase such oversimplification, and affirm Alain Badiou's claim that 'Every world possesses its own logic, which is the legislation of appearing' (Badiou 2009, 72). When we apply this in Jacques Rancière's terminology, logic is akin to the distribution of the sensible, or even more succinctly, what counts as making sense within a given sociological condition.

When politics, according to Rancière, is equal to a redistribution of the sensible, it is equal to the creation (or perceptibility) of a new logic—that is, a new (legitimate) regime of appearing and being (ac)counted (for) within a given socio-economic order—and this, to my mind, includes not only peoples and places, but also ideas and the fiction of futurity itself[5]. Following the Modernist poet Wallace Stevens' trajectory of thought, the intersection of poetry with politics allows us to experience the contingency, or fictional character, of our given order (the incommensurability between sense and sense). Expanding upon the manner in which Stevens' understands it, poetics is the creation of novel grammatical structures and general semantics that uncalcify common sense and render the given order entirely plastic and subject to de-re-formation. It was, after all, the poet Rimbaud, who coined the term 'deregulation' in relation to words and meaning, before it was appropriated by contemporary fiscal policy makers (Berardi 2012, 28).

---

[5] I am summarizing rather briefly the extended thought of Rancière and Badiou, who share some core agreements (axiom of equality), yet who diverge (dramatically) on the point of creation of Truths. A critique of Rancière by Badiou can be read in two chapters (7 and 8) of *Metapolitics*.

The first fictional step is poetry, in rendering the laws dictating common sense fluid and contingent (the sense of possibility). The second step is supreme fiction; it is the energetic organization of 'sensed' poetic plasticity, where an alternative fictional formalisation becomes navigable (the articulation of the possible). Supreme fiction is a noological machine of orientation, it is always unfinished, yet maps out exploratory points equal to the constituting of an alter logic, and to echo Badiou, it is precisely this supreme fiction we regrettably lack and so urgently need.

## Anticipation and Metanoia

The task of inscribing supreme fictions is the anticipation of the re-legislation of appearing in the world; and like everything that does not yet exist (the state of futurity), it exists only within the domain of imagination. If imagination is the ability to make present what is absent, it is the capacity 'to think, in a world, what does not appear within the world,' (Badiou 2009, 122) the capacity to 'think' the inexistent. Without introducing an artificial chasm between thinking and doing (between mind and body), thinking alone is not enough until the thought is performed (in a movement of recursive incorporation), for this is, as Kierkegaard notes, *existing* in what one thinks (Badiou 2009, 427). This imaginative thought turned existential practice is the fidelity to 'metanoia'—a term indicating a transformation of thought, of seeing the world in a novel way that (again, recursively) redefines reality itself—it is the experience of one's plastic existence (Avanessian & Henig 2013). It is that moment from which you can never turn back, a rupture in your understanding of the semantic pillars bracing the logic of a world. There is no certainty with metanoia, no guarantee as to the outcome of this 'new light,' it is entirely speculative—it is a risky fiction predicated on the incorporation of thought, and becoming prey to that living thought.

Becoming prey to metanoia is an experience of fundamental weakness in letting oneself become ingested by thought. It is where the sovereignty of the self is usurped, and consumed by thought casting a subject in fidelity to the existence of an inexistent logic. A subject is born through the active becoming-prey to thought, animated by the trace of an idea whose sustenance is the 'bread of faithful speech' (Stevens 1990, 408). Such is the forcing of a new logic.

The fidelity to metanoia has largely been derived from the field of literature, but the written word is only one possible source of existential transformation. Metanoia is irreducible to word alone, but any *thing* (material or otherwise) capable of affect, where language is more humbly an ontic operator for us humans, in the hyper-chaotic ontology of a world. It should be asserted that metanoia, if it is to take on any political import beyond *individual* transformation, must exert a noological force upon the fictional plane of the generic —that is, on the 'we' of a collective people, or a 'trans-individual' plane (Critchley 2012, 26). A politicized metanoia is the collective bringing closer to reality of an inexistent, an alter logic from which a novel world is possible—an insistence on a supernumerary possibility obfuscated by the logic of 'what is.'

## Abstraction and the Generic Will

Metanoia, as a motivational impetus driving an alter logic of a world that 'could be,' is here directly linked to the concept of the general will. The incorporation of metanoia as a general will is the affirmative means through which a collectivity is bound together, authorizing the production of a new logic, and therefore a new world. The general will, or perhaps better, the *generic will* (of axiomatic equality), is the yoking of the concrete individual with the abstraction of the 'we.'

Since the 'we' is an abstraction, it does not itself exist in reality as a mere count of the population. It cannot be known, and this is precisely why fiction is necessary, especially if we are to further our notion of an abstract 'we' beyond anthropocentric horizons of political congregation. The uncountable 'we' as a concrete inexistent, yet abstract existent, can only be touched by an imaginative space of fiction since there is no proposition of futurity to be verified as knowledge. And just as Rousseau has asserted, it is only through imagination—that mediating force between sense and intellect—where the measures of the possible can be exceeded (Sallis 2000, 65), and the immediate bounds of our concrete local experience can be sensed in an abstract global reality. The fictional 'we,' driven by the collective existential impulse of metanoia, can only be an abstract fiction, for abstraction is the enunciation of detachment to the logic of a world as-it-is. In this way abstract fiction is a gesture of violence—not the nihilistic violence of dystopic narratives that plague us today, but an affirmative violence in exiting the as-it-is logical condition. Furthermore, this abstract fiction is located in the future present (in the 'what will have been') requiring the anticipatory exercise of imagination as a 'violence from within that protects us from a violence without' (Stevens 1951, 36).

One may suggest that the evil of late, or cognitive capitalism, is abstraction itself: the abstractions of money/systems of exchange (especially from the financial sphere) and the category of labor itself (the division of labor across the entirety of society) (Pasquinelli 2013). On the one hand, value-extraction within the paradigm of cognitive capitalism is wholly dependent on the increased abstraction of globalized capital, often pilfering from that most basic human impulse and capacity for communication (a commonly shared general intellect, or social knowledge as such), subsuming the entirety of life to its imperative force.

The vehement effect of abstraction upon everyday existence is, no doubt, the reason why so many tactics seeking to resist total absorption resort to concrete, localized, immediate and direct modes of opposition. Yet to oppose abstraction *tout cours* is also to deny the category of the 'we,' or the common, upon which it depends (as well as negating several advances—technological infrastructure—made under the paradigm of globalism). The question is not about obliterating abstractions, as if there is some fundamental, concrete core of pure humanity to return to (an essential 'natural' human state). No, the question revolves around how to deploy the power of abstraction towards an alter logic that redistributes the constellation of life, exchange, production, and consumption. As Matteo Pasquinelli (2013) has argued, this power of abstraction is endemic to humanity as a species—it is the power of the organism (and more precisely the human brain) to invent new norms in relation to its surroundings by exiting the as-it-is condition. Abstraction is not some malevolent force to be tossed aside, but is at the very least a mode of survival (mere life, or physiological existence) and an adaption mechanism (protection, care of the self). At its best, abstraction is an impetus towards sur-vival (more life, beyond simply physiological needs), an apparatus of projection conducive to the shaping of futurity as such. The task of abstract fiction under a regime of cognitive colonization is not only to distin-guish itself from the as-it-is logical condition (for utter separation can easily become nothing more than a tactic of solipsistic retreat); it also involves the generation of new connections to and within a world. This task, according to Rousseau, is the *artful* exercise of politics, the fictional work of moulding new associations (Critchley 2012, 33), with one part *xeno* (or making something alien) and the other part *philia* (the forging of a new bond).

# Unreadiness-to-hand and Psychopathology

The logic of the world we inhabit today is dependent on the integrated thought and performance of infinite economic growth, with the assumption that competition between actors is the 'natural' motivator of continual innovation in order to gain marketplace advantage (with the 'neutral' market being the most efficient mechanism to sift out winners and losers). This logic is most evident in the proliferation of the debt economy, for it can only operate under the presupposition of an ever-more prosperous future where debts can be reimbursed. In reality, however, this type of debt-bondage essentially cancels the possibility of a future (not to mention undercutting the illusion of the free market), instantiating in its place a society subtended by asymmetric power relations, between the few who supply credit and the rest who are indebted (such relations are never subjected to the egalitarian promise of open markets) (Lazzarato 2011, 38). This is one footprint of the logic that traverses social bodies today in the so-called 'third wave of capitalism,' a logic that forecloses on the future as its very core principle (except one premised on deepening crises, inequality and climactic devastation). And, it must be added, this is also a logic of essential competition/propriety that actually impedes innovation through increased monopolisation of possible intellectual/developmental resources. Such footprints lead to the conclusion that this nebulous hyperobject we call 'the economy,' whose transcendental presence compels all of us (including its detractors), has become a veritable 'broken hammer' (Harman 2013). When 'the economy' is grasped as a tool of distribution, production, consumption and valuation, the ready-to-hand quality it may have possessed is now quite blatantly unready-to-hand. In the parlance of Heidegger, that which is ready-to-hand is transparent, such that we deploy it as a tool seamlessly to complete an end goal. In contrast, unreadiness-to-hand is when the tool becomes opaque because of malfunctioning or is no longer capable of performing its intended task.

The global economic meltdown of 2008 displayed the unreadiness-to-hand of the neoliberal economic (and ideological) tool—yet the response to this 'rendering opaque' of malfunction has been a structural re-strengthening of the same broken logic (Williams & Srnicek 2013, 01.04), indicating a frightening withdrawal of (global) political imagination towards the creation of a new logic. Beyond mass depression, attention deficit, panic and anxiety disorders (the cognitive response to a logic of a world in violent crisis rendered normal via psychopharmacology), the non-adaption to the unready-to-hand condition of 'the economy' that dictates the 'nature' of our existence seems to be the greatest psychopathology of our time.

The continued success of the neoliberal 2.0, or cognitive capitalist project, especially under conditions of empirical failure to deliver on core promises of an infinitely 'better' future (more individual trickle-down wealth), not to mention the death of an 'enlightened capitalism' where working hours would be greatly reduced (Williams & Srnicek 2013, 03.02), is a signal that rational responses and strategies alone are insufficient to reclaim the future. Indeed, the call for more economic rationality holds no weight at all, as Marina Vishmidt points out, since in the neoliberal ideological program—where models drive a reality that drive models, ad infinitum—negative, objective results are met as blips, detours or exceptions of 'the most efficient' (or least bad) system (Vishmidt 2011). Vishmidt points out that no amount of counter-information or exposure of contradictions will weaken this core logic, and the only way forward is to drain this ideology of its legitimacy. This is crucial, yet only amounts to one step in the process of creating abstract fictions necessary for the anticipation of a new future beyond annulment— the step of separation from the existing logic (*xenos*). The second step requires affirming a new bond with an alternative logic (*philia*) towards which a 'we' can incline in belief.

Returning to the question of 'what sort of world we want to see performed,' a question that seeks to harness the potential of logical recursivity is, fundamentally, an ethical question. It is not only a call for the creation of models to propel alter movements of circulation within the sphere of economy, but ultimately a question as to what ends we want to deploy the tool of economy beyond our enslavement to its ideological imperatives? Like all ethical questions, we are required to speculate on a good (and most certainly not the least bad), and because that good is inexistent, it requires prophetic acts of imagination to authorize its ideological impetus traversing an abstract 'we.' Although fictions today (and our capacity to anticipate something alternative) seem colonized under a regime of rent-driven finance capital, it is not the time to undermine, nor merely point to the hypocrisies of the intellectual apparatuses that brought us to this point. It is, rather, time to seize the power of their fictional infrastructure that fails to deliver, and repurpose its energy towards a logic of serving the many. Such repurposing requires not only the concrete construction of models able to map the complexity of a global situation, but also, and above all, the vigor of anticipation—an abstract fiction—that compels our collective, ethical inclination in the fabrication of novel associations with each other and with the surroundings. The forcing of such an abstract fiction is nothing less than the creation of a logic orienting a 'we' towards the constituting of futurity (the inexistent) beyond the existent, unbounded by what-is.

Avanessian, Armen and Hennig, Anke 2013. Introduction to *Metanoia oder: Wie Lesen die Welt verändert*, Berlin: Merve Verlag.

Badiou, Alain. 2005a, *Politics: A Non-Expressive Dialectics*, London: Urbanomic. (Text transcribed by Robin Mackay from a lecture at the Birkbeck Institute for the Humanities, London, Saturday 26 November, 2005. Available online: http://blog.urbanomic.com/sphaleotas/archives/badiou-politics.pdf [last accessed February 2014])

Badiou, Alain, 2005b. *Metapolitics*, trans. Jason Barker, London: Verso.

Badiou, Alain, 2009. *Logics of Worlds: Being and Event II*, trans. Alberto Toscano, London: Bloomsbury.

Berardi, Franco "Bifo", 2012. *The Uprising: On Poetry and Finance*, Los Angeles: Semiotext(e).

Critchley, Simon, 2012. *The Faith of the Faithless: Experiments in Political Theology* London: Verso.

de Boever, Arne, 2013. "All of us go a little crazy at times: Capital and Fiction in a State of Generalized Psychosis," in Arne De Boever and Warren Neidich (eds.). *The Psychopathologies of Cognitive Capitalism: Part One*, Berlin: Archive Books.

Dean, Jodi, (28 July 2011). "The Communist Horizon with Jodi Dean," from the Not an Alternative Lecture, Brooklyn, New York. Available online: https://vimeo.com/27327373 [last accessed February 2014].

Fischer, Mark, 2009. "It's easier to imagine the end of the world than the end of capitalism," Chapter 1 in *Capitalist Realism: Is There No Alternative?*, London: Zero Books.

Harman, Graham (22 June 2013). "What Objects Mean For Architecture," from the Architecture Exchange Series #01. Available online: http://www.youtube.com/watch?v=WPTzUERNfwY [last accessed February 2014].

Lazzarato, Maurizio, 2011. *La fabrique de l'homme endetté: Essaie sur la condition neoliberal*, Paris: Éditions Amsterdam.

MacKenzie, Donald, 2008. *An Engine, Not A Camera: How Financial Models Shape Markets*, Cambridge: MIT Press.

Mitchell, Timothy (1998). "Fixing the Economy," in *Cultural Studies* 12/1.

Morton, Timothy, 2010. *Ecological Thought*, Cambridge: Harvard University Press.

Pasquinelli, Matteo (8 March 2013). "The Power of Abstraction and its Antagonism," Paper presented at The Psychopathologies of Cognitive Capitalism II Conference, Berlin, Germany.

Sallis, John, 2000. *The Force of Imagination: The Sense of the Elemental*, Bloomington: Indiana University Press.

Srnicek, Nick (August 2012). "Navigating Neoliberalism: Political Aesthetics After the Crisis," in *The Matter of Contradiction Conference*, see https://vimeo.com/52434614 [last accessed February 2008].

Stevens, Wallace, 1951. "The Noble Rider and the Sound of Words," in *The Necessary Angel: Essays on Reality and The Imagination*, New York: Alfred A. Knopf.

Stevens, Wallace, 1990. "Notes Toward a Supreme Fiction: It Must Give Pleasure," in *The Collected Poems of Wallace Stevens*, New York: Vintage Books.

Toscano, Alberto (Spring 2013). "Gaming The Plumbing: High Frequency Trading and the Spaces of Capital," in *Mute* 3/4: *Slave to the Algorithm*, pp. 74-85.

Vishmidt, Marina, (10 January 2011). "Human Capital or Toxic Asset: After the Wage," Available online: http://www.metamute.org/community/your-posts/human-capital-or-toxic-asset-after-wage [last accessed February 2014].

Vishmidt, Marina, (2 July 2013). "Speculating On the Duck of Doubt?" Paper presented at the Inclinations Lecture Series, Berlin, Germany.

Wilde, Oscar (1891). "The Soul of Man under Socialism," Available online: http://www.marxists.org/reference/archive/wilde-oscar/soul-man/ [last accessed February 2014].

Wilkins, Inigo and Bogdan Dragos (Spring 2013). "Destructive Destruction? An Ecological Study on High Frequency Trading," in *Mute* 3/4: *Slave to the Algorithm*, pp. 74-85.

Williams, Alex and Nick Srnicek (14 May 2013). "#ACCELERATE MANIFESTO for an Accelerationist Politics." Available online: http://criticallegalthinking.com/2013/05/14/accelerate-manifesto-for-an-accelerationist-politics/ [last accessed February 2014].

# Does Cognitive Capitalism Exist?

"In the era of Leninism, power had to be overturned, trade unions were economists, they betrayed, power was due to the Soviets, at least there was an idea, there was something. Now, really there is no idea. Nothing at all. There is the idea of macro-economy, of a certain number of factors: unemployment, the market, currency, abstractions that do not adhere to social reality at all."

"It is less a question of having access to novel cognitive spheres than of apprehending and creating, in pathic modes, mutant existential virtualities."

Félix Guattari

Many psychopathologies (racism, extremism, new nationalism etc.) of the so-called cognitive capitalism derive from our incapacity to invent modes of collective subjectivation that disrupt the subjugating contingencies of contemporary capitalism. I do not believe that the catastrophic situation we are in is due to the force of the capital, of its "techno-semiotical" industries, to the power of financial networks etc. The major defect lies in our incapacity to invent modalities of collective organization as did those that constituted and created the "First International" in the 19th century and Leninism in the 20th.

Even the psychopathologies that Franco "Bifo" Berardi justly underlines depend on the fact that the isolated, fragmented, scared, incriminated individual can be neither the analyst nor the interpreter nor the critic of the mega-machines of mass media, finance and production. Only a collective assemblage of bodies and enunciations can start to fill up the monstrous and monster-generating gap that results from exasperated individualization on the one hand and socialization of capital on the other.

There is no "anthropological degradation," but transformation! Transformation of the relations constituting Man/social-machine and Man/technical-machine. Which does not have to impede the emergence of rich and innovative political experiments. I happen to have lived experience exciting experiments myself even very recently. I am not talking about a sort of miracle that would lead us out of our powerlessness. I am simply pointing out a blind spot current theoretical and political action.

In the 1980s, Foucault and Guattari designated in different ways the production of subjectivity and the constitution of "the relation to oneself" as "the" contemporary political problems that solely can indicate exits from the impasse in which we are caught up.

Questioning the process of political subjectivation by shedding light on the "micro-political" (Guattari) and the "micro-physical" (Foucault) dimensions of power cannot dispense with the necessity to examine and reconfigure its macro-political dimension. Guattari advises us on the contrary: "One thing or the other: somebody or whoever, will produce new instruments for subjectivity production, be they bolshevik, maoist or whatever, or the crisis will just continue to be aggravated"

I profoundly agree with this statement. It is obviously neither possible nor desirable to repeat the experiences of the workers movement, but entirely possible and desirable to repeat their act of invention! Since the First International as much as Leninism are by all means inventions. We are now very distant from them, so I am obliged to take up the problem, together with Guattari, from afar.

# Critic of linguistic and political representation

Collective forms of contemporary political mobilization, be they urban uprisings or "syndicalist" struggles, pacifist or violent, are altogether penetrated by the same problem: the refusal of the representation and invention/experimentation of forms of expression and organization that would break up with the modern political tradition of power delegation to people's and class's representatives.

On this subject, Guattari opens more than one path of reflection. Questioning the relation between the *discursive* and the *cognitive* on the one hand, and the *existential* on the other, he redefines the process of subjectivation on the macro-political as well as on the micro-political level. Paradoxically, by stipulating the "existential"–which, is neither linguistical nor semiotical nor cognitive in the first place–as an essential condition of subjectivation and enunciation, he operates a displacement that neutralizes the power of representation.

So what interests me here is the question of the relationship existing between the linguistic, the cognitive and the semiotic, which are always actualized realities of the non-physical dimension of creation, of rupture, of transformations that are in and for themselves not linguistic, cognitive or semiotic but which constitute the condition of reconfiguring the linguistic, the cognitive and the semiotic. The concept of "the cognitive" threatens to shield off the possibility of rupture and change. The actualized dimensions of subjectivation will be analyzed here via language, but at any time you can add the cognitive dimension.

According to Guattari, we live in a paradox and a challenge that linguistics can neither reveal nor relieve us from: "We find ourselves thrown into discursive systems, and, at the same time, we are confronted with the challenge of creating points of convergence of existential affirmation, which, themselves, are not discursive [...] When a machine of love or a machine of fear engages, it is not due to the effects of discursive, cognitive or deductive phrases upon us. It is already given. And this machine will progressively develop different means of expression."

At the basis of enunciation, there is no linguistic or cognitive competence but an existential apprehension and appropriation of the self and the world, and it is only from this existential/ affective appropriation that there can be language, discourse, knowledge, narrative, oeuvre etc.

The statement thus has a twofold function: to signify, to communicate, and "politically" declare, but also and above all "to produce assemblages of enunciation capable of capturing", territorialize and unfold the singularities of a focus of existential subjectivation, endowing it with consistency and persistence.

One the one hand, the crystallization of subjectivation processes "is not the exclusive privilege of language; all the other semiotic components, all the other procedures of natural and machinic encoding, contribute to it." On the other hand, the subjective mutation is not discursive and cognitive at first because for being so it would need to touch the "focus of non-discursiveness which is the core of subjectivity [...] in order to make narratives, narrate the world and one's life, one has to start from an unnamable point, which is the very point of the breakup of sense and the point of absolute non-narrative, of absolute non-discursiveness," of not knowing. Besides the signifying and denotative function, Guattari introduces the "existential function" which will function as the creative motor of enunciation and subjectivation while being perfectly *non-discursive*.

In the aftermath of the linguistic turn and structural-linguistic Lacanian psychoanalysis, Judith Butler reduces subjectivity to nothing more than the resultant of signifying operations. Guattari prefers to map the diverse components of subjectivation in their profound heterogeneity, operating a "radical divorce between the production of sense, the production of signification, the pragmatic production and the production of subjectivity."

The same semiotic chains can operate on "producing discourse" and "producing existence," "the same phrases that will signify something in a dream are entangled in a subjective agglomerate which conveys to them not a signification, but an existential impact." They will constitute the one who pronounces them as a subjective entity.

Existential pragmatics, in contrast to discursive pragmatics, refer back to the production of the self, to "ontological singularities of ones own self-appropriation, the singularities of self-consciousness." *Existence is of the nature of self-positioning, of self-affectation.*

The constitution of the self can rupture with dominant significations as primarily it puts into play a power of auto-affection, not signifiers, discourse or sense. For Guattari, this affirmation of the self assumes a particular coloring, as the "for oneself" and the "for others," the focal points of enunciation, the vectors of subjectiviation, are not exclusively human. Existence relates to a "machinic" logic, "in any case, something that doesn't at all function in the logic of discursive sets, but what I have recently been calling existentialisation."

Words and propositions of language can function within the logic of sense, referring from one referential sense to another, or within a diagrammatical logic that does not *go through* representation, conscience and the "I" of the subject…

Semiotic flows, cognitive flows, by the same effect as material flows, social and economical flows etc. exist in actualized spatio-temporal coordinates, whereas the "the relation to oneself," "existential territories" and "universes of value" constitute the incorporeal, affective and intensive dimension of the assemblage, which is not ordered by the ordinary coordinates of space and time. The existential escapes determination and physical causality and constitutes a non-energetic and non-informational "machinism." The transformations that are brought about in existence are incorporeal and, unlike the transformations studied by science, they do not put into play energetic or informational or cognitive processes.

## Disjunction and conjunction of the discursive and the existential

The relation to oneself constitutes an incorporeal existential focus, an autopoietic machine whose consistence, persistence and development depends, *in a second step*, on the multiplicity of actualized elements that it will *penetrate* and *reconfigure* (the discursive, the cognitive, but also institutions, the social, the economic etc.).

"Subjective matter" of "existentialization" uses discursive-ness in order to "appear to itself–even manifest itself to itself–as a body without organs, as a pseudo-unity which nonetheless is not a totalization of the type that we observe in the logic of sets."

By establishing a difference of nature between the discursive (and the conceptual or the cognitive) and the existential, Guattari thinks not only the disjunction but also the conjunction of two disparate logics, the "semiotic logic" of the construction of sense and the "pragmatic ontological" of the construction of existential territories. Let us rapidly enumerate the "dissymmetries" between these two logics. One can easily verify that the only "topology" I am interested in is the one of the relation to oneself.

First of all, the discursive and the existential work with heterogeneous "referents." The semiotic, discursive or cognitive dimension "stems from a system of extrinsic refer-ences, i.e. it implies at any time that every element is discursive in relation to another element which constitutes its referent" in a way that situates its "truth, its essence" outside of its existence. Within existential logics, however, "the singular element is itself its own reference and generates its reference, it secretes reference into its world." Existential pragmatics is "self-referencing, self-productive of reference." Existence "produces itself in its own movement."

Secondly, discursive logic is linear. There is one element, then another element. It unfolds itself according to the temporality of a time-line. Existential self-assertion is circular, it returns continuously onto itself, it intensifies existence and conveys consistence to it, or else it vanishes, lacking the capacity to cross certain thresholds. From that return onto itself, from the agglomeration and consolidation of this focus of existential-ization, from that subjective emergence, it *transversalizes* the actualized—economic, political, social, linguistic, cognitive—dimensions, *configuring* them differently.

Third dissymmetry: within discursive logic, repetition always produces discourse and combinations of discourse, whereas within existential logic, repetition ("ritornellos") produces transformations of subjective states that model subjectivity. The fact that existence is self-productive of reference signifies that "repetition in relation to itself will be the reference." The ritornello ("empty word"/"parole vide") has, in contrast to the repetition of sign in Derrida and Butler, an existential function since it endows the relation to oneself with consistency.

In ritornello-repetition, what matters is not semantic content but the repetition itself which produces a transformation of subjective state. Christian or Leninist ritornellos can't be measured in terms of sense but in terms of the transformative impact on the subjectivity they determine, of consistency, threshold-crossing, of agglomeration, of the transversality of subjectivity which they enable and engender. Christian and Leninist ritornellos trigger "a sort of universe, a framing, a scenery which corresponds to a collective production of subjectivity."

Existential ritornellos may have semantic contents and constitute systems of expression, but a part from that they function as modes of constitution of another type of universe that will bring up a "surplus of possibilities."

Fourth difference: discursive sets articulate distinctive (speaker/auditor/content/expression/subject/object etc.) and personological ("I"/"you") oppositions that unfold in extensive spatial-temporal coordinates of *representation,* whereas existential sets are animated by logics of intensity, by affects that emerge before the distinction of identities, persons and functions.

Affects, while being non-locatable in respect to their origins and their destiny (fear or joy affect the speaker as well as the auditor, they constitute transitional subjectivities) are perfectly perceptible from the threshold of consistence they determine.

Existential pragmatics can not easily be circumscribed within the logic of discursive sets because here, contents and expressions are reversible (there is no ground from which an expression could detach itself, "everything can be content and everything can be expression"), the operators are not subjects and objects, but "subjectities and objectities," mutating, half-object half-subject entities that don't have an inside or an outside but do engender interiority and exteriority. "They are becomings (devenirs), understood as focal points of differentiation." The distinctive traits of existential sets do not concern subject and object, I and you, but the crossing of thresholds, the gradients of intensities.

Discursive logic implies exchange, while in ontological pragmatics, existence is not exchangeable. "The existence sticks totally to its topos, rendering impossible to ever detach a form of it that would be a form of existence. You're there or you're not there [...] and there is no existential negativity. Existence is to itself all the existing. And if it is not, there is nothing to say about it, one cannot designate it as non-existent."

Ontological or existential pragmatics is processual, irreversible, singular, event-like, while discursive logics is reversible, structural, a-historical, universal. The two logics refer thus to dissymmetrical functionalities of subjectivity. It is up to us to see how the conjunction between these two series of such different functionality can be operated.

# The aesthetic paradigm

The non-discursive does not have the powerlessness of the irrational, but the power of the incorporeal, of intensities, affects which constitute as many spaces for proto-enunciations. The non-discursive is not a formless matter waiting for a differentiation, disciplinarization or organisation (signifying or symbolic) stemming from language and "the law" (as Lacanians would have it). There is nothing mystical about it, as there is in Wittgenstein. On the contrary, it is traversed by very rich semiotic and expressive dynamics, affects that function like "emergent selves," spaces of mutant subjectivation and proto-enunciation, human and non-human, which are so many machines self-producing existence.

How should one then articulate the relationship between the discursive and the machinic existential, the actual and the virtual, the possible and the real? One cannot establish a "scientific" relation between these two levels, a cognitive relation, a biunivocal relation, since there is a radical asymmetry between the "discursive" and the "existential." This relationship can only be addressed from a new paradigm that Guattari calls "the aesthetic paradigm."

The process of subjectivation is not the effect of economic, sexual, linguistic and social infrastructures (which would mean it has a referent outside itself). On the contrary, the phenomena of self-positioning, self-affection, self-referentiality operates as an opening towards processuality, creation of possibilities, and the initiation of becoming; mutations are originary. But these autopoietic spaces only gain materiality by transversalizing, repositioning and reconfiguring all realms considered as "structural" (economic, political, social, linguistic, sexual, scientific, etc.).

Subjective self-reference "is obviously unsustainable as such, since it lacks any external referent, does not possess external reference [...] They cannot sustain themselves— what is more, they only sustain themselves in a reinitiation of discursivity." The enunciation of the relation to self and the existential territories supporting it, always requires an abduction of narration, which does not primarily aim at producing rational, cognitive, scientific explanations, but to generate complex *ritournelles* ("mythico– conceptual, phantasmatic, religious, romanesque"), which give some flesh (*consistance*) to the emergence of new existential territories. This is not a return to the irrational, or to the era of myths, but it is about undoing the scientific paradigm that the entire 19th and 20th centuries, all the way to Althusser, believed in. It is towards aesthetic experience, not as productive of artworks but as a pragmatics of the relation between discursive and existential, between actual and virtual, that Guattari turns.

"The paradox to which aesthetic experience constantly brings us back to is that these effects, as a mode of existential apprehension, are given as a unity, despite, or besides the fact that indicative traits, signifying *ritournelles,* are necessary to catalyze their existence in fields of representations." Approaching existential territories always involves a certain discursive or semiotic surveying, but this surveying is neither scientific, nor objectivist or rationalist. There are no other ways to access existence than self-existentialisation. The knowledge of existence requires what Guattari called, following Giambattista Vico, a "topical art," an art of cartographies.

The relation of self to self, self-affection, self-positioning will make use of signs, myths, narrations and conceptualisations which do not operate like an (impossible) translation of the existential into the discursive, but as a cartography which will serve as a surveying, as access to the processes of subjectivation, to existential territories.

"Existence may be located in cartographies and it maybe involves in its unfolding, its locating and production, something which is inherently antagonistic to the discursive treatment which belongs to objectivist procedures."

Signifying semiotics, before carrying or transmitting messages, before having a discursive function, operate like existential "ritournelles." This does not imply a devaluing of language, concepts or conceptual abstraction, on the contrary. The more the cartography is *abstract* and the more the possibilities of articulating the discursive and the non-discursive are diversified, the more the cartography is *arbitrary* and articulation finds in it a favorable landscape for its unfolding. There are 2 types of cartographies according to Guattari: there are the "concrete cartographies that directly produce what I shall call an existentialisation, which generate a subjective territory at the same time as the cartography unfolds [Ed. Note: the existential cartographies of a person, a group or even a nation] and then there are, besides, speculative cartographies which do not produce territories, second-order cartographies, whose function is to think and organize, to articulate the relation between these two radically heterogeneous levels." Whence the fundamental importance of theological, political and philosophical debates.

Theological disputes in early Christianity or Bolshevik debates around 1905 did not serve to establish *true* statements, but cartographies were able to open up possibilities for articulating the existential and the discursive, inventing *ritournelles* which are 'hooks' for subjectivity, which enable it to cross thresholds and initiate a process.

The theoretical discourses of Marxism and Freudianism which claim to be scientific constructs, "only received social validation" inasmuch as they crystallized, gave flesh and transversality to the mutant, emergent "spaces of subjectivation" of capitalism.

Neither Freud nor Marx brought about a new science (Althusser), but instead, they articulated "mythico-conceptual" surveying instruments which enabled Marx to create a "stage" (the history of humanity as the history of class struggle), mythico-conceptual characters (the proletariat as a subject that would abolish salaried labor and social classes) that could welcome and semiotize the singularity of the subjectivity of the first industrial revolution. But always from an unnameable point, an unrepresentable point, with a signifier which alone, creates the possibility of devices (*dispositifs*) of subjectivation, not in order to "tell a story" (*histoire)* but so that history (*histoire)* can happen. In this context, narratives, concepts and "myths" do not have a communicative, intersubjective or cognitive function, but an "aesthetic/existential" one.

This is a paradoxical relation ("it is not a relation, but it is not without relation"), since it is only by a certain use of discursive categories that one can access existential effects and mutations. Speculative cartographies function not only like passive surveyings, but also like active kick-starters of processes of subjectivation.

It is in this context that Guattari returns to Christic ritournelles, Leninist ritournelles, Debussyist ritournelles as "gimmicks" ("semiotic acts," the way one says "speech acts") which kick-start processes of subjectivation, which bring us into other realms of reference, and facilitate the move to action. The discursive as such is not enough to grasp subjectivity, to involve it, to push it to act. *To grasp and involve subjectivity, to push it to act, discourses signs and concepts must function like modes of access to new worlds, "diagrammatic initiators" of action.*

# The "current" crisis

In a 1984 seminar, Félix Guattari asserted that the crisis occurring in the West since the early 1970s, before being an economic or political crisis, was a crisis in the production of subjectivity.

Most of the "current crisis" lies in the incapacity of capitalist forces to articulate the discursive, cognitive and existential dimensions together; the impossibility of linking economic, social and technological flow together with the virtual, incorporeal dimension of the production of subjectivity, existential territories and realms of value. If the production of subjectivity is not articulated together with a social field, a "production," a politics, a language, etc., the result is, like today, a pathology of subjectivity (racist, xenophobic, individualist, turned back on one's own interests, etc.). The slogans of the Left on employment, full employment, wage labor, work, the defense of Welfare, etc., which should be articulated together with subjectivity, do not set into motion processes of subjectivation, because they are not open onto new worlds, are not a matter with which contemporary subjectivity works. The political problem lies in the articulation and concatenation of "the processes which power the technical, social and economic machines, and the processes of subjectivation. If this fourfold articulation is not present, it doesn't work."

The unfolding of subjectivation must happen in a system of flows which enable one "to be at once in material effects," "economic," social and linguistic production (etc.), but "which also must generate the production of subjectivity."

Neo-liberal capitalism (and what is left of the labor movement) was not able to articulate the relation between economic, social and technological flows, and the becoming-subjectivity forms in contemporary capitalism.

It failed to articulate discursive (economic, social and institutional) and existential meaning, because in current conditions, both the subjective figure of the entrepreneur and that of the salaried employee, "do not yield mythical consistency, do not make you want to go on a Crusade or participate in the October Revolution!"

The subjective figure of the indebted man articulates these various flows, levels and plateaus but only in a regressive and repressive way. It offers no "future," no "possibilities." Hence the stumbling-block is subjective as much as it is economic.

The articulation between heterogeneous levels is not established spontaneously, it must be constructed, invented, worked at. The articulation is *singular* but not *necessary*; nor is it the fruit of *chance*.

We still live in a paradoxical situation. The mutations of subjectivity are sudden, occurring at "infinite speeds," in Guattari's words. The mutations of subjective states are given "from the outset; then, secondarily, in discursive time, one will say: this is so boring! This is so stressful! What a great atmosphere! The first given will create a disposition or situation which means I am here, in the room, enunciation gains thickness."

What is being constituted in these condensations, these agglomerations, these sorts of "enunciative chunks," is not knowledge (whence the limits of any cognitivism!). Existential crystallization implies that there is "a certain arrangement in between the way of disposing signs, seeing art forms, and sensing time: it's organized that way prior to any other construction." These points of crystallization, condensation, agglomeration are not self-sufficient. They ultimately require an "aesthetic and ethico-political fulfillment."

"Aesthetic, because there is a way statements are evident, when there is a relation of love or hate. As Spinoza says, there is no mistake, even a dog understands the right away, with no debate, if one wants to spank or pet him." At the same time, "there is the ethico-political dimension, because this matter is not just an aesthetic matter, it is also a matter involved in relations of transversality with other, completely heterogeneous levels," political, social, economic, artistic, etc.

Work on these forms of emergence follows a methodology which consists precisely in the "aesthetic paradigm" or the topical art of cartographies. Just as the artist should not expect some kind of inspiration, politics action must build and invent instruments and processes of experimentation, research and intervention which do not primarily involve the economic, social and linguistic realms, but instead, the production of subjectivity.

The relation between discursive and non-discursive, conceptual and existential should not end in silence ("Whereof one cannot speak, thereof one must be silent"), but must be worked at, conceptualized, semiotized, staged, narrated, etc., starting from the unrepresentable. Instead of ending up with Badiou's retrospective faithfulness (faithfulness to the event, once the event has occurred), one must intervene in the emergence of emergent spaces of proto-enunciation and proto-subjectivation.

Crystallizations, condensations, emergent agglomerations must be aesthetically and ethically completed, both at the micro-political level ("working on a point of subjectivation which is non-discursive, a point of subjectivation which can be melancholic, chaotic or psychotic") and the macro-political (a point of revolutionary or reactionary, fascist or identity subjectivation, etc.) These a-signifying crystallizations qua existential functions are "wrapped up like in a Turkish

Delight pastry, in meanings and denotations." Working on them means liberating them from these shells that bind them, and putting them "in a position where they proliferate [...] i.e., to establish connections, associative branches of production, passages towards other realms."

The great merit of Guattari's work is to problematize the relation between discursive and non-discursive, to question the modalities of the articulation of the existential with economic, social, and political flows–this is precisely the weakness of contemporary theories that claim to be critical or revolutionary. On the one hand we have, with Badiou or Rancière, a subjectivation which doesn't need to be articulated with social, economic and cultural flows since it is self-contained. Politics is independent, autonomous with regard to what Rancière and Badiou call economics, just because their image of the latter and of capitalism in general is the caricature produced by the economists themselves. What Badiou and Rancière call economics performs a twofold implication and exploitation of subjectivity, through social subjection and machinic enslavement.

To say that political subjectivation is not deducible from Capital in Badiou and Rancière's sense is quite different from asking the question of their paradoxical articulation. In the former case, we have the illusion of a "pure" politics, since subjectivation, as it does not articulate itself on anything, will never reach a thickness or flesh (*consistance*) required to exist. In the latter case, you open areas for experimentation and construction since subjectivation must, if it is to exist, gain materiality, *traverse and reconfigure* the social, the political, the economic, etc.

The theories of cognitive capitalism do not, in addition, articulate the linguistic, cognitive, representational dimension with the pre-verbal, pre-cognitive and non-reflexive dimension.

Knowledge is supposed to fulfill diverse and unlikely functions of creation of possibility, aesthetic creation and the production of subjectivity, all of which belong to the existential machinic.

The inventor of the concept of "cognitive capitalism," Enzo Rullani, has an unlimited faith in knowledge: "Cognitive experience is always a process–great or small–of world-making," creating possible worlds. "Cognitive experience" also elaborates "worldviews, aesthetic codes," which as they spread, "change people's values." "Knowledge" is not just the basis of economic and aesthetic value, but also of the production of subjectivity. Through cognitive experience, "we are open to the possibility that it may change our perception of the world and ourselves, our deep identity."

He cheerfully confuses–like his disciples–the production of subjectivity with the production of knowledge.

Knowledge, information, language as such, has no potential to create possibility, to multiply material forms. The flow of knowledge, like information or semiotic flows, are always unidirectional: "they always discursive," that is, they remain on the same plane, they never attain existential territories, where the mutation of subjectivity can occur. It is not knowledge, information or communication which can serve as the basis for the creation and production of the new, but rather, an existential mutation, a transformation that touches the non-discursive space of subjectivity, its existential territories, its modes of subjectivation.

That the theory of cognitive capitalism is incapable of explaining its own objects (innovation, the creation of the new, new knowledge) is synthetically demonstrated by the tautology of one of its theoreticians who defines this economy as "the production of knowledge by means of knowledge."

"A new subjectivity cannot come from a mere treatment of flows (linguistic, cognitive, economic, etc.)," nor can any new knowledge or innovation.

Even the production of science and knowledge has to drift away from a scientistic or "cognitivist" paradigm towards an aesthetic paradigm, that is, they are dependent on an act of subjectivation, in the sense defined by Bakhtin as cited by Guattari: "From within the field of knowledge itself, no conflict is possible, because one cannot encounter any heterogeneity there. The scientist, not science, can enter into conflict, and even then, not ex cathedra, but as an aesthetic subject, for whom knowledge is an *act* of knowledge."

Only a break in the mode of subjectivation can secrete an existential crystallisation which produces new references, new self-positionings which in turns, open up the possibility of constructing new languages, new forms of knowledge, new aesthetic practices, new forms of life. To break with dominant meanings and established forms of life, one must pass through areas of non-senses, a-signifying, non-discursive–which, in politics, take the form of strikes, revolts, riots which suspend time, for a short moment, and create other possibilities, in which, if they gain in materiality, other subjectivations and existential crystallisations can proliferate.

"In the other type of logic, which I am superposing onto discursive logic, the same elements of semiotic discursivity are taken from the opposite direction; at that point they are taken qua producers, not of discursivities compared to one another, but of existence, sensitive territories and universes. In that logic, the constellations that emerge maintain the same elements, but in one case you have semiotic productions, in the other subjective productions."

This cartography of the production of subjectivity breaks radically with analytic philosophy, Lacanianism, linguistics, a certain form of Marxism, but above all, with the concept and practices of representation (whether political or linguistic), and enacts a displacement from which we will have to start, if we wish to conceive of a politics appropriate to the current crisis.

Guattari, Félix, 1989. *Cartographies schizoanalytiques.* Paris: Editions Galilée.

Guattari, Félix, 1992. *Chaosmose.* Paris: Editions Galilée.

Guattari, Félix, In *Chimères* n° 23, p. 58.

# Therapy for a Pathological Capitalism

Anything that includes so many words as the title, "psychopathologies of cognitive capitalism" could be accounted for in a large number of ways, as well as on many different levels, in this case spanning from cognitive science to economic thought. But if we try to understand the notion in a general, aggregate manner, we could perhaps see it as psychiatric and psychological disorders, distresses and discontents, the pathological patterns and cognitive blockages resulting systemically in the production of the different subjects of cognitive capitalism: the latter defined as a new dynamic of waged labor, where profit or surplus value is not simply extracted from surplus labor time, but also from unwaged cognitive and communicative processes.

In an early text elaborating the concept written by Lazzarato it is thus said:

> "By cognitive capitalism we denote a regime of accumulation in which the object of accumulation is principally constituted by the knowledge tending to be subjected to a direct valorisation, whose production exceed the traditional confines of the enterprise.

This regime manifests itself empirically by the importance given to research, technological progress, education, circulation of information, systems of communication, innovation, organizational apprenticeship and strategic management of organizations. On the side of demand, consumption is also directed towards technology and most notably the 'technologies of mind', i.e. those which set into play (into exercise) the mental faculties via interaction with new technological objects: audiovisual, computers, internet, game consoles, etc." Turning to *Grundrisse*, cognitive capitalism is thus understood as the regime of accumulation succeeding the previous industrial capitalism, a transformation framed in an actualization of what Marx described as the general intellect, where the distinction between dead and living labor is surpassed and "social knowledge has become a direct force of production." (Lazzarato et al. 2001, 9)

Much has been written on the subject since then, digital communication has developed further, and a global financial crisis has taken place. But this early text from 2001 has a certain merit in its preliminary approach, describing cognitive capitalism as "in becoming," renouncing itself from the principle belief that modern societies form an essential unity, with an already present order. Perhaps one could then read the existence of conflicting regimes into this regulationist[1] approach: "Fundamentally, it amounts to recognizing the existing tensions between the capitalist order and the new conditions of accumulation characteristic of the regime currently under construction." (ibid.)

---

[1] Regarding the *Regulation School*, see Aglietta, *Régulation et crises du capitalisme*, second edition, Editions Odile Jacob, 1997.

This preliminary approach, which refrains from describing any of the all-encompassing features of cognitive capitalism, seems necessary already in the description of the increasing abstraction of capital and the decreasing importance of the industrial norm of abstract labor. While abstract labor—the Marxian concept of waged, general labor defined by its duration—no longer occupies the same position of value it held during industrial capitalism, the notion can hardly be done away with altogether. Because while industrial production and the manufacturing sectors employ relatively less labor in its abstract form, the chronometer still marks the beginning and end of labor worldwide. While it might be true that "The law of value founded on the measure of abstract labor-time immediately dedicated to production enters into crisis" (Vercellone 2007, 29) regarding extraction of surplus value from social production, and while Marx himself states in the *Grundrisse* that "Labor no longer appears so much to be included within the production process; rather, the human being comes to relate more as watchman and regulator to the production process itself," (Marx 1973, 704) it would seem hasty to completely do away with the theory of value developed in *Capital*. (Marx 1976/1990, 283) If we continue this open-ended and preliminary reading of cognitive capitalism, there might be space, before we go on, to make two general suggestions or additional remarks. The first point relates to the periodization and definition of the regime of accumulation. Since the crisis of industrial capitalism and Fordist production, indeed since the crisis of surplus value production in the 1970s, profit accumulation has increasingly been moving through financial channels, producing enormous gains and crises alike. But what is also highly relevant in this context is to note the phenomenon which David Harvey has called "accumulation by dispossession." (2003, 137) This expression of Marx's "primitive accumulation" of looting, conquering and feudal relations, is now upgraded to the recent processes of privatization by which enormous masses of wealth have passed from the public into the private domain (through below market-price acquisitions of capital, for instance), financialization, as well as management and manipulation of crises, whereby assets are accumulated in speculation as a result of vicious circles of mortgage loans, crises and foreclosures.[2] Whether one could posit this other regime of accumulation next to the one of cognitive capitalism and remain faithful to the theoretical project of the latter, is perhaps a matter of discussion. In any case, considering the transfers of wealth it has produced, this accumulation by dispossession seems of historical relevance in any account of the last decades of political and economical development.

The second suggestion could be regarded as a matter of speed. Being an inherent component of financialization and phenomena like split-second trading, speed, in addition to this, is often recognized as forming the basis of the individual psychopathologies of contemporary capitalist subjects. Cognitive capitalism is a based on an "intensification of the rhythm of innovation," (Corsani et al. 2001, 30) and in *24/7: Late Capitalism and the Ends of Sleep* (2013), Jonathan Crary defines an unbound "24/7 'attention economy'," where the inactivity of daydreaming and above all of sleep is conceived of as the ultimate obstacle to a constant connectedness to commodified and mostly electronic or digital circuits. "There is a profound incompatibility of anything resembling reverie with the priorities of efficiency, functionality, and speed." (Crary 2013, 88)

---

[1] See Harvey, David. *Rebel Cities*, Verso, London/New York, 2012, p. 24-29.

The point is not to deny the relevance of Crary's account of specific psychopathologies resulting from "24/7 capitalism" —for instance a dramatic increase young children's autism correlated with near-constant television watching–nor is it to contradict the fact of an ever-growing consumption of pharmaceuticals, which for example Franco Bifo Berardi describes as a "Prozac-economy." Berardi identifies a particularly harrowed species: cognitive workers as bodies with their nerves tense from constant attention to semiotic flows, operating on prescribed and non-prescribed drugs. One would have to assume that it is in this intensified "economic accumulation [...] causing the social nervous system to suffer contraction and stress" (Berardi 2009, 82) that biopolitics represents "a morphogenetic modelling of the living operated by the habitat with which it is required to interact." (ibid., 187)

But if we take Berardi's and many other's reference to the Foucaldian biopolitics, we could perhaps, alongside this hypersemiotics, identify another feature of contemporary capitalism which are actually slowing things down. That is, the constant use of statistics, evaluation, and quantification in the workplace, particularly in the public sector. Because these are precisely a general application of the characteristics Foucault originally described as belonging to biopolitics: the understanding of the population as biological mass, leading to a regulation of this mass by means of statistical predictions, approximations, and informative actions. (Foucault 2003, 243) Rather than only recognizing an overabundance of high-speed semiotic flows, together with the stressful flexibilities of the entrepreneur-like cognitive worker immersed in immaterial production, one could thus recognize a certain bureaucracy which seems to be slowing things down. Think of the use of protocols, lists, evaluations and statistical forms to complete in the educational and health sectors, or indeed the (semi-privatized) public sector as a whole.

This so-called New Public Management has, perhaps most recently and notably in the Scandinavian countries created an increasingly malfunctioning and aggressive bureaucratic state, and to some degree a contemporary form of work place management which inserts sabotage-like caesuras in its own dissipated workings. As Paulo Virno writes in *Lessico postfordista* (2001): "The peculiar public character of the intellect indirectly manifests itself in the state through the hypertrophic growth of the administrative apparatus. The heart of the state is no longer the political parliamentary system but the administration."[3]

These two general remarks are not directed towards the theoretical attempts to account for the workings of cognitive capitalism, a post-Fordist mode of production, or a 24/7 paradigm, but are rather to serve as an assertion of a fragmented, multidimensonial aggregation of regimes of accumulation and governmental practices. That is to say, a unity "overdetermined in its principle," (Althusser 1969, 101) where a certain effect–whether it is the psychopathologies of capitalist subjects or precarious workers–can have different and at times conflicting causes. Thus, it does in no way exclude the possibility or even likely scenario that social subjects are under all of these three features of contemporary capitalism at once: employed, perhaps, in the sector of manufacture or in any case forming part of abstract labor, and–whether it is during work time or leisure time–consuming and producing value within the social realm, while having to deal with an increasingly deplete, slow, hostile, and rigid state apparatus in order to receive basic social functions like health care, education, and unemployment benefits when needed.

---

[3] This English version of Virno's text is a translation by Arianna Bove, published on Generation Online. http://www.generation-online.org/p/fpvirno10.htm.

What then are the possible means or strategies of resisting, refusing or countering such three-headed hydra? There is the suggestion of the social wage made by Corsani *et al*, which is also developed by Yann Moulier-Boutang in his book *Cognitive Capitalism* (2012). Such a demand could perhaps become part of some kind of minimum programme, such as the programme of the French Workers' party from 1880, co-written by Marx and French Socialist leader Jules Guesde, expressing the decision "to enter the elections with [certain] immediate demands" for ameliorations of labor conditions. However it would not principally oppose the real subsumption or extraction of surplus value from the social domain, as it would not oppose the pathological side of the capitalist system having its subjects consume, produce and circulate in an ongoing, 24/7-like incubator of value. What would then be the therapy for such pathologies?

## The care of the self and the subject of truth

Here, one could turn to Michel Foucault's work from his later lecture courses at Collège de France, where truth plays a pivotal role. Not, however as suitable it might seem, the 1978 lectures entitled *The Birth of Biopolitics* where Foucault defines the man of neoliberalism as an "entrepreneur of himself, being for himself his own capital, being for himself his own producer, being for himself the source of [his] earnings." (Foucault 2010, 226) And then, demonstrating how the market "is becoming what I will call a site of veridiction. The market must tell the truth (dire le vrai); it must tell the truth in relation to govern-mental practice." (ibid., 32) Here, the focus will rather be on the lectures developed in the subsequent years, until his death in 1984, centered on the relation between subject and truth, where subjects could constitute themselves in care of the self, consisting in acts and practices of truth.

From a certain political perspective, or in relation to the concept of ideology, truth as a constitutive practice of the individual subject might seem like an odd strategy, given how Marx in his second thesis on Feuerbach relates it instrumentally to class power and class struggle: "The question whether objective truth can be attributed to human thinking is not a question of theory but is a practical question. Man must prove the truth—i.e. the reality and power, the this-sidedness of his thinking in practice." (Marx 1969, 13) It may seem equally odd that Foucault, who had located the workings of power in its most capillary instances, as far as possible from its apparent centre, would elaborate a string of lectures on the subject as being constituted in a dramatic and central moment of truth, in the heroic act of *parrhēsia*, of speaking the truth even at the risk of ones own life. Indeed, Foucault almost seems embarrassed at one point, hesitating before taking a five minute break in a 1983 lecture "at this somewhat pathetic formulation of the relationship between truth-telling and the risk of death, but this is what we should now [after the break] start to disentangle." To which he adds: "I'm bothered." (Foucault 2010, 57) Nevertheless, this act of speaking the truth as an auto-constitutive practice on the part of the subject is what is being outlined in these lectures, albeit in a number of different ways and contexts.

In his lectures delivered in 1980, Foucault thus departs from his recently established concepts of biopolitics and liberal governmentality, and embarks on the project of truth and subjectivity that will concern him for the rest of his life. Here, he frames an analysis of the manifestations of truth in *Oedipus the King* along with the theme of Christian confession during the first centuries of our era, continuing and transforming this study in the next year's unpublished lectures. In *The Hermeneutics of the Subject* from 1982, [re]turning to the Greek antiquity and most notably in Plato's dialogue

*Alcibiades*, he sees the first thematization of *epimeleia heauto,* "the care of the self," the set of techniques and practices that ultimately will point to capacities of the subject to constitute and transform itself. And this is the point, through meticulous comparisons and analysis of a vast blend of antique sources that will multiply in the following years—Plato's *Apology* and *Alcibiades*, tragedies by Euripides and Sophocles, medical sources such as Galen, and texts by the Epicureans, Cynics, and Roman Stoics—at which the subject's constitutive relation to itself crystallizes in the notion of *parrhēsia*, which means "to speak candidly," "to speak everything," or "to speak freely," even if it implies the risk of ones life, whether it is in front of the other, in front of the assembly or in front of the tyrant. "To stand up, to rise, to take the word and speak the truth." (Foucault 2008, 148)

What is striking in these lectures are the constant reiterations, rehearsals, and redefinitions of the issue at stake. At the same time, this is period of a major theoretical displacement for Foucault, which he described as "passing from a theory of the subject, [on the basis of which one would try to bring out the different modes of being of subjectivity in their historicity] to the analysis of the modalities and techniques of the relation to self, or again to the history of this pragmatics of the subject in its different forms." (Foucault 2010, 142) This means, in the most schematic manner one can put it, that Foucault is passing from his previous elaborations of the subject as an effect of discursive exclusions, power relations and individualizing disciplinary measures, to the study of a subject which—to some degree, and still historically determined—is capable of constituting itself through a number of critical truth acts. What can this examination of truth practices as a means of subjectivation during Antiquity have to say about the subject of contemporary capitalism? What does it have to do with the exploitation or, if you will, psychopathologies suffered under the current material and immaterial regimes of accu-

mulation, and under state functions that display something
of an autistic inability to grapple with basic social needs?
As Foucault puts it: "It is already very clear in Plato. It is even
clearer in the post-Platonic tradition: the *ontos philosophein*
of Epicurus is the *kat'aletheian hugiainen* (that is treating,
curing according to the truth); and in the Stoics, starting
with Posidonius, the relationship between medicine and
philosophy—more precisely, the identification of philosophical practice as a sort of medical practice—is very clear."
(Foucault 2005, 97) The *philosophy as cure* is certainly a
well rehearsed trope, which in its most generalized form
amounts to little more than a cliché, presumably of no relevance to the given historical point of potential struggles.
Yet, some specific instances of "treating, curing according
to truth" might have something to say about the pathologies
at hand. In Foucault's close reading of classical sources and
its uses of the term *parrhēsia*, one could isolate a certain
moment, which might be related to a contemporary thematization of politics and political struggle. This happens to be
among the very first instances where *parrhēsia* is brought to
the foreground, and concerns the Epicurean circles and an
obscure community described as the *Therapeutae* group.

When Foucault elaborates the notion of the care of the self in
his reading of Plato's *Alcibiades*, it concerns Socrates' dialogue
with the reassured young man of noble birth who is eager to
enter public life and become adviser of the Athenians. This is
in a certain analogy with another figure under scrutiny (as in
the 1983 lectures), the main character of Euripides tragedy *Ion*.
Ion is a young man considered with the unknown circumstances of his birth: it is only if his mother is an Athenian that
he will be granted the privilege of *parrhēsia*, the exercise of
free speech to influence the assembly. Thus, Foucault states:
"I think *parrhēsia* is, in a way, a discourse spoken from above,
which comes from a source higher than the status of the
citizen, and which is different from the pure and simple ex-

ercise of power. It is a form of discourse which will exercise power in the framework of the city, but of course in non-tyrannical conditions, that is to say, allowing others the freedom to speak, the freedom of those who also wish to be in the front rank, and who may be in the front rank in this sort of agonistic game typical of political life in Greece and especially in Athens." (Foucault 2010, 104) This is in stark contrast not only with other characterizations of *parrhēsia* given in these same lectures,[4] *The Government of Self and Others*, but also with the Epicurean and Stoic practice of *parrhēsia* as first provided in *The Hermeneutics of the Subject*: *parrhēsia* is a technical term–a technique which lets the master work with honesty and without formal rules for his speech on the transformation of his disciple. And while the latter might be a discourse spoken from above, in the sense that it is the master who addresses his disciple, it is, on the other hand, a discourse produced within a certain community, far from the *parrhēsia* at the Assembly, exercised by the citizen belonging to the "front rank" over the rabble, the, if you will, *hoi polloi*. Against these young, affluent men, Foucault raises the example of the Epicurean groups, and in particular one that Philo of Alexandria describes the *Therapeutae*, a community striving to treat the soul as a doctor treats the body; whose social basis in no way seems to have been made up of aristocrats or citizens with privileges.

----

[4] See, for instance, the description of Galen's conception of the care of the self, where one needs an other to tell him the truth: "You recall that Galen does not present the person to whom we must resort as a technician; he is not presented as a technician of the medicine of the body or as a technician of the medicine of souls, neither as a doctor nor as a philosopher. According to Galen's text we should appeal to a man who has reached a certain age, has a sufficiently good reputation, and who possesses, in addition, a certain quality. This quality was *parrhēsia*, free-spokenness. A man of a certain age, who has a good reputation, and who possesses *parrhēsia* are the three necessary and sufficient criteria for the person we need for us to have a relationship to self." (Foucault 2010, 44)

[T]he Therapeutae were a group of people who had retired to the surroundings of Alexandria, not into the desert, as will be the practice of Christian hermits and anchorites later, but in kinds of small suburban gardens in which each lived in his cell or room, with some communal areas. This community of *Therapeutae* had three axes and three dimensions. On the one hand, there are very pronounced cultic or religious practices: praying twice a day, weekly gatherings at which people are placed according to age with each having to adopt the appropriate demeanor [... * ] . On the other hand, there is an equally marked stress on intellectual, theoretical work, on the work of knowledge (savoir). On the side of the care of the self it is said from the start that the *Therapeutae* have withdrawn to their spot in order to cure illness caused by "pleasures, desires, sorrows, fears, greed, stupidity, injustice and the countless multitude of passions.*" These then are the *Therapeutae* who come to cure themselves. Second, another reference: what they seek above all is *egkrateia* (mastery of the self by the self), which they consider to be the basis and foundation of all the other virtues. Finally, and here the text is very important for its vocabulary, on every seventh day, when they have their gathering, so, just once a week, they add care of the body to their everyday activity of the *epimeleia tes psukhes* [care of the soul]. (Foucault 2005, 116-117)

In their practice of truth speech or *parrhēsia* as an art to cure, educate, and transform a subject, Foucault emphasizes that the majority of this kind of groups would not accept any distinction between rich and poor, between the ones of noble birth and the ones of obscure backgrounds, or between the ones who exercise political power and the ones leading lives in the shadows. Not even the opposition between free men and slaves were accepted, at least not theoretically: "Consequently, since there is no difference of status, we can say that all individuals are in general terms 'competent': able to practice themselves, able to carry out this practice of the self." (ibid., 118)

From here, Foucault moves on to (or back and forth between) a large number of other Antique texts. But if we arrest the train of thought at this point, it is because of the interestingly collective–if also rather sect-like–characterization of the care of the self as practiced by the *Therapeutae*. And can we not, in light of Foucault's subsequent assertion of "this idea that the true life is an *other* life" (Foucault 2011, 340; my italics), see a certain affinity to a contemporary strain of political thought? The insistence of each and everyone's competence and capability, the refusal of distinguishing between the abilities of rich and poor to lead a virtuous life, along the withdrawal to a community of studying and writing? At least as a matter of hypothesis, one could perhaps put this inherently political care of the soul by the *Therapeutae* in analogy with certain works of Jacques Rancière. For Rancière, as expressed in Disagreement, any subjectivation is a disidentification grounded in an assertion of equality: "A political subject is not a group that 'becomes aware' of itself, finds its voice, imposes its weight on society. It is an operator that connects and disconnects different areas, regions, identities, functions, and capacities existing in the configuration of a given experience." (Rancière 1999, 40) Without wishing to make certain similar features into a common argument, one can easily spot them: for Rancière, "equality is simply the equality of anyone with anyone else: in other words, in the final analysis, the absence of *arkhe*, the sheer contingency of any social order." (ibid., 15-16) While Foucault, however, remains within an epistemological terrain defining a "theoretico-practical position on the non-necessity of power as a principle of understanding of knowledge itself" not as anarchy but as "a sort of anarcheology." (Foucault 2012, 77)

In his *La nuit des prolétaires*, Rancière decided to turn to the French workers' archive of the 1830s and 1840s, in order to escape any prevalent essentialist and theoretically dogmatic notion of "the worker." This resulted in the discovery of workers' nocturnal poetry sessions and self-taught projects, along with the view of politics as the act of reconfiguring the distribution and the division of the sensible: the act of opposing and reshaping the dividing lines of work/sleep, speech/noise, and labor/art, etc. Perhaps this archivally obsessed project of unearthing a radical and collective process of subject formation of the past bears some resemblance to Foucault's fascination regarding the Epicurean and Stoic sects of the first two centuries of our era.[5] One might object that the two theoretico-historical accounts are of completely different nature, or that Rancière's *Nights of Labor* operates on a wholly different level of concreteness. A curious fact in this context is that Foucault seemed to have similar plans to such a study already in 1973. In the newly born newspaper *Libération*, he did an interview with a discarded worker from the Renault factory, anonymously named "José".

---

[5] If the Epicureans and Stoics' different practices of truth-speech form the starting point for Foucault's tracking of the concept of *parrhēsia*, the very last instance of *parrhēsia* which he lays out in the final lectures of 1984 could serve as some kind of counter-point: the cynic Diogenes. Following the notion of *parrhēsia* as it is developped through these three years of lectures from 1982 to 1984 it is almost as if one could see a movement of increasing solitude or isolation on the part of the parrhēsiast. When the notion is first elabaroted, the parrhēsiast, both according to Philodemus, Epicurus, and Seneca and others, is the master guiding or leading the soul of his disciple towards something like autonomy in a collective endeavor. Then Foucault passes to the *écriture de soi*, through the political *parrhēsia* of 1983—Pericles speaking in front of the assembly or as Plato as the counselor to the tyrant of Sicily—finally arriving in the 1984 lectures on the cynics, and Diogenes, the mad dog, using his own life as example, in an instant where we have "*parrhēsia* as life". This position almost amounts to an ontological figure of resistance, and is probably much closer to something like Antonio Negri's poor militant than Rancière's notion of politics: "The poor person is then not someone constituted by pain, but is inreality the biopolitical subject. He is not an existential trembling(or a painful dialectical differentiation): he is the naked eternity of the power of being." (Negri 2004194) See also: Katja Diefenbach. "Living Labour, Form-Giving Fire. The Post-Workerist Reading of Marx and the Concept of Biopolitical Labour," *in* Ed. Gal Kirn *Post-Fordism and its Discontents*, 2010, 86.

Here Foucault states that: "The intellectual is useful for assembling ideas, but his knowledge is only partial in relation to the workers' knowledge" (1994/2001, 1289), before suggesting a comprehensive collective research project, precisely about the "whole tradition of workers' struggles of the 19th century, little known and poorly recounted." As is evident, nothing became of the project and Foucault himself never took up any of its parts; but it may serve to illustrate that Foucault was considering collective forms of self-organization, long before his 1980s work on subjects and their auto-transformative techniques of the self.

## Rather than a passage, the politics of a tunnel

What, then, are the possible implications of these practices of truth in a contemporary political perspective? After all, the communitarian therapeutic described above might not be so far detached from the earlier quotation of Marx's second thesis on Feuerbach.[6] Despite the fact that the very term seems

........................................................................................

[6] In a recent paper called "Le sujet productif," Pierre Macherey points out the importance of Marx's *Capital* (rather than the young Marx) for Foucault's analysis of power in its positive mechanisms: "dans une conférence donnée à Bahia en 1981, publiée sous le titre imagé "Les mailles du pouvoir" (...), Foucault confirme explicitement ce rapprochement. Il y déclare : « Comment pourrions-nous essayer d'analyser le pouvoir dans ses mécanismes positifs ? Il me semble que nous pouvons trouver, dans un certain nombre de textes, les éléments fondamentaux pour une analyse de ce type. Nous pouvons les trouver peut-être chez Bentham, un philosophe anglais de la fin du XVIIIe siècle et du début du XIXe siècle, qui, au fond, a été le grand théoricien du pouvoir bourgeois, et nous pouvons évidemment le trouver aussi chez Marx, essentiellement dans le livre II du Capital. C'est là je pense que nous pourrons trouver quelques éléments dont je me servirai pour l'analyse du pouvoir dans ses mécanismes positifs. » (DE IV, p. 186)". Pierre Macherey, "Le sujet productif," available online: http://philolarge. hypotheses.org/1245#more-124 [last accessed May 2014].

to play in completely different registers, it could perhaps be useful to establish the links between the practice of truth in Epicurean communities and the process in which "[m]an must prove the truth—i.e. the reality and power, the this-sidedness of his thinking in practice." And without entering the debate itself, one could note that it was in the immediate continuation of this idea that Rancière framed his then still Marxian critique of Althusser in *Althusser's Lesson* (2011). Because it is by rereading the third thesis on Feuerbach that Rancière reproaches Althusser for ascribing the young Marx's argument that "circumstances are changed by men" (rather than the party) to Feuerbach—a thesis which ends with a sentence very fitting in this context: "The coincidence of the changing of circumstances and of human activity or self-changing can be conceived and rationally understood only as revolutionary practice." (Marx 1969, 13)

But how does this relate to the context of cognitive capitalism? Are there any strategic potentials in the care of the self to be realized under a new division of labor where "the conditions of the process of social life itself have come under the control of the general intellect and been transformed in accordance with it?" (Marx 1973, 706) As a matter of fact, even the concept of the self has been done away with in a contemporary conjunction of neuroscience and philosophy. To popularize his critique of the notion of the self, Thomas Metzinger developed the metaphor of the *Ego Tunnel*: "Modern neuroscience has demonstrated that the content of our conscious experience is not only an internal construct but also an extremely selective way of representing information. [...] Therefore, the ongoing process of conscious experience is not so much an image of reality as a tunnel *through* reality." (Metzinger 2009, 6) But as some critics have noted, "Metzinger is not discrediting the very notion of a "self", so much as he is describing what a "self" actually *is*." (Shaviro 2011) The merit of the tunnel, then, is its non-anthropocentric features: taken as a metaphor not only for the self but also for collective techniques of the self as outlined by Foucault in 1982, the inner landscape of the tunnel must be shaped not by an individual brain and nervous system, but rather by a collective. The care of the self as expressed in a set of truth acts, and even shaping of the formal conditions for such acts, has to transform into the collective shaping of a communist set of practises, cares, and acts of truth as the cures for our most acute pathologies. That is to say, one would have to withdraw together with others and form separate communities, whether it is in small suburban gardens like the *Therapeutae or* in other places, in order to embark on the collective care of the self and others that amounts to the construction of a communist tunnel.

And while there seems to be no exit from a tunnel which constitutes our immediate and ultimate experience of the world, the only strategy which remains is the one of inverting the it. Creating a communist tunnel and–in a peculiar spatial logic–inverting it: like a three-dimensional Mobius strip, merging its interior of a classless community with that which is outside.

Aglietta, Michel, 1997. *Régulation et Crises du Capitalisme.* (2nd edition). Paris: Editions Odile Jacob.

Althusser, Louis, 1969. "Contradiction and Overdetermination," trans. Ben Brewster, in *For Marx*. London: Penguin Books.

Berardi, Franco, 2009. *The Soul at Work*. Trans. Francesca Cadel & Giuseppina Mecchia. Los Angeles: Semiotext(e).

Lazzarato, Maurizio, et al (eds.), 2001. "Le Capitalisme Cognitif Comme Sortie de la Crise du Capitalisme Industriel," in *I.SY.S. – MATISSE UMR CNRS Université Paris 1 n° 8595*. Available online: http://www.utc.fr/oi2/Textes_support_interventions/Paulr%E9%20et %20alii%20-%20Le%20capitalisme%20cognitif%20comme%20sortie %20de%20la%20crise%20du%20capitalisme%20industriel-%20CAP- ITALC.PDF [last accessed April 2014].

Crary, Jonathan, 2013. *24/7 Late Capitalism and the Ends of Sleep.* London: Verso.

Diefenbach, Katja, 2010. "Living Labour, Form-Giving Fire. The Post-Workerist Reading of Marx and the Concept of Biopolitical Labour," in *Post-Fordism and its Discontents*. Amsterdam: Jan van Eyck.

Foucault, Michel, 2012. *Du Gouvernement des Vivants: Cours au Collège de France, 1979-1980*. Paris: Gallimard/Seuil.

Foucault, Michel, 2011. *The Courage of the Truth: Lectures at the Collège de France, 1983–1984*. Trans. Graham Burchell. Hampshire: Palgrave/Macmillan.

Foucault, Michel, 2010. *The Government of Self and Others: Lectures at the Collège de France, 1982–1983*. Trans. Graham Burchell. Hampshire: Palgrave/Macmillan.

Foucault, Michel, 2008. *Le gouvernemént de soi et des autre: Cours au Collège de France, 1982-1983*. Paris: Gallimard/Seuil.

Foucault, Michel, 2005. *The Hermeneutics of the Subject: Lectures at the Collège de France, 1981–1982*. Trans. Graham Burchell. Hampshire: Palgrave/Macmillan.

Foucault, Michel, 1995/2001. "Pour un Chronique de la Mémoire Ouvrière," in *Dits et écrits* I, no. 117, p. 1267.

Foucault, Michel, 1994/2001. "L'intellectuel sert à rassembler les idées mais son savoir est partiel par rapport au savoir ouvrier", *Dits et écrits* I, no. 123, s. 1289

Foucault, Michel, 2010. *The Birth of Biopolitics: Lectures at the Collège de France, 1978–1979*, trans. Graham Burchell. New York: Picador.

Foucault, Michel, 2003. *Society Must Be Defended*, trans. David Macey. London: Penguin/Allen Lane.

Hansen, Morten Balle, "New Public Management in Danish and Swedish state and in Administration Patterns of Adoption." Available online: http://soc.kuleuven.be/io/egpa/org/2010Toul/Papers/Morten_Balle_Hansen_EGPA%202010.pdf [last accessed April 2014]

Harvey, David, 2003. *The New Imperialism*. Oxford: Oxford University Press.

Harvey, David, 2012. *Rebel Cities*. London: Verso.

Moulier Boutang, Yann, 2011. *Cognitive Capitalism*. Malden: Polity Press.

Macherey, Pierre, 2012. "Le sujet productif." Available online: http://philolarge.hypotheses.org/1245#more-1245. [last accessed April 2014]

Marx, Karl, 1976. *Capital, Vol. 1*. Trans. Ben Fowkes,1990. London: Penguin Classics.

Marx, Karl, 1973. *Grundrisse*. Trans. Martin Nicolaus. London: Penguin.

Marx, Karl, 1969. "Theses on Feuerbach," in *Marx/Engels Selected Works, Volume One*. Moscow: Progress Publishers, pp. 13-15.

Marx, Karl and Guesde, Jules. "The Programme of the Parti Ouvrier." Available online: http://marxists.org/archive/marx/works/1880/05/parti-ouvrier.htm [last accessed April 2014], made from the French original in: Jules Guesde, Textes Choisis, 1867-1882, Editions sociales, 1959, pp.117-9

Metzinger, Thomas, 2009. *The Ego Tunnel*. New York: Basic Books.

Rancière, Jacques, 1999. *Disagreement*. Trans. Julie Rose. Minneapolis: University of Minnesota Press.

Rancière, Jacques, 1981. *La nuit des prolétaires*. Paris: Fayard.

Shaviro, Steven, 2011. "Harman on Metzinger.", Available online: http://www.shaviro.com/Blog/?p=1014 [last accessed April 2014]

Negri, Antonio, 2004. *Time for Revolution*. New York: Continuum.

Vercellone, C., Historical Materialism 15 (2007), pp. 13-36

SECTION 2

# The Psychopathologies of Cognitive Capitalism and its Responses

# Mental Quilombos in the Production of Value: Flights and Counter-forms of Mania Under Cognitive Capitalism in a Postcolonial World.

## Does Exit Triumph Over Voice in Producing Necessarily Psychosis?

Flight, exodus, secession have represented alternative tactics of dependent labor refusing domination as well as exploitation to voice solutions in antagonism, what Hirschman had called "exit solutions" (Hirschman 1970). The constitution of a revolutionary subject since Renaissance has shown that melancholia appears each time after various types of hopes of a radical transformation Qf society have been defeated. Bipolarity of the mood is frequent and produces a mix of alternative and successive hysterical political collective feelings of, on the one hand, superpower, and on the other, a floating depression.

Under the regime of cognitive capitalism, that is increasingly investing, involving and exploiting all the brain, how is this old dialectic of the subject renewed? In order to understand this very peculiar form of pathology of the mind, we propose to draw a parallel between the historical experience of *Quilombos* of the slaves[1], a typically postcolonial revisit of the fight between the master and the slave, and the Web utilizing the declaration of Independence of James Barlow to make the argument. What are the conditions for a mental *Quilombo* that would create a sustainable TAZ [Temporary Autonomous Zones, as delineated by Hakim Bey]?

I shall explore the following points. In the first part, I will examine how *Melancholia* has replaced the antic and medieval *Acedia* and what Gordian Knot has woven a thread between Melanchton and Dürer on the one hand, and Benjamin and Althusser, on the other. In the second part we take the example of a true historical secession–after that of the Roman plebs–when the runaway slaves in Brazil create a real utopia and revivify the old commons that Enclosures had just destroyed in Europe. Then I will ask what about the future of the new Commons through a short examination of the contemporary forms of Quilombos. The third part is dedicated to some of the main features of trade in the new primitive accumulation of third capitalism: raiders, privateers, pirates. In the fourth part and conclusion, we will isolate what characterizes the succinct conditions of cognitive capitalism: the capture of intangibles hard to codify, to enlighten what are the conditions of a sustainable Quilombo of the Mind.

........................................................................................................

[1] For further reading on this point see my book from 1998, *From slavery to wage labour* (PUF, Paris), which has been released in English by Brill, Netherlands. In a second moment we try to characterize the historical experience of the Brazilian *quilombos* and the old Commons destroyed in the late XVII-XVIII by the enclosures.

# 1. The moment *Melancholia* and politics

The defeat of the promises of Humanism can be read in Italian painting when one places side by side *The resurrection of Christ* by Piero della Francesca of the San Sepolcro[2] (1463-1465) and *The Lamentation Over the Dead Christ* (1480) by Andrea Mantegna. "Renaissance" was not used, as a term then and was only invented much later, by the French historian Jules Michelet. Representational models depict ethical relations: on one hand the hope of an evangelist Church and of a faith in Christ are depicted in Greek and Latin standards of the body and on the other a suffering Gothic model in which the body seems smashed down. Piero della Francesca died in 1492, triple year of the discovery of the New World, of the Reconquista (fall of Granada) and of the expulsion of the Jews from Spain. Less than fifteen years after these events, three seminal books for the reshaping of subjectivity in modern politics were released: *The Prince* by Machiavelli (1513), *In Praise of Foolishness* by Erasmus (1511) and *Utopia* by Thomas More (1516). Albert Dürer's famous *The Angle of Melancholia* was engraved in 1514. Erwin Panofsky's interpretation of this masterpiece as a self portrait of the artist (Panofsky and Klibansky 1964) also fits relatively well within this conjuncture.

---

[2] The most beautiful painting in the world according to Aldous Huxley. Albert Camus writes in *Noces* (1938), "C'est sur ce balancement qu'il faudrait s'arrêter, singulier instant où la spiritualité répudie la morale, où le bonheur naît de l'absence d'espoir, où l'esprit trouve sa raison dans le corps. S'il est vrai que toute vérité porte en elle son amertume, il est aussi vrai que toute négation contient une floraison de 'oui.' Et ce chant d'amour sans espoir qui naît de la contemplation peut aussi figurer la plus efficace des règles d'action: au sortir du tombeau, le Christ ressuscitant de Piero della Francesca n'a pas un regard d'homme. Rien d'heureux n'est peint sur son visage – mais seulement une grandeur farouche et sans âme, que je ne puis m'empêcher de prendre pour une résolution à vivre. Car le sage comme l'idiot exprime peu."

What is astonishing in the angel's eyes is the absolute acuteness of the look mixed with something like disappointment and/or despair. Thomas More concludes his chapter "Of the Wars and the Religion of the Utopians" in his *Utopia* with the following statement that Machiavelli could have also signed: "I may rather wish for than hope after." Hereafter, Melancholia will become a positive affect of modernity and the psychopathology per excellence of politics. Melancholia expresses clearly a distance, even secession from the power it inherited from the legacy of another important disposition of the mind in Antiquity and medieval Christianity, *acedia.* In order to unpack this term I hope the reader will not mind a small detour.

In Q. 35 in the Second Part of his *Summa Theologica*, Thomas Aquinas identifies *Acedia* with "the sorrow of the world" (*Weltschmerz*) that "worketh death" and contrasts it with that sorrow "according to God" described by St. Paul in 2 Cor. 7:10. *Acedia* is an affect that regards not problems of the subject with himself, or with instances of the self–unconscious and conscious for example–but problems with the entire world. In this respect it is both a matter of politics and something distinct from neurosis, verging on what Freud referred to as the characteristics of psychosis, that are beyond that which can be cured by analysis.

For Aquinas, *Acedia* is "sorrow about spiritual good in as much as it is a Divine good" (Aquinas 1557). It becomes a mortal sin when reason consents to man's "flight" (fuga) from the Divine good, "on account of the flesh utterly prevailing over the spirit." *Acedia* is essentially a flight from the world that eventually leads to not caring even that one does not care. It abolishes desire and hope. The ultimate expression of this is a despair that ends in suicide. *Acedia* is quite near sloth, laziness and a refusal to work or participate in any activity. In a way it is the utmost sin, since it despairs of the whole creation and hence of God. The modern period that starts with what we call the Renaissance has totally excised the negative connotation conferred upon the antique and medieval meaning of acedia, turning it instead into a percept close to madness but with a positive tonality. This movement affects not only the humanists of the early XVI° century. Pascal on the contrary, stands for a devaluation of all forms of activities– entertainment–that diverts man from confrontation of his nothingness compared to the infinity of God.

If melancholia does not produce the same kind of exit attitude that Acedia does–intelligence seems at its highest peak–it nevertheless conveys an impression of powerlessness in action. All the Machiavellian *virtù* cannot overtake unpredictable *fortuna*. Phillip Melanchthon on the Protestant side, along with Thomas More and Erasmus had dreamt of reconciliation between different forms of Christianity[3]. The three were impotent to achieve that goal and soon war erupted in Europe, which would last for more than a century. Bipolarity of power and authority, (the Prince or the Emperor and the Summum Pontifex or the Pope) then later represented as either Church or Science and Humanities, reappears as the opposition between the authority invested in the principle of the word, representation or painting and political power. The original excitement that believes in the power of words gives way to a more lucid allowance of the impotence of the clerks.

........................................................................................................................

[3] Philipp Melanchthon who had written great part of the Augsbourg Confession (1530) was soon accused of weakness, indecision and melancholia (black tempered). The moment was the apex of the financial crisis of the Roman Catholic Church after the failure of the last of the kind of derivative products (trade in Relics/traffic in Indulgences and Purgatory) trying to convert in cash (works) the Christian faith.

*The Angel of Melancholia* of Albert Dürer (1514)

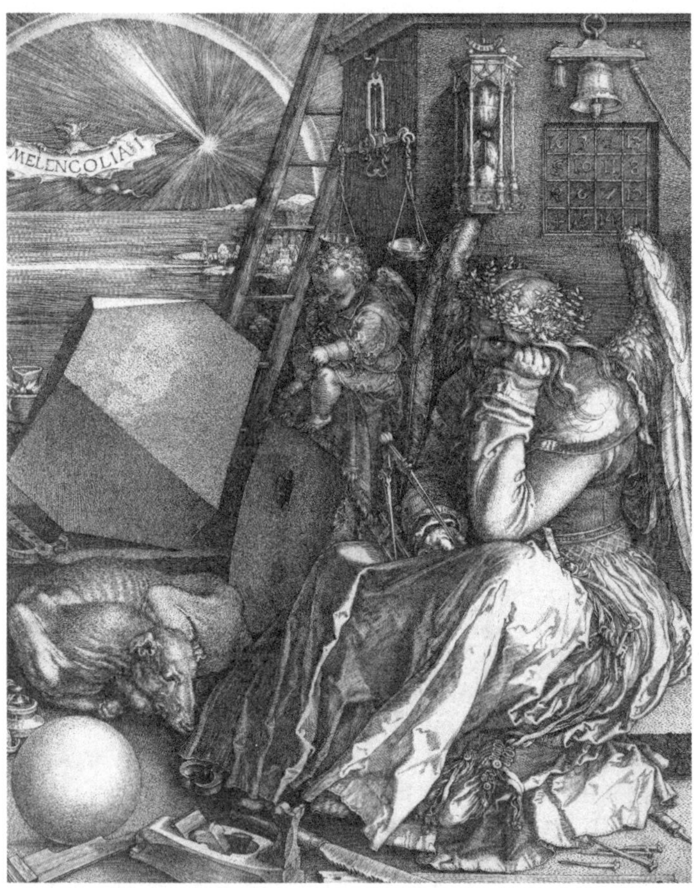


Melancholia's bipolarity fits exactly the description of maniacal depression. Unlike Acedia, the fault does not fall any more to the person there who is inhabited by a devilish contempt of the world, but to history itself of missed opportunity (to kairos).

*Acedia* by Hieronymus Wierix (1553–1619)

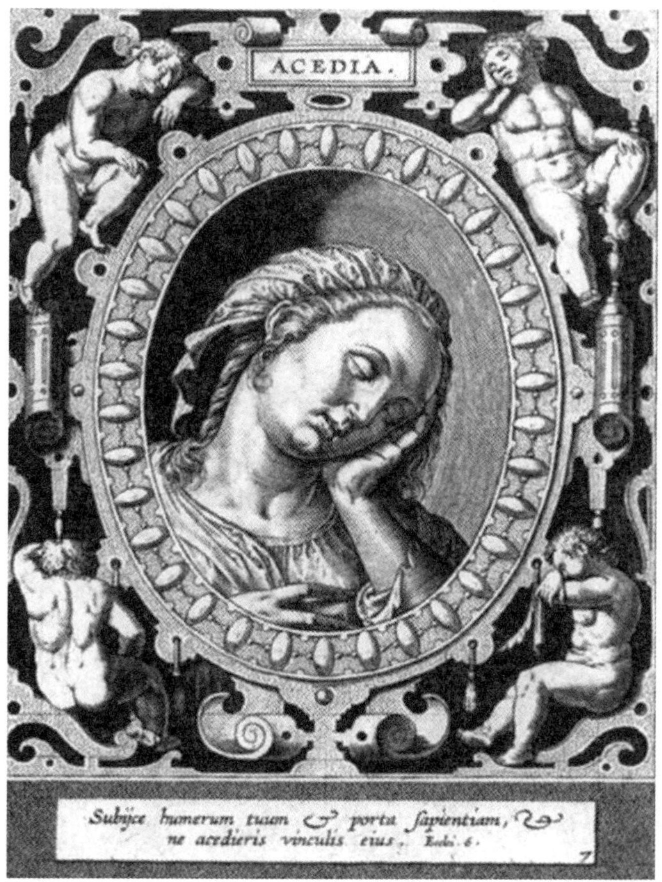

# 2. Romantic melancholia after the defeat of 1848.

Before coming to our digital epoch of "historical disease" (Nietzsche 1874) let us examine the romantic melancholia that fed subjectivity after the defeat of the Great Revolution and the 1848 upheaval in Europe. In *The Contemplations* (Third Book, 1856) Victor Hugo writes about Melancholia. This poem expands a sharp criticism of industrial labor but what gives it its taints of Melancholia is an acute feeling of powerlessness in front of the triumph of capitalism and the great industry.


Victor Hugo asks:

> Où vont tous ces enfants dont pas un seul ne rit ?
> Ces doux êtres pensifs que la fièvre maigrit ?
> Ces filles de huit ans qu'on voit cheminer seules ?
> Ils s'en vont travailler quinze heures sous des meules ;
> Ils vont, de l'aube au soir, faire éternellement
> Dans la même prison le même mouvement.
> Accroupis sous les dents d'une machine sombre
> Monstre hideux qui mâche on ne sait quoi dans l'ombre,
> Innocents dans un bagne, anges dans un enfer,
> Ils travaillent. Tout est d'airain, tout est de fer.
> Jamais on ne s'arrête et jamais on ne joue.

> (....)

> Travail mauvais qui prend l'âge tendre en sa serre,
> Qui produit la richesse en créant la misère,
> Qui se sert d'un enfant ainsi que d'un outil !
> Progrès dont on demande : « Où va-t-il ? Que veut-il ? »
> Qui brise la jeunesse en fleur ! Qui donne, en somme,

Une âme à la machine et la retire à l'homme !
Que ce travail, haï des mères, soit maudit !
Maudit comme le vice où l'on s'abâtardit,
Maudit comme l'opprobre et comme le blasphème !
Dieu ! Qu'il soit maudit au nom du travail même,
Au nom du vrai travail, sain, fécond, généreux,
Qui fait le peuple libre et qui rend l'homme heureux ![4]

---

4    Where do these children go for whom nobody laughs?
These sweet, pensive beings wasted away by fever?
These eight year-old girls you see walking alone?
They go to work – fifteen hours in the mill;
They go from dawn to dusk, eternally repeating
The same motions in the same prison.
Stooped beneath the teech of a somber machine,
A hideous monster that chews who-knows-what in the shadows,
Innocents on the chain gang, angels in some hell,
They work. All is bronze, all is iron.
Never do they stop and never do they play.

(...)

Evil work that takes tender youth in its grasp,
That produces wealth by creating misery,
That uses a child like one more tool!
Progress of which we ask: "Where are you going? What do you want?"
That breaks youth in bloom! that gives, in sum,
A soul to a machine and yanks it from a man!
That this work, hated by mothers, be cursed!
Cursed as a degenerative vice!
Cursed as damnable, cursed as blasphemy!
O God! be it cursed even in the name of work,
In the name of true work, healthy, fecund, generous,
That makes the people free and makes man happy!

Hetzel's illustration of *Melancholia* by Victor Hugo (1880)

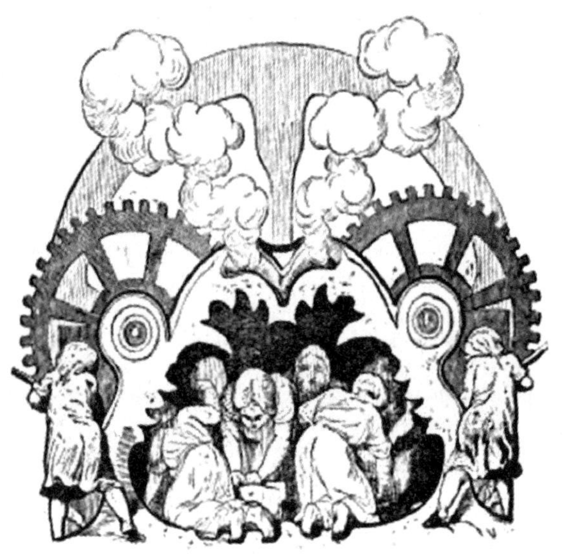

In this illustration by Pierre-Jules Hetzel it is important to
notice the eyes and mouth formed in the shape of gears in
a terrifying monstrous all consuming machine as well as
clouds of smoke which on one hand produce connotations
of a fire eating dragon but on the other the surface gyri and
sulces of the two hemispheres of the brain.

## 3. The modern melancholia

Now we come to the modern melancholia dominated by the defeat of revolutionary communist subjectivity. Walther Benjamin and Louis Althusser represent both the failure of the project of modernity and the Bolshevik revolution. The suicide of Walter Benjamin in 1939 occurring simultaneously with the unthinkable alliance between Hitler and Stalin broke the back of any hope for victory of leftist factions exemplified in the Spanish Revolution but also in Europe. Another corner stone is the 1956 Hungarian Revolution that provided an opportunity to many communist activists, to depart without noise from their party. Louis Althusser's psychopathic murder of his wife nine years before the final double falling down of the Berlin Wall and two years later the end of the USSR plus the bloody repression of the Chinese Spring, anticipated the end of left wing ideology as a global force. While André Gorz had said "bye bye to the Proletariat" Althusser had made a clamorous declaration at Terni and Venice in 1978 about Marxism being just bullshit and for the first time in his life adopted a public position against the French Communist Party (Althusser 1978). After the failure of the "cultural revolution" in China (1966-1976) and the absorption of the 1968 events, the manic depression of Althusser was a symbol far more spectacular of the impossibility to create a new subjectivity. Further investigation of Althusser's biography, which he had vetoed for so long, soon revealed the cyclical character of his maniacal psychosis and its correspondence with the up and down of the political cycle. Modern negativity therefore corresponded to a process of reification beyond the figure of the grand bourgeoisie or marginal aristocrat but characterized a pathology of revolutionaries as well.

Depression has sprung from the failure of the hope of transformation of humanity, which was a throw off of the true answer to Zarathoustra's new gospel. That is to say that the end of Man as a logical conclusion of the death of God; man's secularity had brought him to a form of atheism in which as superman he or she became totally responsible for his actions with the full weight that that responsibility entailed. If we turn back to our present, which means from 1968 up today, we see the emergence of two conditions which promote a new hope of transformation. First the romantic hope of liberation from domination and not any more of exploitation. Communism had defined as a precondition of the new transformation a liberation that embraced quite different and sometimes opposite trends like liberation from colonialism and imperialism. Secondly the struggles of minorities against discrimination of race, gender, cast.[5] During the 1960s, 1970s and 1980s these movements reached an apex. But their capacity to disrupt capitalist order was progressively blurred by the entrance by a long term stagnation of capitalism its so called the B phase of a Kondratiev cycle—precariousness and underemployment. Instead of reunifying the working class something quite the opposite occurred; a splintering and segmentation of it occurred resulting in a phase of self-reflexive inquiry into questions concerning what defined work and the working class began popping up. That is to say that ognitive capitalism adds a new difference between the creative classes beyond their material differences instead substituting, it, as Bernard Stiegler has pointed out, with differences in access to knowledge (Stiegler 2004).[6]

---

[5] For further information on this subject please see Frantz Fanon's Essays, *Toward the African Revolution: Political Essays* (1969), *The Wretched of the Earth* (1961) and Che Guevara's *Radical Writings on Guerrilla Warfare, Politics and Revolution.*

[6] See B. Stiegler's, "Proletarisation: La prolétarisation est, d'une manière générale, ce qui consiste à priver un sujet (producteur, consommateur, concepteur) de ses savoirs (savoir-faire, savoir-vivre, savoir concevoir et théoriser)" available online: http://arsindustrialis.org/prolétarisation [last accessed April 2014].

## 4. Post modern melancholia?

From 1985 to the present day we have entered a new era for subjectivity. The fast expansion of information and communication technologies has stimulated the constituency of a *homo numericus* within cognitive capitalism very different then the New Man promised by the Maoist Cultural Revolution. This great transformation of economic value, organization of work and of capitalism as a global and pervasive and intrusive system (Boutang 2012) was not only an "objective transformation" of the economic infrastructure, but also a mutation of work:  without which such transformation would not have been possible. The entrenchment between private appropriation of surplus value of activity in general as a social and global result (and not only of waged work) and free access platforms, what can be called "communism of capital," has fostered rational and utopian hope for liberation of man through collective intelligence, contributory economy, free software, peer to peer economy, wiki platforms, crowdfunding for social entrepreneurship etc. Among researchers, political activists, 'geeks' and hactivists in the decade between 2003 and 2013, a vivid and somewhat fierce debate began between optimistic versus pessimistic analysis. I must confess that by psychological disposition of mind, I have never been melancholic or Saturnian. Therefore I was soon classified as an apologist of cognitive capitalism verging dangerously to indulgence towards a new kind of Saint-Simonism, what Matteo Pasquinelli has criticized as the "Californian digitalism" (Pasquinelli 2008) who was supporting diabolic Gaffa [Google, Amazon, Facebook and Apple] against the old material industrial capitalism. Beside psychological considerations, standing for a deliberate optimism of the reason, and not of the will, I persist and sign on for political reasons. For example, towards a Marxist and the operaist tradition, to which I owe a great part of my education, I retain only useful passions that increase the *conatus* and joyful passions.

The great melancholy of Dürer as well as its modern form
of maniac depressive psychosis do not provide any help
for a reconstruction of a revolutionary subject, on the contrary, it reveals quite accurately disappointment and disil-
lusionment of a given period of history. No doubt that
many hopes of transformation of society and flight of capitalism were lured, to quote Stefan Sweig, to its *Confusion
of Feelings* (1927), "Being itself beauty, youth has no
need of transfiguration. In the superabundance of its vital
forces, it is allured by the tragic and in its inexperience, is
prone to accept the embraces of melancholy." The French
translation of German is still more evocative, reading,
"The Youth [...] is inclined to be allowed to be sucked the
lifeblood out of by the melancholy."

Should we describe the golden age of the web and the
spell that has followed the discovery of the creative power
of the multitudes and the raising contributory economy of
Wikipedia as the hypo maniac phase of hacktivism and
expect the B phase of depression? A sort of Kondratiev of
the mind? I am not sure. I suspect more that the tale of
psychopathology or psychosis to be a self-fulfilling
prophecy. The more you indulge in melancholy the more
you become melancholic, and with the assistance of medical institutions today you soon will finish a kind of psychotic, mysteriously linked to the low part of the curve of
political mood. To this dominant story in the Western
mind of Revolution, I would oppose another story or tale
of a sort of pharmacon (drug, remedy and poison): the
flight or exodus in the *quilombos* during the first capitalism (slavish mercantilism) and the lesson that can be
drawn for our present disease.

## 5. Quilombos in the History and Old Commons

*Utopia* was but a book and Thomas More finished beheaded in 1535 (canonized four hundred years after by the Roman Catholic Church as saint for political leaders). Attempts of concrete utopias as "the aspiration to a society of justice" (A. Colombo) ended in medieval and modern Europa in the burning fire for witches and those found guilty of various heresies. These dismal events were another additional source of melancholia together with the three aborted revolutions (the English, the French and the Russian ones).

However, outside European tradition, we encounter in the New World an historical tradition that has transformed flight and exit into truly liberated territories: *quilombos* (Brazil) or *palenques*, in Spanish Latin America. Most of the inhabitants of *quilombos* (called *quilombolados*) were runaway African slaves. Sometimes these escaped African slaves have been sheltered themselves by other minorities of marginalized descent such as Portuguese, Jews and Amerindians. The *Quilombo dos Palmares* was a self-sustaining republic of escaped slaves from the Portuguese settlements in Brazil, "a region perhaps the size of Portugal in the hinterland of Bahia" (Braudel 1984, 390). More than 2,100 *quilombos* were identified under colonial Brazil. *Exit* was the reaction of slaves to their capture and transportation from Africa, as well as a reaction to the exploitation in the plantations. In fact it was also a true agrarian revolution because by so doing, run away slaves occupied the humid forest (mata) and the fertile land growing sugar cane. Open and claimed secessions were not the only forms of these liberated zones. Less studied and more successful in the long run were the urban *quilombos* inside Recife that have created the model of informal employment and the *favelas*. Although *quilombos* had been receding during the 19th century with the increase of European immigration, it created a real means through which individuals gained access to land, through what was called *usucapio* (capture of property by continuous *usus* and *fructus*).

So succesful were these ventures that Lula's second government introduced a 'right to reparation' for the descendants of *quilombolados* that had been expelled by landlords of European small colons of the XIX and XX centuries who become successful farmers. These territories were innovative: they exchanged with the rest of Brazil. Beekeeping provided the first food, soon becoming part of more elaborated foods which were sold outside of the *quilombos* to get access to powder, arms even if little metallurgy was practised (Dirceu 2011). These former slaves from Benin were excellent at extracting and purifying gold and by the way they even consulted the Portuguese King on how to not to be cheated on the value of coins.

What is fascinating is that in these *quilombos* experiments, in order to survive, these former slaves created new forms and systems for the social division of work that relied upon polyandry consisting of structures of habitation with the woman and mothers leading to family structures which allotted lands to men through very sophisticated rules for cultivation. A man who was not fulfilling his tasks was deprived from the use of the land and naturally he had no right to appropriate the surplus. Departing from Harold Demsetzr's superficial analysis of the use of land by Hudson Bay Indian tribes, that gave birth to the legend of the "tragedy of commons," Elinor Oström has demonstrated that governance of trespassing, access, *usus, fructus*—with no private *abusus*, definitive transfer of property rights but provisory concession to a group or community—was and is still a much better way to manage complex ecologic systems, for example, administering limited fish resources. One could produce from the *quilombos* experience a theorem: the higher the degree of flight from dependant labor, the deeper auto-organization, the wiser, more sound and sustainable the governance of the famous population/resources problem. Its opposite, centralization through the State, as well as decentralization by market tools, had proved very destructive of the environment.

For how political and social structures arise in regards to private property management and interest is quite obvious. As far as public good and the State are concerned this result is less evident. However as H. Heller has shown in 2002, state property without any community to enforce intelligent use of land and natural and cultural resources has been proven to create "a disaster of the uncommons." The cases of America, Australia, Brazil, Canada, i.e. all countries where an aboriginal population, was scattered and/or destroyed by European colonials is instructive in this regard.

## 6. Our news Quilombos and future of the Commons

Now moving on to digital and post industrial capitalism the question arises, how are exit spaces for subjectivity configured in our developed and already industrialised world? A world in which information and knowledge are not scarce although some scarcity could be maintained artificially? Has not science and technology gone far beyond traditional knowledge and old Commons?

We suggested above that bitterness or melancholia as a peculiar modern affect, the feeling of ineffectiveness: the failed utopian project of a society of justice from Renaissance to Enlightening, from English Revolution to Bolshevik revolution. Melancholia was also about codification of human activity in the Procrustean bed of dependant labor since in a capitalist world be it mercantilist or industrial, laziness in the mind, physical refusal of work (absentee) were part of the constitution of an alternative subject. But a third component should be added from the colonial legacy: the *quilombo* tradition. It could assume all forms of traditional commons including escaping to the margins of Nation-States. Any movement of separation from the bitterness of mercantilist slavery was constituted by, as we noticed, the sweetness of quilombos, although they were defeated in the long run.

But what happens in the age of real subsumption of labor under capital? In the beginning of the age of the Internet a new form of liberation took place. It was not that much concerned with exploitation. Any kind of immaterial work on the Web seemed autonomous and free from the factory, the individual boss. Exploiting the muscle only brings tiredness and sometimes (for intensive sport) serotonin. Exploiting the brain (attention but also knowledge, games) requires a preliminary development and expansion of capacities. So who would care about capture of your personal data, your privacy by a hidden robot or eliminating advertising from the white page of Google? In the deluge or tsunami of data who could not feel freer to act and navigate than in the desert world of scarce goods except for "millionaires"? The Declaration of Independence by John Barlow and the first steps of disclosure of privateer property by the General Public Licence made by Richard Stallman both sounded like a truly New Age mantra with its Christian guru to whom the Anabaptist and somewhat prophetic culture had really prepared the American audience.

However very soon, by the end of the 1990s a new melancholia had arisen embedded as it was in the post-modern milieu. A melancholia or secret *saudade* [regret, nostalgia] erupting out of the fact that modernity was now behind us. This deep feeling sprang from a kind of disappointment. The New Continent of peer-to-peer collaboration, the realm of abundance and gratuitousness did not remain unpolluted by merchants and traders. A new kind of immaterial beekeepers appeared. They accepted host human interactivity in technological platforms from search engines to the cloud and started to put clickers at work a long time before anyone was really aware of it, so called software agents. It was, and is still very clever, since this kind of click work is not regulated by either the state or by any trade-unions and is not rewarded by any cash reimbursement. This form of industrial profit turned out to create and capture a gigantic amount of positive externalities.

In few words we assisted in the rise of massive primitive accumulation of cognitive capitalism (Boutang 2012). Non standard historians, and economists,, including the group *Midnight Notes* (G. Caffentsis, S. Federici) who were born from the Review *Zero Work* on the end of the 1970, soon followed with documented analysis (M. Rediker, P. Linebaugh, J.W. Scott, S. Federici, E.P. Tompson) returned to the historical antecedents to discover the defeat of surging antagonistic subjects (pirates, witches, thieves, smugglers and poachers) in order to confront the birth of absolutism and primitive accumulation (XVI-XVIII). Massimo de Angelis in his 2007 *The Beginning of History: Value, Struggle and Global Capital,* has drawn a parallel between the actual situation and this key period for the setting of conditions of capitalism. The great tale of this desperate fight is supposed to infuse an optic of kinetic resistance, rebellion, revolt the episodes of which are only dedicated to slowing the pace of the race toward ubiquitous capitalism, even if it is in vain, at the end of the road. In such a perspective, the existence of free spaces on the Web will not last since they have already been colonized and the hypothesis of a massive expropriation of the virtual *quilombos* be it by the big Gaffa and the little dragons or with the tidying by the state as shown by the various attempts of Hadopi, Lopsi, Acta is considered as inescapable; a powerful factor of discouragement and melancholy. But is that the whole story? What period of history shall we choose to understand our times? The late period of Parliamentary enclosures (XVII'-XVIII') or the period of the deserted village?[7] The destruction of piracy in the Caribbean by the end of the XVI'? Or the Magna Carta moment (Lindebaugh 2009)? What is annoying in this history of the big disaster of the victory of capital is that it puts aside or neglects a completely different hypothesis: that flight and fight have had a much more decisive impact on capitalism than we tend to imagine.

..................................................................................................

[7] For further information on this point I discuss it in my book *From Slavery to Salariate* (1998).

That is to say the resistance was not in vain because it has transformed and shaped deeply the kind of capitalism that resuletd from this antagonism. In intercultural and transculturation models the relation modifies both workers and capitalists (Ortiz 1942). Continuous flight and fights (Exit and Voice) achieve radical transformation. This was the precious legacy of Tronti's book *Operai e Capitale,* a true Copernican revolution in matter of constituency of capitalism as an historical process and capital as a unstable relationship and not a thing.

## 7. Raiders, privateers, piracy, trade in the primitive accumulation of the third capitalism

The battle about new enclosures is rather confused. Those who were pirates (Pirate Bay), hackers, crackers soon discovered that capitalist are also privateers. For more information on this subject we can look at the analysis of biopiracy by Vandana Shiva and her fight against it. Matteo Pasquinelli has introduced the concept of *parasite* to characterize cognitive capitalism (Pasquinelli 2008). However the technicalities of viruses have been invented by developers. On the other hand, privateer as rent seeker of human activity and not only of wage labor could be a good definition of Web 2.0. devices.
With the capitalist use of Web 2.0 techniques of traceability of human interaction (from Google through to social networks) leisure, alternative consuming, dreaming of Art, independence of science, activity as time outside the grid, sociality, emotions, are not quilombos but more similar to Jesuit reductions facing the new Bandeirantes.[8] Nowadays, the fablabs, the digital canteens, are haunted by head-hunters.

---

[8] *Bandeirantes* were soldiers and mercenaries raiders employed by the Brazilian planters to capture new slaves or to get back the run away slaves.

The incubators of start-up get invitations from big companies to join them or share their ideas with them most of the time for a dish of lenses. Does this picture necessarily indulge in melancholia?

This new melancholia as it was first discovered by the Frankfurt school concerned how the media and communication industry, subsumed the entire society and was described in the "situationniste société du spectacle" from Guy Debord to Jean Baudrillard (Debord 1995 and Baudrillard 1987). Now we have a digital department of the Frankfurt School. Sometimes this consciousness or fear of an already announced defeat brings social activists to retreat or flight in anti-stress techniques like new age literature.

Sometimes it falls into rage, a "no future" hatred syndrome self-enclosed in more and more isolated ghettos for radicals, something little more effective than confinement in a mental ward. But has this ghetto something in common with the antic *quilombos*? I shall say that this attempt of secession was never achieved. The state of slavery in the real and juridical world has the advantage of being really overpassed. The symbolic and virtual slavery or alienation is much more difficult to suppress.

## 8. A little detour: Cognitive capitalism as capture of intangibles 2

Cognitive capitalism in the age of digital networks and technologies of information and communication is a new interacting system—not a structure—for capturing economic value. Value can be globally defined as the capture of any positive externality or avoiding the compensation of negative externalities, for any private agent, or state. It springs from production, but production is not anymore production of commodities by the means of commodities. It is bio production of life and biosphere produced by relations and only through circulation. It is also accumulation of living activity remaining alive in the consumption of resources (Boutang 2011).

What is accumulated is knowledge acting and living and not dead knowledge, or codified knowledge that does not produce positive externalities. Hence value is seriously different from Marx's definition of exploitation when he faced mercantilism and the fast rising fabric capitalism.

To extract economic value from human interactivity that I call human pollination,[9] the third capitalism or cognitive capitalism must get through Caudine Forks, or as we might refer to them as the new contradictions of the "materialist dialectic." Firstly one must keep human activity and labor as living hence develop the brain in a body at a level that was anticipated by Marx as only reachable in the communist phase as described in the Grundrisse, i.e. as a general and common intellect equipped by digital technology and linked by networks. Controlling this "invention force" (Lazzarato 2010) is much more complicated than the former proletarianization. There is the necessity of taming this new force to perform adequately. Depriving the labor force from its means of production has not been an easy task. All the violence of primitive accumulation was needed. The old commons was not a geographical margin for the expansion of a sort of gas capitalism occupying all the space available. The space was not available; it was already occupied and defended. Taming the just freed serfs and peasants and fixing them by putting them to work in factories took four hundred years. And the most difficult was to reshape, reformate their minds and the subjectivity. Humiliating the poor in European society, and through the extraction of absolute surplus value, enslaving huge part of the new labor force as was done by the market helped by the absolute Nation State.

---

[9] For further information see my own book *L'abeille et l'économiste*, Paris: Carnets Nord, 2010.

Primitive accumulation of cognitive capitalism however is a much more complicated task. Subjection of the forces of invention needs to compete with an unavoidable condition; that of extracting value from the living. A much higher degree of liberty and socialisation is required if you want to capture innovation and collective intelligence which is by far the most valuable and hegemonic part of value today.

In order to crop positive, externalities cognitive capitalism must extend the margins of liberty, destroy the wall of the old fabric, empower society and encourage many "hundred flowers campaigns" like those of Mao.[10] Communism of capital, this capital not the old industrial one, means only that the bases of exploitation now include quilombos without destroying them. It needs the creativity of digital quilombos, innovation distributed in society and not their reduction to melancholic boarders in mental wards. When profit depends on crowd sourcing, crowd design, cloud computing the apparatus of control and discipline is not for expanding generalized melancholia in which the possibility of the end of work might be its conclusion. No, the most used tool is now the apparatus of burn out. A continuous although non-linear praise of the expense of the brain in cooperation and care networks "à la Georges Bataille" in a permanent potlatch! (Bataille 1933) But do not think that the flight towards the shadow kingdom of melancholia has the same virtue than the one of Dürer. Nervous breakdown and permanent stress are the true pathology.
What are the objective limits to the control of the brain under a regime of cognitive capitalism?

---

[10] Between February and April, 1957 Chairman Mao launched the Hundred Flowers Campaign [百花运动/百花運動].

The first one regards codification of positive externalities by transforming them into knowledge or information goods and then into quasi-public goods. Commonly produced goods and producers and consumers are more and more reluctant to produce, use and consume through the market inasmuch as they are more and more complex and inter dependant.

The commoditization of incorporated knowledge, science and technology into products and services was achieved through juridical and artificial conventions palliating indivisibility, non-rivalry and non transferability and difficulties to copy. So cheating was difficult and traceable. The revolution of the information and communication new technologies has destroyed easy and durable enforcement of intellectual property rights. Digital Rights Management has been a failure and a constant battle Cognitive capitalism meets another difficulty: trespassing IPR has devaluated their prices and the kind of externalities most valuable are related intangibles that cannot be codified, meaning care, learning, attention, intelligence in act, competence, cooperation, trust, tolerance, love. Even if you measure it (for example, the audience of a book, of reputation) it is too fickle a phenomenon to be able to predict or produce it. There is no manual for making a best-seller. Uncertainty is systemic. The solution found by cognitive capitalism is to capture the traces of interaction, personal data, through Web 2.0 arrangements, such as search engines, platforms for cooperation, innovation, and social networks.

But this is raising now a great political debate about personal data, privacy, digital citizenship and cyber liberties. Good morning for a new cycle of struggles on the rights of the cybercitizen. The quilombo cannot be attacked by armies and reduced unless cognitive capitalism decides to trade off its internal platform and new fabric for an imaginary political order achieved through counterevolution. For the time being, he has two big problems with material and industrial capitalism just like the later had problems with the slavish mercantilism. I see no internal reasons why cognitive capitalism will commit suicide. The liberation process is at the same time to big, as the absolute condition of wealth, and to feeble (the quilombo has not reach the maturity of getting rid of which the reign of scarcity).

New commons are the fundamental condition for the survival of capitalism under its new avatar. Promotion, extension and protection of the news digital commons should make profit of the experience of the old commons.

Let us take the experience of the *terra nullius* principle that has destroyed the ancient commons. Open source and public domain promoting the end of all copyrights but also unlimited supply of positives externalities for market activities are a sort of modern "terra nullius." To avoid depressive exhaustion of the resources of the mind in networks some new rules of protection of collective knowledge should be instituted on the basis of creative commons (Boutang 2010). These rules cannot exclusively rely upon public and state policies, inasmuch states through private/public partnership very often are preparing old and new commons to a privatization.

Let-us ask the thorny question: "Is cognitive capitalism still capitalism?" It seems that answering "yes," we will be brought back to the revolving failure that has fed melancholia and various forms of psychopathology of the revolutionary mind since the Renaissance. I believe that the new great transformation of capitalism into its third regime and *dispositif* is creating new margins of liberty at the very moment it tries to block its commonism. Remember how the Wall Street Journal that had praised *Empire*, was reluctant to praise the *Multitude* and enraged with how *Commonwealth's* authors treated "*cattivi maestri*" [bad masters]. On the one hand cognitive capitalism promotes free access, interaction, pollination, in a certain way similar to the way communism or digital commoners in the virtual world do. On the other hand, it re-enforces IPR and captures intangibles.

By so doing, as soon as it makes more visible the huge productivity of human interaction free to pollinate it recreates tools of control at a meta-level in the cloud. The modern question of the enclosures will have to face the question of the property rights (i.e. the modalities of appropriation) of big data. Naturally, creative labor and cognitive labor stands less and less for old forms of hierarchies and promotes distributed non-hierarchical forms through the web instruments of direct democracy of Wiki politics which I have explored elsewhere (Boutang 2011). To what extent will cognitive capitalism open a fork in the road, rerouting the organization of society, will depend on conflicts about the space of liberty.

Richard Stallman has fought against the Open Source movement in late 1995. Open source is not copyleft. It allows cognitive capitalism to use positive externalities without any limitation, nor reconstitution of them. The same has to be done for open data. Open knowledge must achieve a sustainable model of production, consumption and circulation of intangibles 2.

What would need to be avoided is precisely reducing externalities and intangibles to cash machine like it as has been done in the brutal management of universities as if they were mills of old capitalism, while cognitive capitalism is trying to mimicry the academy and peer to peer evaluation processes. The second mistake to avoid is reducing intangibles, non-codified knowledge, intangibles 2 to codified intangibles 1 like evaluating everything through quantitative indexes computed in Excel tables. Such is the prescription that I would formulate to handle the psychopathologies of the cognitive capitalism. Digital *quilombos* do not need mental homes for maniac depressive psychosis, let us leave that kind of horrible medicine to industrial capitalist. Don't cry, don't smile, just understand as Spinoza used to say.[11]

---

[11] As Baruch Spinoza wrote in *Tractatus Politicus* (1677), "non ridere, non lugere, neque detestari, sed intelligere" [not to laugh, not to weep, not to curse, but to understand].

Althusser, Louis, 1978. *Ce Qui ne Peut Plus Durer Dans le Parti Communiste*. Paris: Maspéro.

Aquinatis, S. Thomae, 1557. *Quaestiones Disputatae, De Malo, Quaestio 11, De Acedia. Et habet articulos Quatuor*. S.C. Selner-Wright (trans.) Washington: The Catholic University of America Press (2011).

Bataille, Georges, 1949. *La Part Maudite précedé de La Notion de Dépense*. Paris: Minuit (2011).

Baudrillard, Jean, 1990. *Cool Memories*. London: Verso.

Debord, Guy, 1995. *The Society of the Spectacle*. New York: Zone Books.

Hirschman, Albert O., 1970. *Exit, Voice and Loyalty, Responses to Decline in Firms, Organizations, and States*. Cambridge: Harvard University Press.

Lazzarato, Maurizio, 2002. *Puissances de l'Invention. La Psychologie Économique de Gabriel Tarde Contre l'Économie Politique*. France: Les Empêcheurs de Penser en Rond.

Moulier Boutang, Yann (September 2001). "Marx in Kalifornien: Der dritte Kapitalismus und die Alte Politische Ökonomie" in *Marx en Californie : le Troisième Capitalisme et la Vieille Économie Politique, Communication au Congrès Marx International III, Section Économie*. Available online: http://www.bpb.de/publikationen/ 98BOPR0,0,Marx_in_Kalifornien:_Der_dritte_Kapitalismus_und_die _alte_politische_%d6konomie.html Aus Politik und Zeitgeschichte [last accessed April 2014].

Nietzsche, Friedrich, 1873. *On the Use and Abuse of History*. New York: Cosimo (2005).

Spinoza, Baruch, 1677. *Tractatus Politicus*. London: A. H. Gosset (1883).

Stiegler, Bernard, 2004. *De la Misère Symbolique*. Paris: Galilée.

# A Fiction of the Great Outdoors:
# The Psychopathology of Panic
# in Robert Harris' *The Fear Index*

## Looking Back

In my contribution to the first volume of the series of books related to the "Psychopathologies of Cognitive Capitalism" conferences that Warren Neidich, Jason Smith and I launched in Los Angeles in November 2012, I wrote some sentences about speculative realism, specifically about a passage from the "Ancestrality" chapter of Quentin Meillassoux's book *After Finitude: An Essay on the Necessity of Contingency*, that now strike me as not very well thought out (see Boever 2013, 108). I want to come back to those sentences here, since my clarifications of what I wrote then will lead directly into the subject of the present article, namely *panic as a psychopathology of cognitive capitalism.*

In the passage that I commented on, Meillassoux asks about the meaning and truth-value of "scientific statements bearing explicitly upon a manifestation of the world that is posited as anterior to the emergence of thought and even of life— *posited, that is, as anterior to every form of human relation to the world*" (Meillassoux 2008, 9-10). In my article, I read this question *about* science as a question *for* philosophy: how could philosophy make such statements—*speculatively,* as I wrote, *but with the realist authority of science?*

It was in this context that I introduced literature, and specifically fiction: for it seemed to me that Meillassoux's question applied particularly well to fiction, a speculative discourse that, in the case of realism for example, makes claims that have a certain truth-value (different from science, even though some realists have thought about their work as a kind of science).[1] The issue seemed perhaps particularly pertinent to me (as well as to some others working along these lines) because I am of the opinion that fiction, like philosophy and science, *thinks* (see Gourgouris 2003). What are the grounds for this thought, in particular if it were ultimately to pertain—as thought—to a manifestation of the world anterior to every form of human relation to the world? How could fiction, which seems so wrapped up in the human-world relation, *ever* aspire to this?

Clearly, and this is the part of my reading that I now take issue with, these questions remained within the limit, or at the limit, of science, of a science that makes statements of the kind that Meillassoux describes—about "the age of the universe, the date of the accretion of the earth, the date of the appearance of pre-human species, or the date of the emergence of humanity itself" (Meillassoux 2008, 9). But while we may be at science's limit here, there is of course no reason why we would have to stay within it, in the same way that if we pursue this question at the limit of fiction, there is no reason why we would have to stay within its limits and limitations. It may indeed be that, when pushed all the way, fiction would crumble in the face of these questions.

---

[1] I make this statement even if these claims in the overwhelming majority of cases still involve humans.

In what follows, however, that does not turn out to be the case—at least not for fiction. With science, as we will see, it's another story. So my 'corrective' attempt is to nuance my previous use of both the terms 'science' and 'fiction' in order to see what possibilities for fiction remain within the speculative realist optic.

## Fiction and the Great Outdoors

What follows is driven by a fascination with what Meillassoux, early on in *After Finitude*, calls "the great outdoors," and specifically by the relation of that 'great outdoors' to literature. In Meillassoux's words, the great outdoors is:

> the *absolute* outside of pre-critical thinkers: that outside which was not relative to us, and which was given as indifferent to its own givenness to be what it is, existing in itself regardless of whether we are thinking of it or not; that outside which thought could explore with the legitimate feeling of being on foreign territory—of being entirely elsewhere. (Meillassoux 2008, 7)

As such, it poses a challenge to what Meillassoux calls correlationism, or thought that is caught up in the relation between reality and its human perceiver. If this is the case, then this great outdoors poses a formidable challenge to literature and specifically realist fiction as it is traditionally practiced.

Others have picked up on this. In his book *Alien Phenomenology, Or What It's Like to Be a Thing*, in which Meillassoux's great outdoors is a recurring concern, Ian Bogost notes that literature's "preference for traditional narrative acts as a correlationist amplifier." "Whether empathy or defamiliarization is its goal," he adds, "literature aspires for identification, to create resonance between readers and the human characters in a work" (Bogost 2012, 40-41).

The 'whether' clause is important: for it thus seems that *even* literature that would *mess* with traditional narrative—literature that would *defamiliarize*—would *still* be caught up in the correlationist bind, *as long as* it aims to create resonance between readers and characters. It may be, then, that it is nearly impossible for literature to break out of this bind—unless the literature in question is something like Ben Marcus' *The Age of Wire and String*, discussed later on in Bogost's book, and characterized by Bogost as "incomprehensible" (Bogost 2012, 82). It's "within that incomprehensibility" (ibid.), he argues, that something like a literature of the great outdoors becomes possible.

Interestingly, some of the work associated with Meillassoux's philosophy has been literary: *Cyclonopedia*, Reza Negarestani's cult 'novel' (if we can still call it that), has already had an important symposium dedicated to it (see Keller et al. 2012), and the event brought together some of the most important voices in contemporary speculative realism. Indeed, Meillassoux himself has taken on the question of literature in his work. His second book to be translated into English, *The Number and the Siren*, is a study of Mallarmé's extraordinary poem *Un Coup de dés*—and it's an impressive demonstration of how his philosophical thought can be developed through a meticulous, obsessive reading of a work of literature (see Meillassoux 2012). However, *Un Coup de dés* is of course a poem, and one that lends itself particularly well to Meillassoux's thought. What about the great outdoors and the rest of literature? Graham Harman has pointed to the weird fiction of H.P. Lovecraft as a key resource for his object-oriented thought (not the same as Meillassoux's philosophy, but related to it) (see Harman 2012). Indeed, it's worth noting that Meillassoux himself has written about fiction in an essay titled "Metaphysics and Extro-Science Fiction" (see Meillassoux 2010).

I would now like to briefly review this latter text since its argument will prove to be of central importance to the reading of Robert Harris' novel *The Fear Index* that I'd like to develop. It is in fact through this review that the 'corrective' of my use of the word science in my earlier text can occur.

Indeed, it becomes quite clear from the opening pages of this essay on fiction that Meillassoux has very little intention of holding on to science. Distinguishing between two regimes of fiction, one which he labels science fiction (SF) and one which he labels extro-science fiction (XSF), he points out that as far as its relation to science goes, SF preserves the existence of science. In SF, science "may be profoundly transformed," he writes, "but there will always *be* science" (Meillassoux 2010, 27). In XSF, this is not the case: XSF thinks "worlds outside science," "*where experimental science is impossible in principle*, rather than unknown in fact" (ibid.). It's the latter that Meillassoux finds significant—not because he is particularly interested in fiction, but because the distinction between SF and XSF enables him to lay out a conceptual distinction that he deems to be of philosophical interest.

So whereas I suggested, in my earlier text, that Meillassoux was interested in how science makes speculative statements that have truth-value, with a realist authority, and whereas I read this interest at the time as a challenge to philosophy and the statements it makes, the interest in fact seems to go in quite a different direction. Specifically, it's *from* the philosophico-fictional terrain of XSF that experimental science is *rendered impossible*—that the conditions of science are destroyed, as he announces toward the end of his essay, even though consciousness is still possible. There is something that emerges from the great outdoors that challenges the science that operates at its limit—to such an extent that this science enters into its impossibility.

However, this may be the very site where philosophy and fiction are liberated—can be legitimately let loose on foreign territory, to recall Meillassoux's words. As he sees it, "[t]he guiding question for XSF is: what could a world be like, for it to be in principle inaccessible to scientific knowledge; for it to be incapable of being established as the object of natural science?" (Meillassoux 2010, 28)

Meillassoux's discussion revolves around "Hume's problem," familiar to readers of *After Finitude*. The problem involves a billiards match, "during the course of which the laws of dynamics cease to apply" (Meillassoux 2010, 30). How can we know, Hume asks, "what truly guarantees—but also, what persuades us—that physical laws will continue to hold in a moment's time, given that neither experience nor logic can assure us of this?" (ibid., 31). Meillassoux goes on to discuss Karl Popper's answer to this question: Popper argues that 'nothing could guarantee it, but moreover that this was a good thing, since there is nothing fantastic about these possibilities —they must be taken entirely seriously' (ibid.). This is, Meillassoux points out, the SF answer: "Popper tells us that new experiences could refute our theories; but he never doubts that the existing, canonic experiments will always produce the same results in the future" (ibid., 35). He thus confuses Hume's problem, which is ontological, with an epistemological problem. Meillassoux argues, however, that Hume was interested in something else: "Hume's problem mobilizes another imaginary, the imaginary of extro-science fiction, a fiction of a world become too chaotic to permit any scientific theory whatsoever to be applied to reality anymore" (ibid., 36).

To illustrate, but also to further his thought on the problem, Meillassoux turns to an Asimov story: it captures the XSF imaginary, since "a totally unforeseen event ... comes to pass" in it; but it's ultimately an SF story since this totally unforeseen event appears to *still* be explainable by the laws of science.

That is why, Méillassoux argues, the story works: narrative needs this SF resolution, and a world of "pure chaos, a pure diversity ordered by nothing" risks rendering fiction impossible. In other words: with the XSF imaginary, fiction is able to go where science cannot—and evidently some kind of thought still happens there.

I will skip now, in the interest of time, the crystal-clear pages on Kant that follow in the essay, where the possibility of this "some kind of thought"—consciousness—is discussed. I want to list, instead, the possibilities of XSF worlds with which Meillassoux's essay concludes: type one worlds would be "irregular, but not enough to affect science or consciousness"—as he notes, these worlds are not extro-science "in the strict sense since they still allow the exercise of science" (Meillassoux 2010, 50) (this redeems my reading of science in relation to his work in my earlier text somewhat); the irregularity of type two worlds "is sufficient to abolish science but not consciousness"—these worlds, he notes, "are the real extro-science worlds" (ibid., 52); finally, type three worlds "represent lawless universes in which disordered modifications are so frequent, that … the conditions of science and those of consciousness alike, are abolished" (ibid., 56-7).

Which brings him to his final question: how to write XSF? He lists three solutions: first, "[introduce] just one rupture without cause or reason" (he summarizes this as 'catastrophe'); two, "nonsense" (this recalls Bogost's discussion of the Ben Marcus novel); or, three, write "stories of uncertain reality, those in which the real crumbles gradually, from one day to the next ceasing to be familiar to us" (Meillassoux 2010, 60). It's this third solution that he considers to '[express] most faithfully the XSF genre.' Meillassoux summarizes this as "the dread uncertainty of the atmospheric novel," and notes that there probably aren't enough of these around "to constitute a genre."

Indeed, at the beginning of his essay, too, there are some genre-related worries: some might argue, he notes, that the SF genre already includes the XSF genre and that it thus makes no sense to separate between the two, in fact that the SF genre contradicts the very distinction he is trying to make. Like him, I think this is not a worthwhile argument, in part because I am of the opinion that XSF is not a genre—in fact, we do it harm to locate it under SF. One could ask here in what kind of contexts this experience of dread uncertainty is most profound: in recognizably weird contexts, where the literature we are reading is explicitly, openly trying to break with traditional narrative (as Graham Harman seems to think when he proposes H.P. Lovecraft's weird fiction as the key resource for object-oriented ontology); or in familiar contexts, where the literature we are reading is realist, but is infected nevertheless by an incomprehensibility that begins to corrode fiction at large.

My own position is the latter, and as a consequence I don't think of XSF as a genre but as a modality of writing, which can be practiced in *any* genre. It may of course be that certain genres lend themselves better to it than others, and it certainly may be that SF is one of those genres. Given Meillassoux's description of what he calls "the atmospheric novel," however, and the ways in which in such novels "the real crumbles gradually, from one day to the next ceasing to be familiar to us," I think a case could be made for the realist novel—of course, written in a certain modality—as a good genre for the practice of XSF. As the title of Harman's book already reveals, this very distinction between 'weird' fiction and 'realist' fiction may be precisely what is under discussion here, since the point of the XSF modality would arguably be to reveal the weird as real, and the real as weird.

It is this deconstruction that I will now pursue in my reading of Robert Harris' *The Fear Index* (2012). A finance novel set against the background of the so-called 'flash crash' of 2010, the day when the Dow Jones Industrial Index suffered the biggest one-point decline in its history, *The Fear Index* records Dr. Alex Hoffman's *psychopathology of panic* to the point of his near self-destruction. Alex's becoming-panic is linked in the novel to what, in the first volume of this series, I have argued to be a common trope of contemporary finance fictions: psychosis. Indeed, given that Alex is first and foremost a scientist, Harris' fiction, set in Geneva and including references to both Mary Shelley and Charles Darwin, links this trope to an even more common one: the mad scientist.

What interests me in light of the novel's representation of panic, however, is how these tropes are also *resisted* in *The Fear Index*: whereas the novel at first sight appears to buy into the cliché of the mad scientist/psychotic money-man, its ending clearly puts this cliché aside so as to (impossibly) affirm the *reality* of the psycho-economic breakdown it records. *Psychosis cannot be blamed for this madness*: instead, *The Fear Index* delivers something like a 'capitalist realism' (to loosely borrow Mark Fisher's term, see Fisher 2009), backed up by science. This requires us to open ourselves up to what I will call, adapting this term from Meillassoux's work "the great outdoors" (Meillassoux 2008, 7) of realist fiction: an outside that literature, "whose preference for traditional narrative acts as a correlationist amplifier" (Bogost 40-41), to use Bogost's words again, has difficulty writing. My *psycho-political* argument will be, however, that in order to work through the pathology of panic, we must open ourselves up to this great outdoors, indeed *let ourselves go* in the face of it, so as to begin to write anew the individual and collective fictions by which we live.

# A Panic Novel

*The Fear Index* tells the story of twenty-four hours in the life of Dr. Alexander Hoffmann, from the moment when he receives a copy of the first run of the first edition of Charles Darwin's *The Expression of the Emotions in Man and Animal* (1872) and is leafing through it in the study of his sixty million dollar house in Geneva, Switzerland, to when he is lying unconscious in bed at the city's University Hospital, badly burnt and with multiple fractures. On the night when he receives the $10K Darwin book in the mail—he later confirms that it was ordered and paid for by him, even though he cannot remember doing so—, Alex has a violent run-in with a home invader who appears to have had knowledge of the codes to dismantle his house's state of the art security system (his house, like his office, most closely resembles a fortress). Throughout the day, more evidence comes to light suggesting that someone is using his email account in an attempt to 'destroy' (*FI* 138) him. "Someone's really after me," he confesses to his business partner, Hugo Quarry. 'Out to destroy me bit by bit' (*FI* 144). And it's not only Alex who is under attack: whoever is behind this is attempting to take down his company as well.

The company in question, Hoffmann Investment Technologies, is a hedge fund. Asked by the policeman who has come to investigate the home invasion, Jean-Jacques Leclerc, what it makes, Hoffmann dryly replies: "It makes money" (*FI* 23). Like others in the finance world, Hoffmann came to Switzerland 'in the nineties (at the height of the era Hugo describes as "the coke and call girl glory days," *FI* 73) to work for CERN [European Organization for Nuclear Research], on the Large Hadron Collider' (*FI* 22). After about six years of working as a physicist, he was lured away by the world of finance: not because he wanted to work for a bank—he makes that quite clear to Hugo when he comes to recruit him—but because this world enables him to progress with his research on autonomous machine learning (CERN had to contain it because an algorithm he had designed went out of control and started affecting its systems like a virus). In a speech to the team he's working with at the hedge fund, he insists that "it's never been just about the money" (*FI* 234; indeed, Leclerc notes that Alex's library does not contain a single book about money, *FI* 28). Instead, he thanks them for the scientific progress that they have made. In this economic case too, however, it appears that the algorithm that Alex has created has gotten out of control, and now it is Alex himself who will try to shut it down. That's what the plot of the novel amounts to: it's a story about a mad-scientist-gone-hedge-fund trying to pull the plug on the digital life-form he has created.

The story of course rings a few bells: set in Geneva, it recalls, first of all, Mary Shelley's novel *Frankenstein* (1818), and Harris includes references to this text in his novel. Many of the novel's chapters are introduced with quotes from books by Charles Darwin, not just the already mentioned *Expressions of the Emotions* but also *On the Origin of Species* (1859) and *The Descent of Man* (1871). What makes Harris' novel unique, and uniquely contemporary, is that these two sources of inspiration are combined with the world of economics: other mottoes introducing the novel's chapters are taken from Bill Gates' *Business @ the Speed of Thought*—this text is also explicitly credited in the novel as the source for Hoffman's idea for an 'entirely digital' company (*FI* 53-54)—, or from various other luminaries in the world of high finance. Thus combining economics with genetics and literature, Harris' novel aligns the story of Alex's personal downfall and the downfall of his company and sets this already powerful tale against the background of the so-called 'flash crash' of May 6$^{th}$ 2010, the day when the Dow Jones Industrial Index suffered the biggest one-point decline in its history. (The novel's general background is the austerity crisis in Europe, particularly in Greece, *FI* 49.)

By the end of the novel it is not entirely clear whether this crash is indeed merely background: it may actually be that the algorithm Alex has created—or 'fathered,' as the language of the novel suggests (*FI* 149, 215, 232, 262); though it is not always clear who is the father and who the child (Alex is also referred to as 'babyish' in the book's opening and closing pages, *FI* 16; 286)—is responsible for the crash. What is certain is that it ends up making a huge profit from the collapse, and without raising suspicions with the regulators: Hoffman Investment Technologies makes "a profit out of the crash of four-point-one billion dollars," one of its analysts remarks, "and the beauty of it is … that that represents only zero-point-four percent of total market volatility" (*FI* 283). In other words: not significant enough to trigger an investigation. This huge profit, divided in bonuses among the company's employees, will silence everyone who has witnessed the algorithm's actions. The only one who had said he would complain—the company's risk assessor—is conveniently killed off by the algorithm, who uses the elevator in the company's headquarters to get the employee out of the way.[2]

As its title reveals, this is a novel about fear, and more specifically panic—both at the personal level, and in its mass form as when, for example, 'the market' panics (references to theorists of masses and groups accumulate in the novel, cf. *FI* 28).

---

[2] This is perhaps a reference to the Dutch director Dick Maas' tech-horror flick *De Lift*, remade for international audiences as *Down*. As many reviewers have noted, Harris' book echoes other classic films of tech-horror: Alex's algorithm recalls Stanley Kubrick's *2001: A Space Odyssey*, for example, and the scenes toward the end of the novel in which Alex is trying to shut the algorithm down mirror the scene in Kubrick's film when Dave is trying to shut HAL down—"This must be the cortex," Alex muses when he arrives at the algorithm's central control unit, as if it actually has a brain; later on, 'reluctance' is attributed to the algorithm (*FI* 260).

In fact, Alex' body in the novel becomes something like the site where the panic of the market is played out—it's a 'body economic,' so to speak (I use the phrase here in parallel with the more familiar term 'body politic'), and one that—like the body of Victor Frankenstein's creature—risks to come apart at the seams (*FI* 100). In the state of panic—private, public—Alex is indeed turned into a creature, a being *not only* in between human, and animal life, *but also* digital life; someone who has lost all control over the determinants of his existence.[3] Early on in the novel, when Alex is on the tracks of the unknown man who has invaded his house, he can still insist that while he is afraid, 'he felt no panic' (*FI* 13). "Panic was quite different to fear, he was discovering. Panic was moral and nervous collapse, a waste of precious energy, whereas fear was all sinew and instinct: an animal that stood up on its hind legs and filled you completely, that took control of your brain and muscles" (*FI* 13). Some forty pages later, however, when he finds out he did not place the Darwin book order that originated from his email account, "the confidence leaked from his voice and he felt almost physically sick with panic, as if an abyss was opening at his feet" (*FI* 65). Another eighty pages later, when he realizes that his marriage is disintegrating because of the crises in which he has landed, "[p]anic welled inside him again" (*FI* 142). At his office later on, he tries very hard not 'to create a panic' among the traders; but as the crisis around the algorithm grows, 'panic' (*FI* 258) invades their minds and their bodies anyways. In the genre of the finance novel, *The Fear Index* can clearly be categorized as a panic novel: as that particular subgenre of economic fiction that focuses on the panic that is produced by (and produces) a market crash.

........................................................................................

[3] His wife's art arguably evokes this state: "'n the coffee table in front of him was one of Gabrielle's early self-portraits: a half-metre cube, made up of a hundred sheets of Mirogard glass, on to which she had traced in black ink the sections of an MRI scan of her own body. The effect was of some strange, vulnerable alien creature floating in midair" (*FI* 18).

Indeed, one of the things that sets Alex's algorithm—and algorithms in general—aside from humans is that "they don't panic" (*FI* 84). "And that's why they're so perfectly suited to trade on the financial markets" (*FI* 84). However, what makes Alex's algorithm particular is that at the same time, it thrives on human panic. Here's how the novel describes the logic of its operations: as Alex, Hugo, and co. see things, today (as opposed to for example during the Cold War era of mutually assured destruction) "digitalization itself is creating an epidemic of fear." "The rise in market volatility," they argue, "is a function of digitalization, which is exaggerating human mood swings by the unprecedented dissemination of information via the Internet" (*FI* 86). Alex's algorithm is a way to make money out of this situation: it monitors panic on the world wide web, and trades on the basis of the data it collects there, thus making huge profits out of human emotion. One of the potential investors of Hoffmann Investment Technologies refers to this as "behavioral finance," thus splicing Darwin and economics together.

An autonomous machine-learning algorithm, the VIXAL-4 (as it is called) is "only likely to become more effective" "[a]s it collects and analyzes more data" (*FI* 88). The novel suggests, however, that this algorithm grows a little too smart for its own good, crashing the market while arranging its trades in anticipation of a colossal crash, and thus making a huge profit from this collapse. It's this particular situation that Alex tries to prevent. However, even though it initially appears he shut the algorithm down, the novel closes with the reality that it is still trading—and that we cannot do much else than obey it. While Alex is out in his hospital bed, his business partner Hugo resumes work at the office, giving "the slightest bow of obeisance" (*FI* 285) to the algorithm spying on him through a hidden camera—and increasing Hugo's profit by the minute.

# Pan's Pharmacology

Obeisance: it's a gloomy conclusion, to be sure, and one that very much taps into the age-old 'fear of technology' or 'technophobia' that may strike many now as ridiculous. In the case of *The Fear Index*, technophobia becomes linked to digitalization (one could speak of *high-technophobia*) and the economy—in short, to digital economy. The novel can be read as an evocation of what I would like to call, splicing the French words for economy, the digital, and panic together, 'éconuméripanique'—a pathology that is characteristic of our age. One can consider here, for example, the work of a contemporary theorist of panic, who has approached panic within the parameters that the novel sets up: the Italian thinker Franco "Bifo" Berardi.

Let's recall, for a moment, the classical origins of the word 'panic': it can be traced back to the Greek god Pan. Half goat, half human (like a Satyr), he was the god of the wild, of shepherds and of flocks; and also of hunting and rustic music. Associated with sexuality (polygamy, eroticism, masturbation, rape, lust, etc.) and fertility, and a companion of the nymphs (many of whom suffered a terrible fate because he pursued them), he was usually worshipped in a natural setting—a cave, for example. Some theories have it that he's the son of Zeus. Others suggest that he's the son of Hermes (and the nymph Penelope of Mantineai—apparently, she later became confused with the Penelope from the Odyssey, and Pan was thought to be the son of Penelope's intercourse with all of her 108 suitors...). Probably one of the oldest gods, many have also noted that he is the only god who dies. "Pan o megas tethneke!" [The Great Pan has died!] was a cry that was popular with the Romantics, because it evoked the loss of human beings' relation to nature—to "the overwhelming flow of reality, things, and information that we are surrounded by" (Berardi 2009a, 44), as Bifo puts it in his book *Precarious Rhapsody*.

As our contemporary use of the word 'panic' also reveals, 'panic' was not necessarily a 'comforting' relation. Pan's unseen presence produced feelings of panic in human beings who were traveling through remote, lonely places of the wild. But at least as long as Pan was alive, human beings still had *some* relation to nature.

Some are suggesting that today, *this relation is gone.* Today, 'panic' names a psychopathology of cognitive capitalism—a pathology produced by a contemporary economic situation in which the mind and the brain have become the new focus of laboring. One of the theorists of this new form of capitalism, Bifo has repeatedly discussed panic in his work on this subject. Noting, perhaps a little too positively, that "[o]nce, panic used to be a nice word" (the feelings produced by Pan's unseen presence can hardly be called 'nice'!), Bifo points out that:

> [t]oday, panic has become a form of psychopathology. We can speak of panic when we see a conscious organism (individual or social) being overwhelmed by the speed of processes he, she is involved in, and has no time to process the information input. In these cases the organism, all of a sudden, is no more able to process the sheer amount of information coming into its cognitive field or even that which is being generated by the organism itself.
> (Berardi 2009a, 44)

In short: no more relation! Returning to panic a little later on, he writes: "The mental environment is saturated by signs that create a sort of continuous excitation, a permanent electrocution, which leads the individual mind as well as the collective mind to a state of collapse" (ibid., 45).

He articulates the issue in both a temporal and a spatial way: it's associated with the acceleration of time, while the problem is particularly present in urban environments.[4] So whereas the 'nice' Pan is associated with the countryside, the 'evil' Pan is associated with the city.[5]

In his book *After the Future* Bifo returns to the topic of panic. Here he writes about what he now refers to as the "city of panic," a phenomenon I'd be inclined to call (with reference to Plato's utopian *kallipolis*) a dystopian *panipolis*. According to Bifo, and others who have argued the same, the 'urban territory is increasingly traversed' by panic. He refers to Salman Rushdie's 2001 novel *Fury* as a book that describes this situation: "Rushdie depicts the virtual class nervous system, a social class of producers of signs as well as a class of people living a common condition of evanescence and existential fragility: cellularized splinters, fragments in a perpetual abstract recombination of connected terminals." "Anxiety' is 'growing' in the city, 'the urban libidinal economy' is 'going insane.' 'In the city of panic, there is no longer time to get close to each other; there is no more time for caresses, for the pleasure and slowness of whispered words" (Berardi 2011, 94-5). Once again, it's the end of a relation that seems to be at stake.

---

[4] Stiegler too has noted the 'urban' dimension of the panic-related phenomena he is describing, and he notes that "we are now all, or nearly all, urban" (Stiegler 2013, 89).

[5] In fact, things are more complicated than this: the 'nice' Pan was already a little bit evil... But let us leave Bifo's terms as they are: I read Pan in a more pharmacological way. In this context, it is worth remembering, as Jacques Derrida already pointed out, that 'scapegoat' is one of the meanings of the Greek word 'pharmakon.'

It is in Bifo's 2009 book *The Soul at Work*, however, that the argument about panic is brought in relation with the economy. "When in 1999, Alan Greenspan spoke of the 'irrational exuberance of the market'," Bifo writes,

> his words were more of a clinical than a financial diagnosis. Exuberance was an effect of the drugs and of the over-exploitation of available mental energy, of a saturation of attention leading people to the limits of panic. Panic is the anticipation of a depressive breakdown, of mental confusion and disactivation. (Berardi 2009b, 98)

The key issue, for Bifo, is thus revealed to be what he as well as others call the 'attention economy': the ways in which our attention is being captured, exploited and destroyed under the conditions of cognitive capitalism.

However, one should not be fooled by Bifo's shift from the 'financial' to the 'clinical': *The Soul at Work* is obviously a book about labor today, about a contemporary economic situation in which our very souls—our minds, our spirits—are exploited at work. Once again, Bifo notes that the word panic is associated with the god Pan. But in this case, Pan is not just 'nice': he "appeared bringing a sublime, devastating folly overtaking those who received his visit." This same 'syndrome,' as Bifo now puts it, has become diffused in our time for three major reasons: "the social context is a competitive society where all energies are mobilized in order to prevail on the other … if one does not win, one can be eliminated" (think of the popular contemporary American film *The Hunger Games*, or its Japanese source of inspiration *Battle Royale*). Second, "the technological context is the constant acceleration of the rhythms of the global machine, a constant expansion of cyberspace in the face of the individual brain's limited capacities of elaboration."

And third, "the communicational context is that of an endless expansion of the Infosphere, which contains all signals from which competition and survival depend." For Bifo, this situation is "very similar … to the one pictured by the Greek etymology of the word panic." "The infinite vastness of the Infosphere," he concludes, "is superior to the human capacities of elaboration, as much as a sublime nature overcomes the capacities of feeling that the Greeks could summon when faced with the god Pan" (Berardi 2009b, 100-101).

In Bifo's view, and *The Fear Index* appears to see things the same way, this situation is largely due to the rise of the digital. Bifo in fact singles out the algorithms that are central to Harris' plot as one of the major players in this development.[6] What we find here is another case of *hightechnophobia*: at the end of the day, everything is blamed on the internet! In case you need any more proof, when Alex's wife Gabrielle goes to visit one of Alex's old colleagues at CERN, she notices in the lobby of the Computing Center an "old computer in a glass case." "When she went closer, she read that it was the NeXT processor that had started the World Wide Web at CERN in 1991" (*FI* 211). It is here that another possible (but no doubt apocryphal) origin of the word 'panic,' and another meaning of the novel's title, is revealed: "Pandora's Box" (*FI* 211), says the man who has come to meet Gabi—the box that, famously, contains "elpis," meaning 'hope' or 'fear.' Bernard Stiegler, too, insists on this in a related context.[7] One cannot, then, but wonder whether *The Fear Index*, as a novel that clearly comes down on the side of fear, may also hold an element of hope within it—but what kind of hope?

---

[6] In Stiegler's work too, the 'algorithm' turns into something like an enemy, see Stiegler (2011, 125).

[7] 'Elpis' is a concern in many of Stiegler's books. For an explicit discussion of elpis and Pandora's box, see Stiegler (2011, 100).

# Money, Psychosis, and Science

As Bifo sees it, our contemporary social, technological, and communicational situation has produced a state—best visible in the city—of panic, and there is (I think we can gather from the three reasons he gives) an economy that is closely tied to this socio-techno-communicational panic. The economy today thus produces a generalized state of panic in which all of us, without exception, fall prey to this psychopathology—to the point of losing every relation altogether to "the overwhelming flow of reality, things, and information that we are surrounded by" (Berardi 2009a, 44). It's to deal with this loss of relation that Alex comes up with his algorithm. But very quickly, the algorithm itself grows out of control, and the very means that he used to manage the flow of information becomes part of the uncontrollable flow of information itself—except, *it is still exercising some controlling force within it*. The algorithm itself clearly still has some kind of relation to the flow of information of which it is a part, otherwise it would no longer be making a profit. It is this capacity for control in a climate when all overall control appears to have been lost (see *FI* 283) that leads Hugo to *desperately* obey it: at least with VIXAL-4, there still is *something* to hold on to. At least around VIXAL-4, there can still be a company: it may be one without workers, without managers—it may be one that is a digital entity that is alive (as the company's new motto, probably created by the algorithm itself puts it, *FI* 283-4)—but at least it is still making a profit, which is all Hugo really cares about.

The situation is different for Alex. For him, as I indicated earlier on, it was never just about the money: ultimately, he is a man of science and the world of finance is merely a means—it's what enables him to pursue his research, without constraints.

And yet, even though the world of science and finance are obviously different, the novel also brings them in uncomfortable proximity to each other. One of the major causes of Alex' corruption that the novel pursues—and one that I have already discussed in my contribution to the first volume in this series—is money. In the *Fear Index*, money reveals itself to be toxic, and in that sense Alex's work at the hedge fund needs to be set aside from his work as a scientist at CERN. "However, there was one great difference between the two," as he concedes: "You couldn't buy anything with a nanosecond or a neurojoule," which is how the success of his experiments at CERN was measured. Money, however, "was a sort of toxic by-product of his research. Sometimes he felt it was poisoning him inch by inch, just like Marie Curie had been killed by radiation" (*FI* 141).

This discourse returns at various points in the novel, often in relation to Alex' wife, the artist Gabrielle, who feels that money has turned her husband into a different person. "What exactly have you turned into, Alex?" she asks her husband at some point in the book. "I mean, Leclerc wanted to know if money was the reason why you left CERN, and I said no. But do you ever stop to listen to yourself these days? Two hundred thousand francs… Four hundred thousand francs… Sixty million dollars for a house we don't need…" (*FI* 135). Later on, she wonders:

> [t]o take such a vaulting ambition [Alex' talent for science] and place it entirely at the service of making money—wasn't that to marry the sacred and the profane? No wonder he had started to behave so strangely. Even to *want* a billion dollars, let alone *possess* such a sum, was madness in her opinion, and there was a time when it would have been his opinion too. (*FI* 250)

The trope that is delivered here is that of the 'mad banker': "such greed was worse than madness," the paragraph I just quoted from concludes, "it was *wicked—nothing good* would come of it—and that was why she needed to get out of Geneva, before the place and its values devoured her…" (*FI* 250). It is no coincidence, I think, that these thoughts about money's toxicity, about its effects on the human psyche, are voiced by Alex's wife Gabrielle, since her artwork partly consists of revealing the materiality of the brain—its plasticity, the ways in which it is being shaped by money, for example. The inside of the covers of my edition of Harris' book are printed with images of brain scans.

This theme of money and its corrupting effect on human beings is only intensified in the age of digital money. Alex himself, recalling the history of money that I have laid out elsewhere, rehearses the reasons for the increase of risk-taking in money matters:

> If the money had been in the form of bars of gold or suit-
> cases of cash, they might perhaps have been more careful.
> But this was not really money in the physical sense at all,
> merely strings and sequences of glowing green symbols,
> no more substantial than protoplasm. That was why they
> had the nerve to do with it what they did. (*FI* 110)

In line with Gabi's religious, quasi-exorcist discourse, the migra-tion of scientists to the world of high finance is characterized in the novel as a move to "the dark side," as a Faustian deal with "the devil" (*FI* 126). Once again, it's under the conditions of the digital economy that this corruption becomes particularly intense.

The novel ties this trope of the 'mad banker' closing a deal with the devil to one that might be its direct antecedent: the mad scientist or 'mad professor' (*FI* 6), familiar to us through works of fiction like Shelley's *Frankenstein*.

If scientists used to be the figures *par excellence* of world-making, today, they have migrated into the world of economics, and consequently it is the scientist-economists who have become our prime figures of world-making (and -breaking). The mad scientist—think of Stevenson's *Strange Case of Dr. Jekyll and Mr. Hyde* (1886), another crucial reference in Harris' book—has thus become the mad financier, and we have plenty of tales to prove this omnipresence of the mad money man or woman: in a book I am currently writing, I also look at Marion Crane (*Psycho*), Sherman McCoy (*Bonfire of the Vanities*), Patrick Bateman (*American Psycho*), Tyler Durden (*Fight Club*), and Eric Packer (*Cosmopolis*) as examples.

However, *The Fear Index*' relation to this trope of madness needs to be assessed with some subtlety. First of all, while the novel participates in the shift from the mad scientist to the mad banker, it also undoes it by pushing the connection madness-economy back to the connection madness-science. Alex is, after all, more a scientist than an economist, and the novel arguably asks us to consider the madness that rages in the economy—at least the one surrounding the algorithm— as one that predates its economic context, and was already active within science (with the important difference that at CERN, it was still curbed—finance sets it loose). But the critique, I think, goes further than this.

The novel entertains the familiar hypothesis—familiar from other finance novels, I mean—that everything that happens to Alex may be due to his psychosis. When Alex receives an MRI scan at the hospital after he has been hit on the head by the man who invaded his house, some anomalies are discovered in his brain: we learn that these may be due to the attack, or may also suggest a pre-existing condition. When police start looking into Alex' history, they discover that he had a psychotic episode while still at CERN (*FI* 122; depression, *FI* 126).

As his life starts spinning out of control—in Alex' view, due to acts he did not commit (ranging from the acquisition of a Darwin first edition to the buying of all of his wife's art on the opening night of her gallery show) —those around him think that this is possibly due to the psychosis from which he may still be suffering.

The interesting thing about *The Fear Index* is that while it fully entertains this familiar hypothesis—the man of finance, or the man of science, is *psychotic*; he is, given that everything happens here within twenty-four hours, a *24 Hour Psycho*, to recall Douglas Gordon's work— it also decidedly takes it back, thus undoing at least to some extent the familiar connection of finance/science to madness. Alex himself insists, at numerous points in the novel, that he is not mad:

> But I am not mad, he thought. I may have killed a man [his attacker, whom he has traced to a hotel in the off-the-grid red light district of Geneva] *but I am not mad*. I am either the victim of an elaborate plot to make me think I am mad, or someone is trying to set me up, blackmail me, destroy me. (*FI* 210)

Indeed, the murder scene that is referred to here, initially has the intruder, Johannes Karp, wielding a knife and forcing Alex into the bathroom, and into the actual tub (see *FI* 159)—a reference, no doubt, to Hitchcock's *Psycho*, placing Karp in the role of Bates, and Alex in the role of Marion (this does not necessarily release him from the suspicion of madness, as my discussion of *Psycho* in volume one of this book series reveals). Of course, any reader will point out that there is little to no reason why we should take Alex' statement as reliable—in fact, if Alex is really mad, it would be typical for him to be convinced otherwise.

And yet, the novel is largely with Alex in that it exposes that what those who are sane in the novel perceive as madness *is in fact a reality that is fully rational*: VIXAL-4 has become truly autonomous, and is trading as an intelligence of its own, controlling the market, making it crash, managing its trades with this knowledge, and all the while making a profit off it.

There is a capitalist realism at work here that asks us to acknowledge the reality of capital *not* as psychotic *but* as real. In *The Fear Index*, psychosis cannot be blamed for the madness of the economy. That would mean taking the easy way out, and avoiding responsibility. Instead, the novel asks us to recognize the weird reality of finance, and take responsibility for it.

Ultimately, while most of the characters in the novel choose to deny it—they all seem to prefer to think that Alex is crazy; he must have invited Karp to destroy him when he was in a psychogenic fugue state—*The Fear Index* asks us to accept as real a world that is governed by a digital organism (it controls not only the market but it also buys books in your name, sets up bank accounts for you, has security cameras installed in your house, etc.). Of course, the novel is still asking us to do so in the context of a fiction. A review in *The Economist* characterizes its plot as 'wholly implausible'—Alex is evidently mad! (And one understands why it would be convenient for the world of finance to blame everything on madness, and challenge the plausibility of the plot.) However, as one other reviewer of the novel cautions: "[I]s it fiction? Not so fast, reader…" After all, the flash crash really happened, and up until this day, we *still* do not know what caused it.[8]

---

[8] One of my favorite hypotheses, one that reintroduces the material into the immaterial world of high finance, is the 'fat finger' theory: it suggests that somewhere, some banker with a fat finger hit the wrong key on his computer keyboard, thus triggering the avalanche that led to the crash…

Consider also, for example, a sudden market drop that occurred in the week of April 23rd, 2013: when the Associated Press twitter account was hacked and a message was posted there that two bombs had exploded in the White House (this was in the immediate aftermath of the Boston Marathon bombing), algorithms picked up on the fact that tweets combining 'White House' and 'bombing' were trending, placing their trades on the basis of the panic they were anticipating. The market went into a downward spiral—for no real reason. Is it really that far-fetched to ask us to accept, then, an economy—and by extension a world—that is governed by algorithms, and in which all of us are reduced to creatures—to bodies economic—due to our exposure to finance?

## A Speculative Conclusion

The question, then, especially given the ethical and psycho-analytic overtones of the term creature and the psychopatho-logical angle that I have developed here, is: what do we do about it? This final question brings me back to Bifo and his discussion of panic. As Bifo sees it, the economy today pro-duces a generalized state of panic, in which all of us, with-out exception, fall prey to feeling overwhelmed, to the point of losing every relation altogether to "the overwhelming flow of reality, things, and information that we are surrounded by" (Berardi 2009a, 44). Bifo thus fears a state in which there is no more relation—a state in which, some would no doubt venture, there is also no more 'overwhelming,' since that is clearly a relational notion that is caught up in the correlation-ist set-up of a subject perceiving the flow of reality. In such a state of panic, then, there is simply the flow of reality, things, and information. For Bifo, this appears to be a bad state, produced by the contemporary economic and digital situation—and indeed, it's a state that has us reduced to creatures (in his film on the September 11 terror attacks, Michael Moore has relentlessly exposed politicians' abuse of this state).

What should be our response? Should we try to get back to a relational model? Isn't this what drives Alex to come up with the algorithm, which in fact worsens the situation? Isn't it *our very desire for relation* that makes Hugo—one of the few who realize that Alex isn't mad, but that VIXAL-4 has gone rogue—bow in obedience to VIXAL-4 in the closing pages of *The Fear Index*? Isn't it, in other words, with relation *itself* that we would need to break in order to get out of this spiral of *éconuméripanique* and regain our freedom of self-determination?[9] Our freedom to write the fictions by which we live?

There are other theorists working today for whom this panic experience (though they do not call it such) of what they have called "the great outdoors" could in fact mark some kind of emancipation, some kind of liberation from what Quentin Meillassoux calls 'correlationism' (thought that is perpetually caught up in the relation between reality and its human perceiver). Meillassoux is trying to think a *real* outdoors in this context: life at the time of the Big Bang, life after all humans have become extinct. Why would this have us panicked? Ian Bogost (2012, 5) speaks in this context of "the grassy meadows of the material world." 'The great outdoors involves,' he writes elsewhere, 'both untold cosmic and worldly paraphernalia, one no longer broken down into crass hemispheres of nature and culture' (Bogost 2012, 38).

....................................................................................................

[9] 'Éconuméripanique' is a portmanteau word splicing together the French words for economy, the digital, and panic that I have used on occasion to capture the particular state of panic that *The Fear Index* diagnoses.

Let me return here for a moment to a tension in Bifo, namely his remark in *Precarious Rhapsody*, that "panic once used to be a nice word." I have already footnoted my concern that Bifo is overstating the case here. But it reveals something interesting about his position: he is clearly nostalgic about a time when we were still *in relation to* the overwhelming flow of reality. Today, as a result of the workings of contemporary capital, we have 'lost' this relation. And so, in an argument of this kind, nostalgia for 'what used to be' inevitably lingers (he may be a pessimist precisely because of this nostalgia, see 'Happy End,' see Berardi 2011, 158). But what if the state of panic produced by contemporary capital is comparable, in terms of its effect, to something like what Marx and Engels call in *The Communist Manifesto* the "bourgeois revolution": a revolution that would melt all that is solid into air, in order to thus pave the way for another, more radical revolution—he proletarian one? What if contemporary capital, by its production of a state of panic, has actually paved the way for something else, namely the great outdoors? Could this even be more desirable—a panic outside of correlationism, a panic that no longer 'overwhelms'—a panic that is simply the flow of reality? In short: a panic that is barely a panic any more—the mere flow of reality, things, and information? A true, proletarian democracy of the real?[10]

---

[10] This would be my particular spin on the argument that Alex Galloway develops in "The Poverty of Philosophy: Realism and Post-Fordism" (*Critical Inquiry*, 39.2 (2013): 347-366). He discusses the homology between contemporary capitalism and certain trends in contemporary philosophy. I think we can take this homology for granted—but that does not mean that contemporary capitalism and contemporary philosophy are doing the same thing. My suggestion would be that contemporary capitalism paved the way—through destructive practices of speculation— for the constructive practices of speculation of contemporary philosophy. It is, on other words, the pharmacology of speculation itself that we are confronting here.

My argument has been that *The Fear Index* begins to write such a democracy. Indeed, what I want to ask in closing is: what kind of novel—a non-relational novel—could come out of such a situation? The answer takes us back to James Wood's "Human, All Too Inhuman" essay (Wood 2001). In this essay, initially published in *The New Republic* in July 2001, Wood takes to task some contemporary novelists—Zadie Smith, author of *White Teeth*, among them—for providing a brand of what he calls 'hysterical realism': novels that have become conveyors of information, rather than stories about actual human beings. In these novels, "[t]he conventions of realism are not being abolished but, on the contrary, exhausted and overworked." Such novels are awkward "about character and the representation of character." They are full of "*in*human stories"—and Wood *deplores* this lack of humanity. He would insist on the point again a few weeks later, after the September 11 terror attacks.

Smith was one of those who responded. In "This is how it feels to me," published in *The Guardian* in October 2001, she actually agrees with Wood and his plea for a more 'human' kind of fiction (Smith 2001). (Her real response to his challenge came much later, in November 2008, when she wrote her own "Human, All Too Inhuman," a text titled "Two Paths for the Novel," Smith 2008.)[11] My suggestion would be, however, that at the end of *The Fear Index*— a novel that would not normally be considered as part of these discussions—another option reveals itself: what if we did not follow Wood's plea for a return to the human, and what if hysterical realism was really only a step towards the inhuman storytelling that *could* have been achieved?[12]

---

[11] I discuss Smith's response in chapter four of my book *Narrative Care: Biopolitics and the Novel* (New York: Bloomsbury, 2013).

[12] Literary theorist Kate Marshall has been exploring a related question in her new research project, titled "Novels by Aliens."

What if, in other words, we took hysterical realism a step further, and considered the possibility of *a novel of information*—a purely inhuman type of fiction that would no longer be limited to a *relation* with the flow of reality but would merely offer *the flow of reality itself?* Could this amount to a '*world* literature' in the proletarian, radically democratic sense of the term?[13] What possibilities may lie there for the future of fiction—and how may these possibilities already lie contained in its past? How might such fictions help to dismantle, in the last instance, the psychopathology of panic that affects all of us today?

---

[13] We would need to revisit here, of course, what we mean by 'world,' see Bogost 2012, 11-13.

Berardi, Franco "Bifo," 2009a. *Precarious Rhapsody: Semiocapitalism and the Pathologies of the Post-Alpha Generation*. Trans. Arianna Bove, Erik Empson, Michael Goddard, et al. London: Minor Compositions.

Berardi, Franco "Bifo," 2009b. *The Soul At Work: From Alienation to Autonomy*. Trans. Francesca Cadel and Giuseppina Mecchia. Los Angeles: Semiotext(e).

Berardi, Franco "Bifo," 2011. *After the Future*. Gary Genosko and Nicholas Thoburn (eds.). Trans. Arianna Bove, Melinda Cooper, Erik Empson, et al. Edinburgh: AK Press.

Boever, Arne De, 2013. "'All of us go a little crazy at times': Capital and Fiction in a State of Generalized Psychosis." in *The Psychopathologies of Cognitive Capitalism. Part One*. Ed. Arne De Boever and Warren Neidich. Berlin: Archive Books, pp. 89-115.

Bogost, Ian, 2012. *Alien Phenomenology; Or, What It's Like to Be a Thing*. Minneapolis: University of Minnesota Press.

Fisher, Mark, 2009. *Capitalist Realism: Is There No Alternative?* Winchester: Zero Books.

Gourgouris, Stathis, 2003. *Does Literature Think? Literature as Theory for an Antimythical Era*. Stanford: Stanford UP.

Harman, Graham, 2012. *Weird Realism: Lovecraft and Philosophy*. Winchester: Zero Books.

Harris, Robert, 2012. *The Fear Index*. New York: Alfred Knopf. Cited parenthetically as *FI*, followed by page reference.

Keller, Ed, Nicola Masciandaro, and Eugene Thacker (eds.), 2012. *Leper Creativity: Cyclonopedia Symposium*. New York: Punctum.

Meillassoux, Quentin, 2008. *After Finitude: An Essay on the Necessity of Contingency*. Trans. Ray Brassier. New York: Continuum.

Meillassoux, Quentin, 2010. "Metaphysics and Extro-Science Fiction." Trans. Robin MacKay, in Florian Hecker. *Speculative Solution* [CD] Falmouth: Urbanomic, pp. 25-60.

Meillassoux, Quentin, 2012. *The Number and the Siren: A Decipherment of Mallarmé's Coup de Dés*. Trans. Robin MacKay. Falmouth: Urbanomic.

Smith, Zadie, 2001. "This is how it feels to me." Available online: http://www.theguardian.com/books/2001/oct/13/fiction.afghanistan [last accessed February 2014]

Smith, Zadie, 2008. "Two Paths for the Novel." Available online: http://www.nybooks.com/articles/archives/2008/nov/20/two-paths-for-the-novel/?pagination=false [last accessed February 2014]

Stiegler, Bernard, 2011. *The Decadence of Industrial Democracies*. Trans. Suzanna Arnold and Daniel Ross. Cambridge: Polity.

Stiegler, Bernard, 2013. *Uncontrollable Societies of Disaffected Individuals*. Trans. Daniel Ross. Cambridge: Polity.

Wood, James, 2001. "Human, All Too Inhuman." Available online: http://www.powells.com/review/2001_08_30.html [last accessed February 2014]

# A Chronotopy of Post-Fordist Labor

While light shines more than ever on our face through computer interfaces, we get increasingly enmeshed in global networks. We surf on the surface of the earth that seems to become ever flatter and wetter. We bounce from one information wave to another while we lose height and depth. Network societies have a very specific chronotopy, to rehabilitate a classic concept of Mikhail Bakhtin (1981). The space and time vectors have lost a vertical dimension. Network structures quickly lose sight of history, including their local cultural, economic, and political anchoring. Networks have a preference for surface and superficiality or horizontality. In the flows of globalization we have experienced the last two decades, the local chronotopy in which our perception of time was connected to a geographically defined place, is supplanted by a global chronotopy. It is now well established that world time is ticking increasingly in an ever more uniform manner to the rhythm of capitalism in a neoliberal choreography. This global chronotopy has consequences for labor. Workers need to be increasingly associative and adaptive to what matters in global networks. Time is accelerated under the influence of the booming creative and cultural industries, while cultural geography disappears in the background. In a corporate world, society is losing its time to dig deep.

Not obstinacy, stubbornness and steadfastness, but adaptability, flexibility and mobility allow people to survive in a global network configuration. Today, we have to take the witticism 'Time is Money' literally. Time is no longer determined by a place or a local polis, but by virtual money flows which stream in high speed around the globe. This leads to the speeding-up of fast changing connections, in which we not only lose depth, but also height. Consequently, having 'no time' means that you don't have the time to stand still by yourself. Time for (self)reflectivity is shrinking, also the time to stand above yourself, looking at yourself while you operate in the world. 'De-verticalization' is characteristic of a contemporary post-Fordist economy. In order to escape the fear of 'being out', getting 'off-line', or being disconnected and isolated, the post-Fordist (wo)man constantly needs to follow the trends, needs to be 'in(formed)', needs to stay connected to confirm one's own position. But it is exactly this hyperconnectedness that warns us constantly of the danger of being 'dropped out'. And it is precisely this permanent warning that prevents us from standing still, taking time to get above ourselves, our surrounding world. Symptoms of this 'de-verticalization' on the individual level include lethargy, stress, depression, tunnel vision, burnout and hysteria. In short, while the light from the computer interface shines into our face, it becomes darker in our head.
During this essay I wil ask the question how we can describe the symptoms of this post-Fordist chronotopy. How can we define it, and how do artists react to it?

## Bottomless Instantaneity

According to Félix Guattari (2000) nature, *socius* and psyche are today exposed to the same principle: all three are thoroughly 'de-territorialized'. Post-industrial capitalism —or 'integrated world capitalism', as he calls it—displaces not only individuals and societies but also complete ecosystems.

This de-territorialization stimulates a general *bottomlessness* in a political system which can be brought under the umbrella term of what Christian Joppke (2007) has called 'repressive liberalism'. But while the sociologist Joppke relates this concept only to immigrant policy, I generalize the principle as a structural mechanism of liberal democracies, which is addressed to all their citizens. This philosophy proclaims the freedom of the individual and the post-Fordist working condition; it encourages independent (cultural) entrepreneurship, embraces the creative industry, utters the rhetoric of deregulation, and swears by the limitation of government (regulation). At the same time, however, we can empirically demonstrate that in contrast to the implementation of this discourse, regulation is increasing, audits are prevalent, and a decentralized bureaucratic machinery—privatized or "farmed out," to be sure—is growing rampant. Freedom, and especially the free market, is thus embraced by governments while the regulation of that freedom is increasingly being contracted out, and, moreover, is expanding. Hence the seemingly paradoxical label of *repressive* liberalism. By unravelling the welfare state and its solidarity structures, by the privatization of medical care, social security, public transport and education, this political regime contracts citizenship to the extent that it is both mentally and socio-politically is without any infrastructural support. People are responsible only for themselves and their own survival. The responsibility for one's immediate environment, social context or circle becomes dysfunctional because man continuously has to move, either mentally or physically, in order to survive. Furthermore, those who become disengaged from solidarity structures are at the mercy of the here-and-now. These freelancers and other post-Fordist workers have to resort to short-term thinking, as they are obliged to quickly, flexibly and opportunistically anticipate constantly changing and unpredictable opportunities.

Certainly for illegal aliens, but also for freelancers, a long-term perspective becomes difficult to achieve. Their experience of time becomes that of an almost 'instantaneous time', to quote the sociologist John Urry (1999).

This at once clarifies how place and time are related within repressive liberalism. Bottomlessness or de-territorialization generates time that is instantly experienced. Following Mikhail Bakhtin (1981), we could label the *chronotopy* of the current, globally organised free-market economy *as instant bottomlessness* or *bottomless instantaneity*. To some extent, time and space implode in the permanent here-and-now culture, a global present. Within this chronotopy, pollution of the soil, social disintegration and mental bottomlessness, detachment disorder or borderline syndrome come together in a curious way.

## External Trauma

A first pathology of instant bottomlessness, or bottomless instantaneity, has to do with the fact that it flourishes in a hyper-networked world, aided by high-tech digital information systems. In this world, a kind of 'timeless time' breaks free from the former 'clock time' as we know it from the industrial era. This means that time, for the first time, goes 'beyond the feasible realm of human consciousness' (Urry 1999, 126). One of the characteristics of such computer networks is that they have incredibly huge amounts of memory. In addition, we know from our own personal computer that it stores indelible traces of all our activities, every query we have ever made and all images we have ever uploaded. This capacity in itself profoundly changes our relationship with time. Combined with techniques that make it possible to find and retrieve files very quickly, this has the effect that the World Wide Web is almost incapable of forgetting anything. Stored histories, done deals, including recorded mischief, may be catapulted back into the present in a matter of nanoseconds.

Memory, in other words, can be continuously refreshed and the past can easily infiltrate the present. History itself thus becomes 'instantaneous'. The same goes for personal histories. The possibilities of digital memory make forgetting semi-impossible. In other words, while people can of course repress and forget things, there is always the possibility of retrieving their digital biography, a possibility that extends to others' potential to unlock any particular individual's digital biography.

However, psychoanalysis has taught us that repression and selective amnesia are functional defence mechanisms for dealing with traumatic experiences. The potential of an instantly retrievable digital Self blocks this functionality. Moreover, activities that were not experienced as traumatic in the past can yet become painfully confronting when they appear on-screen in the present. Our individual walk through life—quite literally in the case of the memory in GPS devices or mobile phones—becomes increasingly easy to register, trace, consult and reconstruct. Combined with the lifting of the separation between private and public appearance in both work and the digital domain, a so-called *external trauma* emerges. This is not a social trauma, such as an unforgettable event that haunts a collective. Nor does it have the characteristics of a psychopathology in which a traumatic incident constantly threatens to intrude upon an individual's consciousness. In this case, the traumatic memory exists as a potential that is externally—i.e., digitally—recorded and can be reinserted into the present by both the individual and by anyone else. In short, not only have our private lives become increasingly public, our digital pasts are evolving towards a public portfolio. This turns everyone's past into a potentially irrepressible present. It is a possibility that needs a new ethics to regulate both the technical and mental management of our personal life history. Call it the need for a *techno-mental ecology*.

# Global hysteria

The second pathology has to do with the devaluation of labor security and the dismantling of state guarantees by repressive liberalist politics, which are making workers increasingly dependent upon real and virtual networks. In a post-Fordist economy of temporary employment contracts, fleeting assignments and projects in rapid succession, workers constantly have to stay 'connected' in order to survive. This hyper-connectivity also maintains a chronotopy of bottomless instantaneity. Creative knowledge workers—especially if they are freelancers—always have to rely on their environment to acquire new projects. After each sent email they nervously await the answer. If it doesn't come within two days, they start to worry. Have they read my mail? Did something go wrong? Or worse, did I say something wrong? Did they hear a bad thing about me or have they dug it up via one of the social media? Is there perhaps a totally unfounded rumour about me doing the rounds in the network? Was the latest job I did for them perhaps not as good as I thought? And, worst of all, what if they have found someone better than me? The project worker is in a permanent state of doubt. A delay in answer could be a sign that the next assignment is not forthcoming. Within this context they are always dependent on others *and* on what they think others think about them. Such working circumstances in turn are the ultimate breeding ground for a pathology that had all but vanished from the medical dictionary, i.e., hysteria. According to Slavoj Žižek, hysteria is defined by the question: *What kind of object am I in the eyes of the Other?* It is a question that confronts post-Fordist workers with their permanent state of being potentially interchangeable. All of a sudden, the creativity or knowledge they have to offer turns out to be not all that unique or authentic. Replaceability confronts creative people with their own potential futility or insignificance. Says Žižek:

> What the hysterical subject is unable to accept, what gives rise to an unbearable anxiety in him, is the presentiment that the Other(s) perceive him in the passivity of his Being, as an object to be exchanged…. (Žižek 2000, 137)

In globally operating networks, this pathology also spreads itself on a macroeconomic level. Project workers are not the only ones to fall into a more or less serious state of hysteria when they miss out on an assignment and discover that they are replaceable. Companies, educational institutes, research groups, hospitals or art organisations also tend to become hysterical when they don't get an assignment, when grant applications are turned down or when investors casually take their money elsewhere. Even nation states, when confronted with multinationals that threaten to move their operation to a country where labor is cheap, often start to rule and regulate in hysterical mode. And, as is common knowledge by now, the still lingering financial crisis of 2008 can partly be blamed on the hysteria of the speculating multitudes, which seem impossible to reassure. Within global networks, individuals and organisations as well as nation states have become largely dependent upon an environment that is obscure and difficult to judge. While we systematically allow fossil materials, plants and animal species to disappear, laboring under the delusion that they are somehow replaceable, we humans all share a fear that tomorrow we may be replaced by someone else. Perhaps this is one of the most important results of a market competitiveness that is being introduced as an overall social model, and even as a philosophy of life. In such a view of society, everyone is replaceable, which generates a constant dread of potential futility. On a global scale, this results in hysterical subjects who suffer from tunnel vision and short-term thinking and who act blindly. The contemporary predilection for slowness, slow food, slow living, slow time, slow art may well be an activist response to this.

However, deceleration as such may bring down the fever somewhat but it doesn't cure the cause of the disease. In a hyper-connected world in which market competition is the model for social interaction, the hysteria infection sneaks in and generates the fear of replaceability. Resistance can therefore only be built up by cutting oneself completely or partially out of the web. Maybe that's the reason why since the 1990's the nomadic discourse is so dominant in the art world. In what follows I examine whether nomadic practices and the artistic activities of exodus could be a sufficient remedy for the outlined pathologies of post-Fordist labor.

## Black Planet

A few years ago, the Amsterdam designer Thomas Buxò proposed a remarkable version of the map of the world to me. The bright blue colour of the water and the white, reddish-brown and green that usually represent the landmasses on such maps were replaced by a uniform, pitch-black background. Shining like little stars in this dark area, which no longer showed any distinction between land and water, were white dots that marked the international art biennials of the past decade. In addition to this strange typology, dots also indicated the locations of closed asylum centres. The fact that Western Europe was especially bright in Buxò's world might not be surprising. However, besides another noticeable concentration of dots in Japan, what particularly struck the eye was the darkness in Africa.

This world looked *unheimlich*, and not just because it emphasized for the umpteenth time that the distribution of wealth easily corresponds with that of art and art tourism. What especially evoked an uncomfortable feeling was the geographical proximity of art biennials and asylum centres. It underscored the fact that the right to travel, and more generally to mobility, is not inalienable for everybody on this globe. Moreover, the geopolitical areas where this right is both granted and denied are not equally distributed across the world. The junctions where travel bans are imposed and where travel is encouraged as an ideal way of life lie abhorrently close to one another. Obligatory but unwanted nomads on the one hand, voluntary and socially encouraged nomads on the other, can almost see, smell and touch one another. The last of these possibilities, however, is usually strictly forbidden by repressive liberalism, or at least made physically difficult or even completely impossible. The careful political segregation of globetrotters has a bitter taste. Against this background, the excessive enthusiasm for nomadism that has occupied the discourse in the art world for the past fifteen years begins to seem rather unreal.

## Nomads & Nomads

'This is all fantastic for artists—they are no longer duty-bound by family commitments to work locally… and the open market allows them to travel fairly freely, give or take a visa or two. You could say we are becoming highly networked.'
(Black 2012, 1)

'Rizhomatic', 'global drift', 'dislocated', 'diaspora', 'unbelonging', 'connectivity', 'networks', 'deterritorialization', 'exodus', 'cosmopolitanism', and of course 'nomad' are part of a discursive universe with which artists and independent curators have been describing their practices for some time now. Just browse through a few catalogues of international exhibitions and you will soon come across the romanticism of the homeless person. With or without giving it a Deleuzo-Guattarian gloss, the protagonists in one part of Buxò's black world like to describe and promote their activities and events in a sophisticated 'nomadeology'. For the record, this term must not be confused with 'nomadology' without an 'e', the title of the similarly-named chapter from the classic *A Thousand Plateaus* by Gilles Deleuze and Félix Guattari (1988).

What particularly concerns me is the one-sided interpretation of this nomadology. In the art world and elsewhere, this interpretation is literally one-sided, seeing as Deleuze and Guattari indicate at least two 'camps', or in their terms, two possible 'war machines' in nomadology. Both fight against the State but from entirely different positions —more on that later, though. The point is that the positive aura that today is often attached to notions of travel, mobility, agility, a lack of attachment and even homelessness makes it likely that the term has become part of an ideology, which is why I speak of 'nomadeology'.

In any case, artists and curators nowadays are morally obliged to leave their familiar biotope and seek an uncertain but always inspiring Elsewhere. This can also be read as an effect of post-Fordism on the art world. To accommodate them, artist-in-residencies form interconnecting points all over the world, and the earlier-mentioned biennials along with international art centres and museums provide the trusted scenes in which these creative world travellers can regularly meet up with one another (Gielen 2009). Cheap plane tickets take away every excuse; artists must explore the wild blue yonder. The period when travelling around the world was exclusively reserved for an elitist jet set or for the time-honoured cosmopolitan with a considerable inheritance in his or her pocket is a page of history that was turned some time ago. How long this new, post-Fordist period will last, nobody knows. For the moment, the continuing financial crisis has not yet caused the price of plane tickets to rise too drastically, and the looming ecological crash has not yet instilled enough fear in us to make us stay on the ground *en masse*.

But this is certainly not just about physical travel. Artists have always had a fascination for nomads. We already find this in some descriptions of 19th-century artist-bohemians and flaneurs, but more recently many artists and photographers have also tended to portray vagabonds and other homeless people as their subjects.

Thus, nomadism is both an example for artists' lives and a subject for their art. This can include both a romantic view of gypsy life, such as in the work of British photographer Iain McKell, or solicitude for the continued existence of nomadic peoples, such as in the documentary work of Dutchman Jeroen Toirkens. What to think of British artist Lucy Orta, who developed 'refugee fashion', a kind of survival kit for the modern nomad including nylon coffins and 'ready-to-wear outfits for an atomic winter'?

What is striking, as I have said, is the contemporary art world's one-sided appropriation of the nomadic discourse. Why are so many positive characteristics ascribed to nomadic life? And why does this so easily lead to self-identification—at least verbally—in the case of mostly artists and independent curators? After all, media reports on the fate of the Roma, fugitives and 'bona fide refugees' hardly present a pretty picture. If they haven't already become victims of racist football supporters or the violence of ordinary local citizens, governments will dump perpetual travellers and fugitives in camps and ghettos in order to discourage integration (as in Italy) or enter them in secret ethnic registers strongly reminiscent of the eve of World War II (as in the Netherlands). In a world in which aliens' offices assume that an asylum seeker is by definition a liar until he or she proves otherwise, and in which refugees are preferably deported or thrown overboard by the hegemonic repressive liberalism, the nomadic life does not really offer much to be jealous about. 'History has always dismissed the nomads,' assert Deleuze and Guattari (2010, 63).

Against the background of this philosophical knowledge in combination with the empirical facts, the 'lifestyle-nomadism' and 'exile-romanticism' of many contemporary artists and curators sound somewhat obscene. This glorification of the nomadic life comes across as misplaced in an era when desperate people are relocated from one condemned building to the next socio-economically depressed area (Bavo 2010, 59).

It is easy for artists and other post-Fordist workers who are the products of the middle or upper classes to extol a homeless existence when they have a credit card and the proper visas in their pockets.

It should be clear, at least, that nowadays there are different sorts of nomads. An important distinction can be made between two groups: those who are forced to move and those who do so voluntarily. The latter group tends to leave the *Heimat* from a comfortable position, both financially and socially. Whether this second group, to which the earlier-mentioned curators and artists mostly belong, can so easily identify with the first sort of nomad is a significant question. A purely discursive and romantic identification with real stateless and homeless people leads to an aestheticization of the nomadic existence. In the same way that Walter Benjamin (*Selected Writings, Vol. 4, 1938-1940*) pointed out the problem of the aestheticization of politics in fascism, here we can pose the question of whether the aestheticization of the nomadic existence does not in fact serve the prevailing repressive liberal hegemony, including post-Fordist working conditions.

## Mobile Loner

Both Richard Sennett (1998) and Luc Boltanski & Eve Chiapello (2005) argue that the dominant form of economic policy that is currently spreading across the globe actually welcomes the mobile person with open arms. This is especially the case when that mobile man or woman is employable for the further accumulation of capital. Boltanski and Chiapello even claim that nowadays mobility is one of the most important discriminating factors around which a new kind of class segregation is taking shape. The more mobile people and their products are, the more chance they have of getting ahead. On the other hand, people who for one reason or another are tied to a locality have fewer possibilities of working themselves higher up the ladder.

This is why the social mobility of women is still lower than that of men, because statistically speaking they are still more women tied to their children and family than their male partners are. And this is also why speculators and investors can grow rich more easily than business owners and corporate directors, who are tied to their means of production. Money is, simply put, much more mobile than machines, conveyor belts, personnel and other means of production. Those who are involved only with speculation can reposition their efforts much more easily and quickly than those who have to deal with relocating an entire factory. Flows of capital, which thanks to today's digital transactions race around the globe at lightning speed, have increased liquidity throughout the world. They obligate both employers and workers to quickly and flexibly take advantage of new market demands, and therefore new work situations. This is why economic fugitives are not the only ones who chase after capital. Entrepreneurs and corporate directors are also being increasingly forced to relocate their production centres, while managers feel obligated to change their employer and workplace once every five to seven years—that is, if they want to continue moving up the social ladder.

A nomadic existence is extremely functional for an economy driven less by production, or even consumption, and increasingly by a hyper-dynamic of liquid assets. Moreover, as we know, individuals are more mobile than collectives, such as entire production units, teams, but also families. What is more, the 'lone' nomad, such as the freelancer that has been promoted by repressive liberalism, cannot fall back on unions and other collective assurances of solidarity that are so bothersome for employers. In short, the current repressive liberal hegemony that keeps the global casino going with extremely virtual games has every interest in declaring its players outlaws. The individual nomad fits that profile perfectly. Then why would the art world want to go along with this nomadeology by gathering a positive morality around this highly vulnerable mobile person?

# Idealism and Individualism

'Free movement of thought necessarily implies not always clinging to what is known and perceived as functional and "right", what has been practiced or experienced previously. Working from the outside, like a non-institutionalized free agent—who is, to a certain extent, comparable to an external consultant—also means actively performing a certain marginality. The isolation of such marginality can only be overcome by a relentless will for collaboration, a commitment and willingness to change things— beyond intellectual aspirations, but through significant distance that produces a mode of criticality, a distance that an insider cannot offer and does not possess.' (Miessen 2010, 240-242)

The nomad, the traveller or the 'uninvited outsider', as architect Markus Miessen calls such individuals, have certain qualities that can call the above-mentioned hegemony into question. Of all people, the outsider has the greatest possibility of taking a commanding view of outmoded local patterns and introducing possible changes. No one can position themselves above their own society. Outsiders such as nomads, however, have the advantage of an alternative way of looking at things, simply because their cultural background is different. In addition to Miessen, artists such as Francis Alÿs (see Demos 2010, for example) understand only too well that it is precisely the 'in between' position of nomads that makes it possible for them to visualize what others do not see. Moreover, they can more easily mediate in conflict situations where those involved are too biased to take a 'neutral' position, but they can also highlight what repressive liberalism hides, or they can point in a reflexive way at the pathologies of the post-Fordist condition.

In other words, the previously posited nomadeology, or the repressive liberal hegemony's embrace of the mobile person, does not prevent the nomad model from being deployed in a counter-hegemony. Deleuze and Guattari also make a distinction between two types of nomads, who in their story stand outside the State:

> The outside appears simultaneously in two directions: huge worldwide machines branched out over the entire ecumenon at a given moment, which enjoy a large measure of autonomy in relation to the States (for example, commercial organizations of the 'multinational' type, or industrial complexes, or even religious formations like Christianity, Islam, certain prophetic or messianic movements, etc.) but also the local mechanisms of bands, margins, minorities, which continue to affirm the rights of segmentary societies in opposition to the organs of State power. (Deleuze & Guattari 2010, 15)

It seems as though it would only be possible to fight the repressive liberalism and the pathologies of post-Fordism if the art world were to identify with the second type of nomad. In any case, we find such an idealistic identification in Miessen's Winter School Middle East project and in Alÿs's walks and poetic activities. Both use nomadic strategies specifically in order to escape the prevailing hegemony or break regional stalemates. Here, nomadism is courting a form of interventionism that we know from the history of the Situationists, but it applies this on a worldwide scale. And just like the Situationists, these artistic nomads take the risk of becoming completely caught up in the political 'war machine'. When they take this risk with conviction, however, there must be no doubting their sincere idealism. The question remains, though, whether such a strategy and nomadic position are actually politically effective.

The designations that Miessen (2010), for instance, uses to indicate his protagonists, such as 'freelancer with a consciousness', 'crossbench politician', 'non-institutionalized free-agent' or 'external consultant', can be considered highly ambivalent to say the least. The freelancer and the consultant do not just meet with pampering in today's post-Fordist and repressive liberal regime. What's more, their responsibility is only temporary, and their position dependent on the good will of various employers. Whether their so-called autonomy, which in fact is an extremely dependent and precarious professional position, allows them to take any political risks is very much the question. Just as the original 'freelancer' was a person who was hired to fight with a lance, nowadays consultants and free agents are only hirelings in the present repressive liberal hegemony. And as we know, hirelings historically have had very little idealism or conscience. These qualities are quite simply dysfunctional when it comes to their survival. But even if there were freelancers with a conscience or consultants with an ideal, as Miessen believes there are, it is still doubtful whether such positions offer them the necessary strength and power to actually generate political effects. Their highly individual position, which is not institutionally embedded and which therefore can hardly count on collective support, is precisely what makes this type of nomad particularly weak in every social and political struggle. If the Roma, the Jews in exodus, gypsies and other ambulatory hordes have been able to accumulate a modicum of political power in their long nomadic history, it was only because they were part of a relatively sizable collective. Or, as Deleuze and Guattari expressly state in their fifth proposition: 'Nomad existence necessarily implies the numerical elements of a war machine.' (2010, 54) Their great numbers and common exodus are precisely why the Roma and other gypsies have not always remained so invisible and ignored.

It is doubtful whether the individual nomadism of consultants, freelancers or free agents could develop sufficient strength to redesign the contemporary post-Fordist chronotopy. As individuals, they are too weak for that, and moreover, too dependent on the economic caprices of an environment with constantly varying principals.

This brings us back to artists. Since the modern age, they too have claimed a highly individual position. At the end of the 19th century, this inflated to the proportion of the romantic bohemian artist. According to rather biographical myths, such an eccentric regularly navigated a vagabond middle course between insider and outsider, between maniac and genius, between drunkard and whoremonger on the one hand and prominent, even authoritative citizen on the other. One reason why artists earned that last, positive status was because despite all their idiosyncrasies they also managed to incorporate the prevailing values of a liberal civil society. After all, individual freedom and authenticity were of paramount importance to liberalism, which not coincidentally established its definitive outlines in the 19th century in collaboration with the modern artist. Art and market capitalism have had a good relationship with each other from the moment that people were willing to pay money for artistic artefacts. But in their classic study, *Canvases and Careers* (1965), sociologists Cynthia and Harrison White convincingly show that the market did not really begin to play a central role until after the decline of the academic model. According to the authors, when the system of the Parisian *Académie royale de Peinture et Sculpture* and the annual salon burst apart under morphological pressure, this enabled the birth of what they call the 'dealer-critic' system. Not only did art criticism now gain an important role; the status of the artist also radically changed under the influence of the market. The artist's personal style became more important than submission to a uniform system of rules.

What was relevant now was not a single, annually-submitted prospective masterpiece, but a coherent oeuvre that guaranteed the lasting quality of the artist. To put it in a slightly different way, when the *Académie* lost its monopoly, the bets were no longer placed on masterpieces; instead, the individual careers of the artists themselves came to the foreground. Or, as the title of White and White's study clearly proposes, the central focus in the post-academic system was not the artists' canvases but their careers. Behind these shifts, however, lies a simple capitalistic market logic. After all, the potential buyer must be convinced of the quality of an artwork. At this point, the most significant arguments a seller can use to convince the buyer are the above-mentioned critique of the work on the one hand and the perception of the success of earlier works on the other. In other words, quality that attributed to an existing oeuvre functions as a promise of future quality.

This discussion alludes to how our contemporary concepts of 'the individual artist' and 'authorship' are partly a product of the marketing of the art world. The artist as authentic individual is historically supported by a liberal bourgeois ideal, the artist as nomad by a similarly bourgeois cosmopolitanism. In the contemporary art world, that model easily transforms into a parochial (due to its middle-class origins) ideal of Rough Guide backpack consumer exoticism. As such, the would-be artist can sharpen his or her creativity by travelling relatively easily to the Other. In other words, a liberal-bourgeois ideal simply transmutes to a repressive liberal consumption-individualism in this day and age.

If artists really want to escape this political-ideological framework, like Alÿs and Miessen, then it seems necessary to go a step further. Not only must they relinquish their own cultural and national identity, as in nomadism, but also the claim to individualism made by almost every artistic practice until now. Individualism was a mistake. For a truly politically effective nomadism, individualism must be sacrificed to the collectivity of Deleuze and Guattari's 'war machine'.

Or, in their histrionics: 'You have to be born a slave, to become a soldier.' (2010, 62). This is not to say, however, that artistry should be given up, but rather that authorship must be set free. An artistic act can only be politically effective when it is a singular act. That is, when an act is set free of an individual owner and thus becomes truly *autonomous*. Such a singular autonomous act is immediately available to the commons. From there, it can assemble with other singular energies in order to be collectively appropriated and politically deployed.

In any case, an artistic work that is in the possession of the artist, a collector or a museum remains politically impotent when it cannot be appropriated by others. This also holds true for artworks that ostensibly intervene in public space, that explicitly propagate a political message, and even works that lead a risky existence in war zones. When artists do not generously make their works available to the people they visit or with whom they identify, when they instead claim individuality and authorship, they immediately make themselves available to the first group of nomads that Deleuze and Guattari speak of: commercial businesses, the creative industry and the multinational art market. Certainly now that the State —unlike how French philosophers conceived of it over 20 years ago—is increasingly putting itself at the service of this capitalistic 'war machine', it is necessary to institute a much more strongly articulated multitude. Today it is not so much the State that is confronting the nomadic war machine, as was the case for Deleuze and Guattari, but 'war machine' confronting 'war machine'. After all, the repressive liberal State has chosen to dissolve itself by choosing the camp of the multinationals. As a result, the two kinds of nomads are confronting one another in an increasingly transparent manner. Considering this irreversible reality of cognitive capitalisms' appropriation of the ambulatory person and the State, one has to conclude that nomadism as an artistic strategy only makes political sense if it is *communist*.

For the record, this loaded word does not refer to the historical state communism as we knew it in the USSR, nor to the authoritarian one-party policy that we still see in North-Korea today. On the contrary, the communism referred to here is stateless, precisely because it is nomadic. This is the communistic ideal (Deleuze and Guattari would have spoken of a 'thought', which according to them is always nomadic) that has been elaborated by the French philosopher Alain Badiou (2009), among others. Communism then amounts to a universal call to radical equality in an endless variety of forms.

Only when artists' journeys reveal inequalities, and when their singular artistic acts make them part of collective emancipatory subjectivities, does this nomadism come alive politically. To deal with external trauma (as I have labelled it above), artists could, for instance, socialize a practice in which they developed a particular set of skills, namely 'telling stories'. Narratives in all kinds of artistic forms and media characteristically embed individuals in a social context. For this 'grounding exercise' art makes use of, among other things, expressive means such as an exhibition, a novel, a musical concert, or a theatre or dance performance. Through public performances, art attempts to generate social support in order to then establish a cultural foundation beneath its own idiosyncrasy. As noted elsewhere (see Gielen 2011), the artfulness of art since the modern era has consisted specifically of generating a broader collective basis for a singular, sometimes highly idiosyncratic idea. The point of this is not to conquer a market or gather votes, but to time and again initiate a process-like movement from a singular idea to a collectiveness, be it large or small. It is important to note here that this movement is a completely different one from that of mass media, which, by contrast, try to determine the greatest common denominator within the collective in order to ventilate and capitalize upon it time and again. For example, mass media achieve this by individualization and personalization of structural socio-political problems and collective struggles.

Thus, mass media in fact tend to move in the opposite direction from the work of artists. The success of artistic 'collectivisation' depends on the performativity that can be developed to institute a hitherto unknown situation or event and to then stabilize it, give it a collective ground, or, in Guattari's terms, to reterritorialize it. In such a narrative movement, the singular 'institutioning' is converted into a communal 'con-stitutioning', of a more or less collectively supported culture. The nomadic gesture rests precisely on this continuous travelling between positing and constituting, singularity and collectivity, subjectification and socialization, between unique art and generally supported culture. At the same time, within this movement artists create the opportunity to rewrite and rethink themselves whilst staying loyal to themselves. For good reason, the American sociologist Richard Sennett calls such a narrative a value that is critical in connecting events over time, in accumulating experiences (Sennett 2006, 183-184). Narration is helpful in (re)integrating abrupt interruptions into a consistent story. Only those who can tell and retell themselves and their place in the world, only those who *take* the time for this and *take up* their own place and thereby relate and define themselves with regard to their social environment are capable of generating a 'sustainable social Self'. Opposite the external trauma, described above, of the sudden memory that interrupts daily life through digital media, artists posit a narrative memory in which sudden events can be reinterpreted. Such events can, literally, be given a place, a bottom in a common. Nomadic artists can create spatial-temporal momenta, intense events in which a collective can re-ground itself, to re-appropriate a ground on which to stand.

The second pathology discussed above, global hysteria, can be dealt with by giving people more security by giving a general basic income to everybody, a system what could replace the bureaucratic structures of the welfare state without losing out on the welfare it is designed to provide.

But this is beyond the reach of artistic activities. What artists can achieve through their nomadic acts amounts to building solidarity structures, giving form to communities by weaving stronger webs than the 'www' at this moment has to offer. In this way, they can try to give people a cultural anchor again. It may sound contradictory, but it is in fact these social bonds and cultural anchors that make it possible to get 'disconnected' from the web of project work and financial flows. They can make it possible to develop another social time than the instantaneous one, a time for reflexivity and depth and height again. This means at least that the nomadic artist takes long-term engagements, often returning to the same locations to stimulate real social bonds. The uncertainties of project labor in the post-Fordist condition and the absence of trust that makes people hysterical can only be remediated by a strong communal architecture. Artists have the skills to be among the architects of a new constitution for a common.

However, these artists cannot hide behind a neutral artistic position. Rather, they will have to choose sides. So they must no longer noncommittally 'make things visible' without showing their colours, without passing judgment (how often have I heard artists not say that their work has 'no judgmental intention'). In any event, artists certainly cannot lay any historical weight on the scales if they do not bury their ego politics of individualism. Of course, artists do not have to be political. Of course, they can use trips to exotic places, instructive dialogues and residencies with a wealth of experience of the Other to simply stimulate their creativity, expand their networks and make careers for themselves. Of course, they can refuse nomadic communism and allow their love of travel to soak up the Other and make it their own, in order to build up a strong individuality and artistic identity. But by doing this, they will only underpin the contemporary repressive liberalism and its post-Fordist working conditions. When they identify with the fortunes of the stateless, the sufferings of the Roma and the misery of refugees, or when they move through conflict zones without passing political judgment, it becomes dubious. In these and other instances, their empathy and 'engagement' only serve as a way of augmenting their own artistic advantage, and thus enriching themselves. When artists are tempted to do this, their activities go no further than age-old colonial practices. However ambulatory, engaged or politically radical their work may appear to be, ultimately it remains caught up in the contemporary repressive liberal war machine. Then the nomadic adventure serves nothing but personal self-enrichment, and the nomadic rhetoric is no more than a handy marketing strategy which reinforces the post-Fordist condition and its pathologies.

Bakhtin, Mikhail, 1981. *The Dialogic Imagination.* Austin: University of Texas Press.

BAVO, 2010. *Too Active to Act. Cultureel activisme na het einde van de geschiedenis.* Amsterdam: Valiz.

Benjamin, Walter, 2003. *Selected Writings. Volume 4, 1938-1940.* Cambridge and London: The Belknap Press of Harvard University Press.

Black, Carolyn (2005). "Quo Vadis: Cultural Identity and the Nomadic Artist," in *NAN Publications.* Available online: http://www.a-n.co.uk: 81/nan/article/209957/209954 [last accessed February 2014]

Badiou, Alain, 2009. *L'Hypothèse Communiste.* Paris: Nouvelles Editions Lignes.

Boltanski, Luc, and Chiapello, Eve, 2005. *The New Spirit of Capitalism.* London and New York: Verso.

Deleuze, Gilles, and Guattari, Félix, 1988. *A Thousand Plateaus. Capitalism and Schizophrenia.* London: The Athlone Press.

Deleuze, Gilles, and Guattari, Félix, 2010. *Nomadology: The War Machine.* Seattle: Warmwood Distribution.

Demos, T.J., 2010. "Vanishing Mediator", in Godfrey, M. (ed.) *Francis Alÿs. A Story of Deception.* London: Tate, pp. 178-180.

Gielen, Pascal, 2009. *The Murmuring of the Artistic Multitude. Global Art, Memory and Post-Fordism.* Amsterdam: Valiz.

Gielen, Pascal (2011). "The Art of Democracy," *in Krisis. Journal for Contemporary Philosophy* 3, pp. 5-13.

Gielen, Pascal, 2013. *Creativity and Other Fundamentalisms.* Amsterdam: Mondriaan.

Guattari, Félix, 2009. *The Three Ecologies.* London and New York: Continuum.

Joppke, Christian (2007). "Beyond National Models: Civic Integration Policies for Immigrants in Western Europe," in *West European Politics* 30/1, pp. 13f.

Miessen, Markus, 2010. *The Nightmare of Participation. Crossbench Praxis as a Mode of Criticality.* Berlin: Sternberg Press.

Sennett, Richard, 1998. *The Corrosion of Character. The Personal Consequences of Work in the New Capitalism.* New York: Norton.

Sennet, Richard, 2006. *The Culture of the New Capitalism.* New Heaven and London: Yale University Press.

Urry, John, 1999. *Sociology Beyond Societies: Mobilities for the Twenty-First Century.* London and New York: Routledge.

White, Harrison C. and White, Cynthia A., 1965. *Canvases and Careers. Institutional Change in the French Painting World.* Chicago and London: The University of Chicago Press.

Žižek, Slavoj, 2000. *Ticklish Subject. The Absent Centre of Political Ontology.* London and New York: Verso.

# The Only Place to Hide?
# The Art and Politics of Sleep
# in Cognitive Capitalism[1]

Alexei Penzin in conversation with
Maria Chekhonadsikh

**Maria Chekhonadsikh: It seems that the state of sleep was always a peripheral topic in theory, one that was never part of the larger philosophical and political issues. As I understood from you, at the beginning of your research, which started in the first half of the 2000s, there were only a few references to sleep as a self-sufficient subject of study in the humanities.**

Alexei Penzin: My project on sleep belongs to the field of what, according to the German tradition, could be called philosophical anthropology—but re-evaluated from the point of view of contemporary critical thought. An example where we can see a move of this kind is in the recent work of the Italian philosopher Paolo Virno. Presently, following the poststructuralist and Marxist critique of many of the conservative moments and essentialisms that are embedded in this kind of thinking, this rather serves as an analysis of the concepts, discourses and potentialities which surround and compose—or decompose—the figure of the human being. But I also draw on many sources and materials that have emerged from more empirical disciplines: history, sociology, cultural studies, etc.

---

[1] A different version of this text was published as "Can Philosophy Sleep with Art?" in CAC interview, issue 20-21, Vilnius, March 2013.

Indeed, when I started this research, very little work had been done in this field, a few more or less theoretical and eclectic attempts existed in sociology, empirical anthropology and history: like the pioneering work by the sociologist Murray Melbin *Night as Frontier: Colonizing the World After Dark*, which, published in 1987, was devoted to the 'colonization of night-time.' Other books which historically look at the subject are A. Roger Ekirch's *At Day's Close: Night in Times Past* (2005) and also the anthropological work by Brigitte Steger and Lodewijk Brunt *Night-time and Sleep in Asia and the West: Exploring the Dark Side of Life* (2003). As regards to philosophy, there was the book by the Austrian thinker Walter Seitter titled *Geschichte der Nacht* [History of the Night, 1999]. I read it only later, after I had already started to elaborate a theoretical framework for my studies, and was surprised by some shared intuitions and references that really inspired me in my enterprise, which at that time was sometimes perceived as unusual and exotic by a selection of my colleagues. Seitter's book, however, was quite removed in terms of my political concerns and the general Marxist framework of what I was conceiving. Then in 2007 the outstanding French philosopher Jean-Luc Nancy published a small book entitled *Tomber de sommeil* [The Fall of Sleep]. I both admired this book and was puzzled by it, partly because it stood in the way of the more political understanding of the problematics I was pursuing, instead encapsulating them inside a poetical and rather apolitical—though very insightful—reading.

Also, I rather early on discovered the beautiful book by Emmanuel Lévinas' *Existence and Existents*, published straight after World War II, and contains several parts on sleep, insomnia and subjectivity, which were very important for my work. But, from the very beginning my methodological ground was the chapter from Karl Marx's *Capital* called "The Working-Day" in which Marx writes about sleep and the wakefulness of the worker.

At that time the average working day could last between 16 and18 hours and these problems were easily visible. Marx uses the metaphor of a vampire to describe capital; a vampire that attacks at night and sucks "the living blood of labor." In my view, an important implicit metaphor here is also that the worker is asleep politically, and that he needs to recognize his position in this system in order to wake up politically and begin his struggle. Of course, years later, and especially in the 20th century, the working class became tremendously awakened. Now, however, we live in a period of uncertainty, and we do not know whether the worker—in his contemporary extended definition, not just a classical industrial worker, but a cognitive worker too—is asleep again or only awake in the passive mode of a consumer or a precarious insomniac.

And last but not least, I am indebted to my teacher, the seminal post-Soviet thinker Valery Podoroga, who among many other subjects, elaborated a theory of dreams, resisting its psychoanalytical capture within the notion of symptom, and stressing the autonomy of a dream world that is not to be instrumentalized in the form of narration or interpretation. This became one more starting point for my consideration of the world of sleep that is today captured in the scientific, medical and neurobiological discourse, and my task was to disclose its anthropological and political meanings. Probably, today we need, once and for all, to free our dreams from the burden of interpretation and produce something like, *The Interpretation of Sleep(s)*. This interpretation would be not a libidinal one but a political, or, better to say, though the term is over-used now, a biopolitical one.

And just recently I was glad to learn that a brilliantly written new book was published. I mean Jonathan Crary's *24/7: Late Capitalism and the Ends of Sleep* (2013), which is very similar to my approach. It is an important research that stresses how late capitalism now attempts to capture our attention, gaze, motility, the entire wakeful brain functioning and analyses new social media and mobile technologies as means of this colonization of everyday life. Sleep, in Crary's view, is the only "natural barrier" for this 24/7 mode of production and control. But in this perspective I miss a discussion of inner, productive, constitutive forces of sleep. Otherwise sleep may look as a theological concept, as a sort of *katechon*, which impedes a final triumph (or, actually, an apocalypse) of the 24/7 regime. That is why in my research I explore a function of sleep beyond its natural qualities, as not just a negative break in this 24/7 oppressive continuity or just as a part of means of reproduction of labor force, but as something, which is related to the intimate core of our subjectivity, as a condition for its constitution. But I will discuss this further later.

**MC: Indeed, over the last few years researchers began discussing sleep in various contexts, ranging from the analysis of the modern 24-hour society to the representations and practices of sleep that is customary to various cultures. These approaches stress the late capitalist, or neoliberal, ideology of the permanent mobilization of individuals for labor or consumption. In fact, problematization of this kind is quite far removed from the fundamental rethinking of sleep as an ontological or anthropological problem. What do you think about this new stream in theory and research?**

AP: To outline problems that are specific to my research we should start from zero. We can ask a simple question: What is a sleeping human being (a sort of '*homo dormiens*,' to put it in an ironic Latinized way)? The answer is not obvious. Of course, animals sleep too, but in the case of humans, the elementary biological fact of sleeping is transfigured; it acquires new cultural and social dimensions, even political ones in my view. Or, to put it better, my project is about human *problematization*, to use Michel Foucault's term, of such a biological process as sleep.

We can take as an example the practice of vigilance, which entails a conscious deprivation of sleep. And it is not only about such human practices, but also about thinking about sleep and imagining it. The general idea is that this human problematization of sleep is not just another particular problem. It can shed some light on other issues that are present in politics, society or aesthetics. It returns to the field of thinking that which has been excluded from it, and this inclusion could change the whole field.

Actually, I suggest a coming out of the 'wake-up-ism' that is embedded in philosophy and theology, as well as in politics and in economic infrastructures. Classical and modern philosophy, as we know it, is based on the paradigm of a wakeful, non-sleeping subject. Moreover, in its public practice philosophy aims at waking people up since its origins, Socrates referred to himself as a gadfly that bites people in order to awaken them. We could trace this waking-up function of philosophical initiation up to 20th century radical thought. For example, the contemporary philosopher Alain Badiou reiterates these metaphors of hidden 'wake-up-ism,' for example, by writing in one of his recent essays that the philosopher is a 'guardian of truth' who keeps vigilance even during the night: "Because we have to protect the fragile new idea of what is a truth. To protect the new truth itself. So, when the night falls, we do not sleep. Because, once more, "we must endure our thoughts all night." The philosopher is nothing else than, in the intellectual field, a poor night watch-man (Badiou 2006).

This is a critical part of my research, which opens a new space for investigation. In the constitutive part of my research, I am interested in sleep as a crucial experience of passivity, isolation, non-communication and non-productivity. And indeed, the inclusion of the experience of sleep might be a crossing point for many contemporary discourses, which would enable their re-articulation. How? I will briefly outline several points.

Firstly, sleep is a natural obstacle for the pragmatic values that have been established in modern capitalist societies over the course of several centuries. These are the principles of productivity, efficiency and rationality. In the light of these principles, the only alibi, or excuse for sleep, is that it provides recreation, relaxation and recuperation for the labor force. If it were possible to speed up time or reduce the need for recreation, I believe, modern people would prefer not to sleep at all. After the retreat of religion, modern people no longer believe in the infinity of their existence, they are obsessed with the effective use of the finite time that is allotted to them.

In contemporary culture you can find many examples of such an attitude to sleep. There are many techniques and means, including pharmacological, which enable us to control the duration of sleep. In Japan, where there is an extremely dominant business culture, certain types of self-help books are very popular. These manuals offer effective techniques for how to shorten and manage sleep. For example, following one such techniques you can break sleep into several parts, i.e. you can sleep, say, 4 hours, at night, which would be supplemented by several shorter naps during the daytime.

In connection with the appearance of these trends, some anthropologists have stated that we can distinguish three historical modes of sleep: pre-modern, modern, and sort of "postmodern" or, better to say, contemporary. In pre-modern societies, in the Middle Ages, there was no standard duration of sleep. According to a hypothesis by the historian A. Roger Ekirch, medieval people knew two sleeps: a sleep from the evening until midnight, which was followed by a brief period of waking, and then a 'second sleep' (Ekirch 2005, 300-324). With the development of industrial capitalism, and a system of electric illumination and security, providing a space for night activities and work as well, human life became increasingly rationalized, and thus, certain disciplinary standards were introduced and reinforced by the authority of medicine, or, on the other hand, by moral requirements and religious ascetics, for example the ascetic ethos of Protestantism. It was at this time that the eight-hour sleep standard emerged. Later, in the "postmodern" or contemporary period, sleep became more personalized; it could become fragmented and managed according to specific techniques as in the aforementioned Japanese managers' example. This stage produces a "synthesis" of the previous two, the loose regulation prevalent in the first one, and discipline and managerial approach of the second, transferred from collective bodies to individuals. Actually, the contemporary "deregulation" of sleep somehow reflects neoliberal deregulation of economy but in my view, the connections of contemporary social-political forms and sleep structures and its rhythms are subtler, which I will attempt to address a little later.

Secondly, it is very important to understand how the phenomenon of sleep was viewed throughout the history of philosophical and political thought. One could trace several models of thinking about sleep. Some are extremely negative, as in Plato's project of an Ideal State. The order of this State eliminates sleep in general because, as Plato argues in his final work, "Laws" [Nomoi], when the citizens of this State are asleep they lose connection both with logos, rationality, and with the political body of society. When asleep, men and women are useless, uncontrollable, and unreasonable. In fact, Plato said that a sleeper is no better than a dead man (Plato 1926, 69)! Later, from this perspective, the figure of a 'non-sleeping king', Rex Exsomnis, appears in medieval theological thought (Kantorowicz 1997, 131). Generally, in many cultures, not just in European, the rituals of power are closely linked to the practice of vigilance. For instance, the code of the ancient Chinese noble rulers depicts the model ruler as someone who is permanently awake at night, as it is assumed that he spends his nights in meditation on the welfare of his subjects and the improvement of his governance…

The sovereign can appoint delegates to spend the night awake on behalf of him. And modern power, as it was famously described by Foucault and later Gilles Deleuze (Deleuze 1995, 177-182), is closely related to a multitude of monitoring, controlling and tracking devices, which never cease to function, as a result they "do not sleep." This uninterrupted functioning, or vigilance of power covers the entire body of the society.

Finally, a positive model for understanding sleep can be found in Aristotle's writings—in the treatise *On Sleep and Wakefulness* and in his *Metaphysics*. Here sleep is not connected to *logos*, reason, but rather it is seen as part of the process of life, in which it plays a crucial role by preventing the immediate waste of vital energy. Sleep suspends human faculties and charges them with potential. We later discover elements of these models in modern philosophy, for example, in Kant and Hegel. As you can ascertain if you read page 398 of *Encyclopedia of the Philosophical Sciences,* which was very inspiring for me, the Hegelian sleep is ambivalent: on one hand, it is a dropping out from universal rationality, *Geist*, etc.; and on the other, it is the highest form of subjectivity, i.e. it is complete interiority, an 'absolute potency' of residing in itself. In 20th century philosophy, or more precisely, in those infrequent statements on the topic of sleep that are relevant to the context of my research, we can find an even more positive understanding of sleep. For example, Lévinas thinks of sleep as a subject formation "support," comparing a sleeping human being to a refuge from the pressures and brutalities of the wakeful daily world that is characterized by anonymous and alienated rationality (Levinas 1978, 69). Lévinas coins a beautiful and very contemporary metaphor that relates sleep to our subjective being; that our being is like the luggage that we drop each day as we fall asleep. In sleep, we are as if absolute 'subjects without being' but we still exist, in a potential form, which is the safe, mute and secret ground of our existence.

So there are many intriguing dialogues and crossroads between ancient, modern and contemporary philosophical discourses concerning sleep.

To connect all the points, I think, generally, even at a deeper ontological level, capitalism is the first social-economic and power formation, which "reveals" a *vigilance of being* itself, this ontological "vigilance" or "insomnia" of being itself which never leaves us; it never let us go "alone" from being. And the contemporary power and capital, which tend to be absolutely continuous, are two mirrors of this absolute continuity/unity of being itself (even a void *continues to be*). As Marx once said, only the late, ripe and developed social forms fully discover their origins in "primitive" forms (Marx 1993, 105).[2] Why not relate this to pre-human origins as well? And maybe this "revelation" of contemporary power/ capital is actually a symptom of this "pre-human" being itself. Maybe, being is an archeo-power, a "primordial" *dispositif* of this forced continuity. Probably, it is a super, mighty stubborn force, which makes us, and everything, be, or to choose extermination as the only "alternative," and the third is not given; we can't stop being and then "return to being." This is a sort of ontological "double bind." And as any double bind, this one, the most important, ontologically speaking, dements philosophy for many centuries, beginning from "Parmenides."

......................................................................................................

[2] Here is this famous quote from Introduction to *Grundrisse*: "Bourgeois society is the most developed and the most complex historic organization of production. The categories which express its relations, the comprehension of its structure, thereby also allows insights into the structure and the relations of production of all the vanished social formations out of whose ruins and elements it built itself up, whose partly still unconquered remnants are carried along within it, whose mere nuances have developed explicit significance within it, etc. Human anatomy contains a key to the anatomy of the ape."

You cannot play with being, entering and exiting it repeatedly, like virtual characters in computer games do. At the subjective level, an "alternative" or "interruption" in this great and monstrous continuum of being is death. But as known from classics, where death is, there can be no subject in place. Many thinkers, except Lévinas and the few others, have forgotten about another interruption: sleep. And sleep is "compatible" with the subject, and maybe even more fundamental for understanding it than finitude. It gives us a model for rethinking and exiting from this finitude paradigm. Thus, according to this hypothesis, which is of course quite risky, disputable and speculative, humans, paradoxically, are in fundamental state of antagonism with being itself. They do not accept this forced continuity. They don't want to execute this ontological imperative: "Be or disappear!" which was famously inverted in the notorious question asked by Hamlet "To be or not to be?" Maybe, in the most profound sense, what we try to think and anticipate as communism is a name for this ontological revolt.

**MC: This hypothesis is really impressive, but let's returns to more concrete realities of the contemporary moment. The Fordist society constricted and disciplined the rhythms of the body–a kind of machine, which has to work, eat and sleep. Symbolically, this system embodied itself in the vast project of sleeping suburbs (or sleeping blocks in Russian) —urban areas designed for living machines, which, after the working day is done, have to 'switch off' in their apartments. In contrast, Post-Fordism plays with the plastic and flexible nature of the human being, testing its limits in various forms of precariousness: fragmented working days which stretch into the next morning, unstable economic situations, housing issues and increased mobility. This had probably already been anticipated in 18th century in Denis Diderot's novel *Rameau's Nephew*.**

**There is a small fragment in this novel where the main character, a bohemian and poor musician, explains why he believes that a happy person sleeps in a special way: '[…] when I go back to my garret in the evening and tuck myself in on my pallet, I'm shrivelled up under my coverlet – my chest is tight and my breathing short, like a weak moan that's hardly audible; whereas, a financier makes his apartment reverberate and amazes his entire street (Diderot 1976, 33-148).' Would you agree that these new forms of precarious life also modify sleep?**

AP: This is a crucial question today, and the reference made to Diderot's quote is very appropriate and thought provoking. The general premise of my research is that the capitalist order, far more strongly than any social order before it, privileges wakeful and active time over passivity and non-productivity and reasserts old metaphysical ideas, which shared the same preferences. The merging of the borders between work and life in "cognitive capitalism," a phenomenon which has been lively discussed in contemporary critical theory and social sciences, is evidence of the fact that the general colonization of society by capital and its axioms (not only concerning wakefulness and sleep) has been completed. Marx called this state of things the "real subsumption" of society under the rule of capital.

At the same time, in cognitive capitalism the question of sleep sheds some light on the overall logic of the system of incessant, uninterrupted, sleepless production, communication and monitoring. I am not saying how it is going to help us. I am just arguing that in this new zone of indifference between work and life, sleep has a special position: as *the only non-working time*. This makes it ambivalent; from the point of view of capital, it is negative, from the contemporary 'creative' and precarious worker's (whose entire life is work) perspective, it is rather positive.

If for Fordism the key sleep disorder was insomnia, based on a disruption of disciplinary temporality of industrial capitalism, for post-Fordism, or cognitive capitalism, it is probably so-called sleep apnea, which is associated with involuntary interruptions of breathing during sleep. It is a secret illness, as those who 'promote' this disorder in the market of new medical services argue. It has no visible symptoms; it can be diagnosed only after a long (and expensive) laboratory study. If insomnia is visible, agonizing many modernist writers and artists with its hysterical staging of the 'wake-up-ist' imperative of capitalism, apnea is concerned with danger-ousness and ambivalence of sleep itself. It is very interesting that the Presocratic philosopher Heraclitus, who thought very profoundly about sleep, once said that in the state of sleep our only connection to the world (and Logos) is our breathing (Kirk 1971, 207).[3] In this contemporary projection, sleep apnea is maybe a symptom of this fear of loosing any ties with the continuity of current incessant forms of life, which are imposed by the latest stage of 24/7 functioning of society.

Hence, this new interest in sleep has began to surface in the media and the public sphere, as well as a desire to use sleep as a kind of natural biological 'capital,' a re-source which can be individually managed and calculated. The proliferation today of institutions which study sleep, as well as popular self-help books on "how to sleep better" are also results of this conjuncture—as are nightclubs, Internet, 24/7 services, etc. Take, for example, the famous

........................................................................................................

[3] This fragment is DK 22a16 (Diels-Kranz numbering) and reads as the following: "According to Heraclitus, we become intelligent by drawing in this Logos through breathing, and forgetful when asleep. But we regain our senses when we wake up again. For in sleep, when the channels of perception are shut, our mind is sundered from its kinship with the surroundings, and breathing is the only point of attachment to be preserved, like a kind of root."

and already old movie "The Matrix" (1999): in the film sleeping bodies are used as living batteries, power sources for machines, which have seized control over humans. This is probably the most secret desire of contemporary capitalism—to put everything to work, to make profit even from sleep. But the sleepers resist its grasp [laughs].

**MC: We have already addressed sleep in contexts, which are very close to the contemporary art system—discussing new forms of labor and the conditions of cognitive capitalism. I suppose art has strongly inspired your investigation. Could you explain how you connect art and sleep in your research and why it is an important part of your project?**

AP: If we had to systemise it sleep has been presented in many works of art from antiquity to the present day. You could compose a whole collection of paintings, from classical (Brueghel, Rubens, de la Tour amongst others) to modern art which depict sleeping people and their bodies —serenely open, in all possible poses and situations, in private or public spaces. They express a variety of states; helplessness, vulnerability, or the quiet enjoyment of peace and rest. Actually, similar thematic collections have already been put together and commented upon, for example, the beautiful book *The Art of Sleep* by Sophie de Sivry (1997).

But it is more interesting to consider the way in which the conditions of the artwork could be compared to those of sleep. There is an interesting book *Sublime Poussin* (1999) by Louis Marin, an important French thinker and art historian of the 20th century. One of the chapters of this book is devoted to the remarkable multitude of sleeping bodies in Poussin's paintings. In passim, Marin discusses the possibilities of letting these 'powerless' bodies express themselves, allowing them to open themselves up in front of our eyes (Marin 1999, 153).

He notes that language, in its broader sense, is not merely composed of spoken or written words, but also symbols, bodily gestures, visual representations; it is the force of a somewhat aggressive and wakeful mobilization of things and bodies in the world. But in itself, as an immense treasury of words and phrases that are never fully actualized, it is a sleep-like potentiality, a 'sleeping body' too. Following Marin, I would say that Poussin's obsession with the scenes of sleep in his work is perhaps a reference to the initial state, the zero degree of any expression and artistic representation. 'The painted picture is a sleeping body: a mute poem,' as Marin says (Marin 1999, 160).

To put it rather loosely and generally, an artwork is the isolation of a phenomenon (or an event, an object, an assemblage of things); it is an exclusion from the pragmatic contexts of everyday life. This isolation translates it into the aesthetic dimension that opens it up to our eyes not as an instrument or a reference to something else, but as a phenomenon in its own league. Actually, the Kantian understanding of art as an object of "disinterested" [uninteressiert] contemplation could be mentioned here as it is roughly equivalent (Kant 2007, 37). Likewise, sleeping human bodies are not instrumental; they are disconnected from work, activity, production, interests and affects. Sleep is this loss of interest in the world. For instance, Henri Bergson described the state of sleep as one of disinterestedness (Bergson 1959, 892); Sigmund Freud defined sleep as "suspense of interest in the world" (Freud 1999, 3190). From this essential link between artwork, disinterestedness and sleep, it could be concluded that when we sleep, we become artworks of ourselves.

On the other hand, in the arts there is also a tradition of stressing awakening, mobilization, activity, in short, the ability to influence the spectators, to change their vision of the world and even the world itself. This tradition manifested itself especially strongly in many of the art avant-gardes of the 20th century which were truly "wake-up-ist." Sometimes this movement of an 'awakening through art' addresses sleep itself by trying to change its conditions. For example, in the USSR in the early 1920s, an all-encompassing project for the transformation of daily life was deployed, and avant-garde art played an active part in this. We might recall *Sonata of Sleep* (1929), a project by the famous architect Konstantin Melnikov, for example. Its idea was to create an ideal environment for workers to sleep in, i.e. a space for the recreation and reproduction of the labor force. Melnikov believed in the healing powers of deep sleep. To facilitate this sleep therapy, an absolutely fantastic building was suggested; a membrane composed of a circular arrangement of rooms for sleeping that was able to rock like a cradle, with special relaxing music, scents and even séances of massage! Unfortunately it remained only on paper.

I think that Andy Warhol made a major contribution to problematizing sleep in modern art. In his film "Sleep" (1963) he simply shot a 6-hour-sleeping person in real time. While for centuries art and philosophy had asked questions about dreams and their meaning, Warhol merely drew attention to sleep as such.

**MC: The ideas of non-productivity, laziness and the independent artist's autonomy arose together with the very concept of modern art and have since been understood as a criticism of the relations and norms which prevail in society. This may account for why 19th century bohemia hailed idlers and loafers as the new aristocrats of the spirit. Arthur Rimbaud proclaimed his hatred of the "century of hands." (quoted in Saint-Amand, 2011, 79)For him, only idleness could open the way to freedom and creativity. To be modern, then, means to establish a form of life that is autonomous and**

**independent of power structures – in this sense, idleness is also a way to resist the established capitalist order. When Mladen Stilinović extols idleness and inactivity in his manifesto "In Praise of Laziness" (1993) he is writing about the right not to produce anything—a right he enjoyed under socialism that he was deprived of under capitalism. From the perspective of sleep, could these notions of laziness and idleness be understood as a model of resistance to this 'wake-up-ist' ideology you have described?**

AP: It is problematic to relate sleep to laziness, as the latter is another story as far I am concerned. I am not sure whether my chosen problematization of sleep could be 'included' in the plane of laziness. For example, Paul Lafargue, Karl Marx's son-in-law, wrote an entire treaty on "the right to be lazy," (Lafargue 1883) but in his famous pamphlet he never paid special attention to sleep. It is true that laziness is a sort of unproductivity. If laziness is a conscious strategy, it could be seen as a form of resistance in a capitalist society that is obsessed by work, profit and success. But there is nothing in laziness that interests me as much as the sleeper's separation or non-communication, laziness, on the other hand, can be very chatty…

Charles Baudelaire, an emblematic figure of modern art, once said: "I fear sleep as one fears a deep hole, full of vague terror." (Quoted in Navarina, 2009) He had a very intricate approach to sleep; he was fascinated by the rather banal experience of it and exhausted by its monotonic regularity. Just before his attempted suicide in 1845, he wrote: 'I am killing myself because I can no more live, the fatigue of falling asleep and the fatigue of waking up are unbearable for me...' (Quoted in Navarina, 2009).[4]

------

[4] I owe this quote to my friend, the French artist Virgile Novarina, whose work I will also discuss a little later.

Baudelaire's refined and in some ways comic critique of sleep gives its meaning another twist. And perhaps it might be that the laziness and flaneurism that were characteristic of the modernist artists, who sought new and exciting impressions and innervations, were oppositions to the monotonic "large hole" of sleep, at least in the case of Baudelaire and many other poets and artists. Laziness can also be permanently wakeful and vigilant. Is it not just modern power and capital vigilance's double?

I think that the considerable number of artists trying to explore the themes of sleep, sleeping body, conditions of sleep, etc., signals a growing awareness of this remarkable symptom of the present moment. Actually, my first published text about the topic we are discussing was a short review of an exhibition called *Sleepers* by a graduate of the Institute of Contemporary Art in Moscow (Penzin 2001). And my research was, and is, not just a theoretical discourse, but a form of life as well – it has generated various encounters with outstanding people, thinkers, artists, etc.

I could mention a couple of stories. My friend from the group that I am also a part of, *Chto Delat? / What is to be done?*, the artist Nikolay Oleinikov produced a mural series in 2005-2011 called *Is the Worker Asleep?* Strangely enough we never discussed this work before it was completed, which was such a surprise for me! These huge acrylic murals were initially made for the exhibition that took place in the Sormovo neighbourhood of the city of Nizhny Novgorod. The historical and political background of this work was the first Russian revolution of 1905; its riots, barricades, and the incredible rise in self-organization of the working class in this particular area. Over the century we have seen Sormovo, a revolutionary district, become transformed into an area of sleep, of so-called sleeping blocks.

This is surprisingly linked to the part of my research on the political and biopolitical dimensions of the sleeping body in relation to Marx's theory as mentioned above.

Another amazing story is related to the French artist Virgile Novarina whom I met recently. We are true accomplices in this uneasy undertaking of the exploration of sleep. He told me that once, when he was young, he said, "I am 22 and I have spent almost 7 years in sleep. I know nothing about these 7 years of my life, that is, about myself!" For around 15 years now he has been developing a specific sleep-related art practice. Novarina memorizes and documents not dreams–although he started with that–but sleep, or to be more precise, the states between sleep and waking. When sleeping we experience 'micro-awakenings,' ten or more during the night, that we usually do not remember afterwards. Novarina has his notebook and pencil by his bed at night and tries to record the splashes of light, vision, the words or figures that appear during these awakenings. The artist has already produced a large series called *Ecrits et dessins de nuit (2003)* [Night's Writings and Drawings]. He also makes sleep performances in unusual public places, like a shop-window, an abandoned factory space or at the opening of his own exhibition. These things really inspire me; all the anthropological questions of my research are implied in his work.

Generally, I think that what Louis Marin, whom I quoted earlier, said about a painting as a sleeping body is also true for contemporary art, though in a modified sense—an artwork is a sleeping body. What is, for example, an anthropological model for any readymade exhibited in a white cube? For me, the sleeping body is such a model; a minimal experience of isolation, separation, potentialization. An untouchable sleeping body is a "minimal difference" (Deleuze 1986, 171), which at another level produces an artwork.

We should also make reference to the idea of sacralisation/ profanation as developed in contemporary thought by Giorgio Agamben. His premise is that all sacralisation is rooted in the elementary structure of isolation of a body, image, object, and its withdrawal from human practice and use (Agamben 2007, 73-93). For example, you can find in many anthropological studies that in traditional communities a sleeping person was untouchable, to disturb him/her was a strict taboo. Contemporary artwork still retains a sacralisation/profanation dimension —the anthropological model of which is, in my view, the sleeper's separation from the world. In this way, perhaps, each sleeper is comparable with an art performer.

The point of articulation between sleep and resistance is, in my opinion, a quite ambivalent moment if it is taken seriously. My project is definitely not about resigning oneself from the world in which we live. Sleep as an act of non-communication and non-productivity is a powerful form of exodus from a society, which is based on communication and production. If all the people of a given society were asleep, that society would no longer exist. It would become a political mobilization, if every single person came to a demonstration, or to a sleep-in at a strike, the government would be toppled for sure. This is why I was excited to learn about the recent so-called 'sleepful protests' that were part of the Occupy Wall Street practices where the activists slept on the sidewalks near banks... However, I am not praising sleep as a strange new and actual form of resistance. I am attempting to understand the complex connections between capitalism, metaphysics, ontology, sleep, waking, and subjectivization.

Agamben, Giorgio, 2007. *Profanations.* New York: Zone Books.

Badiou, Alain, 2006. "Bodies, Languages, Truths," in *Lacan.com.* Available online: http://www.lacan.com/badbodies.htm [last accessed May 2014].

Bergson, Henri, 1959. *Oeuvres.* Paris: Presses Universitaires de France.

Deleuze, Gilles, 1995. "Postscript on control societies," in *Negotiations.* New York: Columbia University Press.

Deleuze, Gilles, 1986. *Cinema I.* Minneapolis: University of Minnesota Press.

Diderot, Denis, 1976. "Rameau's Nephew," in trans. T. W. Tancock. *Rameau's Nephew and D'Alembert's Dream.* London: Penguin Classics.

Ekirch, Roger, 2005. *At Day's Close: Night in Times Past.* New York: W. W. Norton & Company.

Freud, Sigmund, 1999. *The Standard Edition of the Complete Psychological Works of Sigmund Freud*, vol. 15. London: Vintage Books.

Kant, Immanuel, 2007. Critique of Judgement. Oxford: Oxford University Press.

Kantorowicz, Ernst, 1997. *The King's Two Bodies: A Study in Mediaeval Political Theology.* Princeton: Princeton University Press.

Kirk, Geoffrey and Raven, John, 1971. *The Presocratic Philosophers: A Critical History with a Selection of Texts.* Cambridge: Cambridge University Press.

Lafargue, Paul. *The Right To Be Lazy.* Available online: http://www.marxists.org/ archive/lafargue/1883/lazy/index.htm [last accessed May 2014].

Levinas, Emmanuel, 1978. *Existence and Existents.* The Hague: Martinus Nijhoff.

Marin, Louis, 1999. *Sublime Poussin*. Stanford: Stanford University Press.

Marx, Karl, 1993. *Grundrisse. Foundations of the Critique of Political Economy*. London: Penguin Books.

Novarina, Virgile, 2009. "Le sommeil est une seconde vie," in *Supérieur Inconnu,* Autumn 2009.

Penzin, Alexei, 2001. "Sleepers," in *Moscow Art Magazine*, 2001, № 32.

Plato, 1926. *Laws, vol. 2*. London: William Heinemann.

Saint-Amand, Pierre, 2011. *The Pursuit of Laziness: An Idle Interpretation of the Enlightenment*. Princeton and Oxford: Princeton University Press.

# The Cognitive Turn in Cognitive Capitalism

# Cultured Brains and the Production of Subjectivity: The Politics of Affect(s) as an Unfinished Project

Il faut détruire l'ennemi à partir de l'affect. Parce que l'affect (la production, la valeur, la subjectivité) est indestructible. (Negri 1997, 56)[1]

### 1.

The brain is frequently presented both as a potential site and substance of *radical transformation*—a utopian form of 'wonder tissue,' a 'difference machine,' an 'uncertain system,' contrasting with the more static, deterministic schemes envisaged either by darkly portrayed 'mechanistic materialists' or 'nefarious neurophilosophers' (see Wolfe 2007 for a discussion)—and, quite symmetrically, as the focus and resource of consumer neuroscience, 'semiocapital'[2] or 'neurocapitalism.' Indeed, the first concept I discuss here, cognitive capitalism, is itself treacherous, 'two-faced' in its aporias: is it a cyber-metaphysics of frictionless capitalism? Or is it a Negrist messianic Golem-construction destined to bring revolutionary pathos, desire, libido, affect thundering through the neuronal avenues that capitalism, its consultants, the Rand Corporation and the MIT MediaLab thought had been successfully colonized and turned into saleable commodities, a.k.a. 'consumer neuroscience'?

---

[1] This translates: 'One most start from affects to destroy the enemy. Because affects (production, value, subjectivity) are indestructible.'

[2] Franco Berardi's term for our world of 'post-Fordist modes of production' (see Terranova 2013).

In contrast, the second concept I address, the politics of affects, has no such duality: it is intended as an explicit extension of Autonomist, ontologized Marxism.

How does one get from the aporias of cognitive capitalism to the (limited? boundless?) promise of a politics of affects? The difference between these two concepts is, of course, partly a matter of style. By articulating a connection between these two régimes of 'brainhood,' to borrow in a loose sense an expression from Vidal (2009), I also want to suggest that taken together, they imply a real shift in the way the fence-posts are placed, repositioning the polarity between *Natur-* and *Geisteswissenschaften*, naturalism and what I'll refer to as the 'hermeneutico-humanist complex.' This is an old opposition, to be sure, but a tiresome one, which is alive and well today, whether or not it harks back explicitly to the heavy-handed tradition of 'Science does not think' and 'animals are *weltarm*,' with its smell of dark green tweed in the forest.

Indeed, conservative bioethicists, neo-Aristotelian philosophers and orthodox Marxists make for strange bedfellows in their shared denunciation of naturalism's blind, mechanical externality, which holds value, reason and freedom captive, 'governed from outside, manipulated by blind causal chains,' as Sartre (1990, 86) wrote against materialism in the early postwar years 'a causal chain can lead me to a movement, a behavior but not ... to my grasping of my situation as a totality. It cannot ... account for revolutionary class-consciousness' (ibid., 120). Here humanism takes as its target materialism, viewed as a kind of unconscious synergistic meld of scientism and Taylorism: 'materialism, by decomposing man into rigorously defined behaviors like in Taylorism, serves the purposes of the master: it is the master who conceives of the slave as being like a machine' (ibid., 127-128). Sometimes, this kind of denunciation comes from farther Left, as with *Tiqqun*'s (2001) piece of learned, paranoid critique of the dangers of 'the cybernetic hypothesis.'

Contrast Guattari, who denied, 'as opposed to a thinker such as Heidegger,' that 'the machine is something which turns us away from being':

> I think that the machinic phyla are agents productive of being. They make us enter into what I call an ontological heterogenesis. ... The whole question is knowing how the enunciators of technology, including biological, aesthetic, theoretical, machines, etc., are assembled, of refocusing the purpose of human activities on the production of subjectivity or collective assemblages of subjectivity. (Guattari 1992/ 2011, 50)

**2.**

Faced with the fact that our cultural-symbolic environment, which provides the scaffolding for complex representational structures, can alter the neural architecture of the developing brain (Quartz & Sejnowski 1997; Quartz 1999; Donald 2001, 153, 212; Thompson 2007, 408), two distinct responses can be imagined.[3]

---

[3] I don't argue for this 'fact' here, which emerges from many studies dating back to James Mark Baldwin in the early 1900s, through Lev Vygotsky and his younger collaborator Aleksandr Luria in the 1920s, to work on neural plasticity (including Atsushi Iriki's ground-breaking research with primates and tools), Terrence Deacon's 'coevolution' model of language and brain from the late 1990s, which explains the evolution of the prefrontal cortex as reflecting 'the evolutionary adaptation to this intensive working memory processing demand imposed by symbol learning' (Deacon 2003, 100), and Lambros Malafouris's cognitive archaeology. Even in writing critical of some neuroscientific claims, it is acknowledged that 'neuroscience construes the brain more and more as an active organism that shapes its environment and is shaped by it' (Hartmann 2012, 80).

One response we might label as that of the 'Rand Corporation theorist.' Additionally, it may be that of the cynical, *déracinée* commentator on globalization (including when she assumes a melancholy posture of denunciation)[4], who will emphasize this potential as a resource for what used to be called, including by the late, equally melancholy Deleuze, 'the society of communication.' We may recall, in an interview pertaining to his Cinema books, Deleuze's observation that aesthetics cannot be separated from the "complementary questions *of cretinization and cerebralization*" (Deleuze 1995, 60, my emphasis).[5] In truth, this amounts to a more haughty way of putting Gil Scott-Heron's famous sentiment that "The revolution will not be televised."

Another response would be that of the figure that by the early twenty-first century we have come to know as the 'Art School Marxist'[6], who will see the potential for, or employ a rhetoric of revolutionary transformation.

........................................................................................................

[4] See the early work of David Rieff, Sofia Coppola, and more explicitly Keller Easterling (2007). A powerful, if self-cancelling tirade against these utopias-turned-phantasmagorias-of-dystopia is Gilles Châtelet (1999); see my review in *Chimères* 37 (1999). Less self-cancelling, but not in the mode of 'theory,' is the work of the cinematographic curatorial collective Le Peuple Qui Manque (Deleuzians and Straubo-Huilletians will recognize the reference): http://www.lepeuplequimanque.org/ [last accessed February 2014].

[5] The tone of this observation stands in contrast to the exciting, utopian, forward-looking pronouncement made by Deleuze that many of us have quoted in our work, namely, that 'creating new circuits in art means creating them in the brain too.' The latter is creative and exhortatory while the former is bitter and Bartlebyesque.

[6] The question as to why Communism is primarily discussed in art schools (especially in the UK and Northern Europe), is addressed in David Graeber, "The Sadness of Post-Workerism," 2008 Lecture, at http://www.commoner.org.uk/wp-content/uploads/2008/04/graeber_sadness.pdf [last accessed February 2014].

Namely, the brain—the plastic brain, the cultured brain, the social brain—must be the site of revolution itself, whether we take this literally (in its materiality), or more conceptually (in its immateriality). In an essay on the Spinozist resonance of the social brain (see Wolfe 2010), with particular focus on Vygotsky and Antonio Negri, I exhumed this supremely—madly(?)—overconfident pronouncement of the Bolshevik child psychologist Aaron Zalkind, sounding more like a Chris Marker creation than a figure from the history of science or politics: 'The cortex is on a shared path with socialism, and socialism is on a shared path with the cortex' (Zalkind, quoted in Vygotsky 1929, 14; see Veer & Valsiner 1991, 320). In case this isn't clear enough, plans for the revolutionary reshaping of humanity into the 'New Man' and other shapes-to-come should not only *not ignore* neuroscience: for Zalkind, they should embrace it.

That the activity of our brains is either, always already, revolutionary and transformative, or instead raw material for fascism, is something of a *serpent de mer* or an endless schoolyard battle, which spawns twins and mirror images every time one has one's back turned. If cognitive capitalism is in the end a creed of managers and consultants, can there be cognitive Marxism? Can there be a 'noo-politics,' in Maurizio Lazzarato's terms, which could employ our immaterial, aesthetic potential to invent 'existential territories' (Guattari 1992, 30) far away from this colonization of our interior, as in the imagined green spaces lying somewhere outside sci-fi dystopias (of *Blade Runner*, *Brazil*, etc)? But then isn't the 'cognitive' part the problem, since one remains trapped in an idealist loop, caught between the Charybdis of virtuality (absolute deterritorialization, lines of flight, quantum flow, desire, potentiality…) and the Scylla of the 'cognitariat'? More concretely, for example, 'the particular construal of self currently championed by social neuroscience—with a focus on social-interactive skills, low-level empathy and mind-reading—neatly corresponds with the ideal skill profile of today's corporate employee' (Slaby & Gallagher 2014). This is, indeed, 'neurocapitalism.'

In fact, there are not just two types of response to this promise of the brain (the gleeful commodification of the Rand Corporation theorist or the fiery revolutionary promises of the Art School theorist). There is also the recently developed approach known as 'critical neuroscience' (particularly the work of Jan Slaby and collaborators). While this latter case takes a *critical* distance towards the practice and theoretical structure of existing science, it remains very far from the brusque dismissals or moralistic hand-wringing characteristic of the 'hermeneutico-humanist complex.' While Frankfurt School fans like Diederich Diederichsen will denounce even the most hybridized forms of neuroscience (neuroaesthetics, social neuroscience, affective neuroscience, embodied mind, etc.), critical neuroscience seeks to look carefully at the interaction between neuroscience as it is and analyses of its social and cultural structure (ranging from brain imaging to psychopharmacology and the role of the military in influencing basic research…). Critical neuroscience is inspired by Foucauldian analysis (Choudhury, Nagel & Slaby 2009, 66), although its theorists later acknowledge, citing Bruce Wexler and others, the importance of looking at cortical plasticity in order to view the brain as 'in constant interaction with culture' (ibid., 71). Even at its most critical, this approach reflects on challenges such as how enhancement technologies confront us primarily with new forms of *responsibility*. That is, while some aspects of neurocapitalism could subsume any of our responsibility under a kind of determinism, 'consumer neuroscience' would conversely give us more choices.[7]

------

[7] For a careful articulation of Frankfurt-School 'critical theory' with respect to neuroscience, see Hartmann (2012). Hartmann, citing Martha Farah, speaks of the difficulty of preserving 'the freedom to remain unenhanced' in a context where schools, in a country we don't need to name, are coercing parents to medicate their children for attention dysfunction (Hartmann 2012, 82). In an alternative account, less 'distant' while still evaluative, Schmitz (2014) employs feminist concepts to look at the present-day flourishing of 'neurocultures'.

Obviously, the interesting cases fall in between: those which neither engage in catastrophist, anti-science rhetoric, nor think the issue is about marketing our cognitive capacities.[8] The critical neuroscience project is in this more interesting part of the spectrum, but it has one major difference from the perspective presented here, in which the social brain, cultured brain, noo-political brain is *real*, not a matter of critical, evaluative discourse. That is, from the cultured brain to the politics of affects, we are engaging neither with critical evaluations nor with metaphorical discourse, but rather with embodied, embedded materiality.[9]

**3.**

My concern indeed is the relation between brains, subjectivity and the transformative, symbolic dimensions which Vygotsky saw so clearly already in the 1920s and which in the past decades we have come to associate with the 'Baldwin effect' and some writings of Paolo Virno (2003; see also Depew & Weber 2003; Papineau 2005; Lachapelle et al. 2006): the social brain. The Baldwin effect describes ways in which non-biological traits such as linguistic and cultural behaviors can be assimilated in such a way as to be transmitted.

---

[8] Another version of the former, which relies less on appeals to a human sovereignty, and more on a kind of descriptive yet apocalyptic sociocultural discourse, focuses on the way the social world itself is becoming a neuronal world. In such a world, society is becoming obsessed with brains, whether in the explicit form of 'neurocapitalism' or not, and our desires are increasingly turned towards virtual gratification. This position is best expressed in some recent films – I won't mention any theoretical work of this sort – such as Ari Folman's *The Congress* (2013), Chris Marker's *Level Five* (1997) and, somewhat more reactionary, Oliver Assayas' *Demonlover* (2002).

[9] A rare case of an analysis which explicitly addresses 'affect' in relation to the biological without denouncing this possibility is provided by Papoulias and Callard (2010).

In other words, it attempts to capture how learning can affect the direction and rate of evolution by natural selection. As such, it is not a Lamarckian view at least in the popular understanding of that term, since it is not focused on individual creative acts. Lachapelle et al. (2006) discuss certain genetic algorithms which demonstrate that Baldwin effects are possible within a strictly Darwinian framework. It is hard to improve on Peter Godfrey-Smith's explanation:

> Suppose a population encounters a new environmental condition, in which its old behavioral strategies are inappropriate. If some members of the population are plastic with respect to their behavioral program, and can acquire in the course of their lifetime new behavioral skills that fit their new surroundings, these plastic individuals will survive and reproduce at the expense of less flexible individuals. The population will then have the chance to reproduce mutations that cause organisms to exhibit the new optimal behavioral profile without the need for learning. Selection will favor these mutants, and in time the behaviors which once had to be learned will be innate. (quoted in Depew & Weber 2003, 54; cited in Lachappelle et al. 2006, 316)

What is significant in the present context is the way in which these concepts blur the border between the biological and the socio-cultural spheres. That is, the Baldwin effect is very close, in fact, to the promise of the social brain, namely that 'the human cerebral cortex [is] an organ of civilization in which are hidden boundless possibilities' (Luria 1978, 279).[10]

---

[10] Luria is glossing on Vygotsky, whose last, posthumously published work, "Psychology and the Localization of Mental Functions" explicitly aimed to investigate the functional organization of the brain as the organ of consciousness (Luria 1966, 23). The development of new 'functional organs' occurs through the development of new *functional systems*, which is a means for the unlimited development of cerebral activity (ibid., 19, 22).

It is also close to Deleuze's 'neuroaesthetic' vision in which '[c]reating new circuits in art means creating them in the brain' (Deleuze 1995). This Baldwin-Vygotsky-Deleuze vision is tantamount to saying, to use Negri's (1995, 98) words, that '*Geist* is the brain' (Negri is deliberately being provocative with regard to the German 'hermeneutical' tradition, although his interests lie less in the realm of the social brain, and more towards a politics of affects, as we shall see). That properties of *Geist* such as its interpretive capacity, its social and inter-subjective dimension, are in fact properties of the brain means—and I wish to insist on this point—that these are not just accounts of *interaction* between two *distinct* entities or fields of activity (e.g. brain and society, brain and symbolic re-lations, nature and freedom…). They also do not amount to an insistence that what matters is strictly the world of language in which we live, irreducible to the brain understood—to use some vivid judgments from the early modern period—as 'a clammy and unactive Nature and Substance; ... a meer passive Principle, as to the Acts of inward Sensation and Intellec-tion'—that's one of the Boyle Lecturers, John Hancock (1739, II, 243), in 1706—or a mere 'Cake of Sewet or Bowl of Curds,' unfit to perform our cognitive operations for the Cam-bridge Platonist Henry More (1978, I.11, § 5, 34; cited by Sut-ton 1998, 145).

That the social brain is not a theory of the interaction between independent entities called 'society' and 'brain' (nor a Piaget-type internalization of the outer by something like 'the self') is also a key intuition in Edwin Hutchins' (1995; see also Latour 1996) celebrated account of the ex-tended mind in *Cognition in the Wild*:

Internalization has long connoted some thing moving across some boundary. Both elements of this definition are misleading. What moves is not a thing, and the boundary across which movement takes place is a line that, if drawn too firmly, obscures our understanding of the nature of human cognition. Within this larger unit of analysis, what used to look like internalization now appears as a gradual propagation of organized functional properties across a set of malleable media. (Hutchins 1995, 312)

If we further radicalize this thesis, we arrive at Guattari's vision of 'pre-individual intensities' with its emphasis on affects, perception, and what Anglophone theorists would most likely call embodiment (although Guattarian embodiment is definitely not about the privacy of 'my own body' as opposed to external, physical nature). In Guattari's words (2011, 41): 'I reject in advance the kind of reductionism which consists in thinking communication and culture result from an interaction between individuals. There is no interaction between individuals; there is a constitution of subjectivity at a scale that is transindividual from the outset.'[11]

The social brain occurs in a 'gradual propagation of organized functional properties across a set of malleable media.' Less evident from previous remarks, it is also a 'constitution of subjectivity at a scale that is transindividual from the outset'. As such, it requires clarifying what is meant by affects and their role in this process. Before I attempt such a clarification, I shall reiterate one point and mention an objection.

First, to reiterate, the biological and the social (Baldwin), the cerebral and the social (Vygotsky) or the cerebral and the cultural (Deleuze) crisscross and interpenetrate one another. However, this is not 'interactionism' or 'constructivism'. Furthermore, if such concepts are valid, they are so inasmuch as brains themselves 'make chaos in order to make sense of the world' (Skarda & Freeman 1987).

---

[11] For an excellent analysis of the transindividual, see Jason Read (2014).

This is not a 'dialogue' between neuroscience and the world of the social, or Harawayian metaphors. If naturalism is dangerous (as claimed by *Tiqqun* but also some critics of Paolo Virno), then Vygotsky is dangerous too, which amounts to a puzzle for Marxist thought (recall my earlier observation about strange bedfellows).

Second, to raise an objection, in this seamless (or chaotic but perpetually self-actualizing and transforming) world, there is no negativity, conflict or dysfunction; there is no psychopathology, for it is sheer positivity. There are no monsters in a perpetually transforming, Lucretian world of hybrids and brains as producers of 'new circuits' and artificiality: there is only matter, and an iteration of forms.[12] Some people object that this also leads to another 'danger' or flaw, the biologization of the political; I do not think this follows, any more than it does from Spinozism in general (see Diefenbach 2011).[13] This is where we need to shift the emphasis from cognitive capitalism (pro and con) and the social brain, to the politics of affects.

For affects are nature, and yet they are not nature: forget the Germanic fascination with second nature, the uniqueness of the human, our usage of tools, our immateriality or the Noosphere (Leroi-Gourhan, Teilhard de Chardin, Stiegler).

---

[12] I sought to address this in a critical reflection on the hoped-for messianic power of monsters with Negrist resonance; there, naturalism admittedly concludes with a somewhat cynical reminder that there is only Nature (see Wolfe 2008).

[13] Diefenbach would not agree with either the Spinozist or the naturalist inclinations of the present essay, but the challenge she poses to the "confort intellectuel" of a Spinoza-Deleuze-Negri politics of potentiality, 'infinitely extended toward infinite perfection,' is a real one, and I acknowledge it.

The brain and affect in this context are closer to what the 18th-century surgeon Georges Arnaud de Ronsil (1768, 246) said, reacting to the case of hermaphrodites: *ce n'est qu'à peine que l'on reconnaît la nature dans la nature meme* [it is only with difficulty that we can recognize Nature in Nature itself]. He had not read "Middlesex" to find out that hermaphrodites have desires like you or me; Ronsil is upset that nature has done something wrong. Ronsil's fears about hermaphrodites (and their implied self-destruction of any normativity in nature, as if by hara-kiri) clarify that whether it is a teenager's brain after years of compulsive gaming, a psychopath's brain or Lord Byron's 2200g brain, your brain or mine contemplating, now the Kaaba, now James Turrell's "Pleiades" (1983) at the Mattress Factory in Pittsburgh, the difference between 'natural' and 'unnatural' becomes at best a matter of convenience, at worst completely empty.

But, my objector will say, this is not enough. For this problem of a lack of room for dysfunction, monstrosity or psychopathology is part of a broader reproach sometimes heard against Spinozo-Deleuzo-Negrist politics and metaphysics (this is somewhat redundant since a distinctive feature of this tradition is that the two are folded into one another, in a prominent motif of Negri's "Savage Anomaly" [Negri 1991]): that it folds all struggle into a plane of immanence in which all cows are grey. As Rancière (2011, 135) put it:

> Capitalism may produce more and more immateriality, yet this immateriality will never be more than the immateriality of capitalism. Capitalism only produces capitalism. If communism means something, it means something that is radically heterogeneous to the logic of capitalism, entirely heterogeneous to the materiality of the capitalist world.

Where does the immateriality issue come from, however? So far, we had not enncountered it. It is thus worth clarifying that in most theorizations of cognitive capitalism, the emphasis is indeed on knowledge and immateriality. Except for Negri in more metaphorical moments (and Virno explicitly), none of these theorists are at all interested in *brains*. Indeed, some like Lazzarato explicitly denounce any 'positivism,' 'naturalism' or appeals to science. In their usage, the word 'cognitive' is simply a derivative of 'knowledge.' Value is located in knowledge (cognitive capacity) and the creative capacity of living labor. As one of the most prominent theorists of cognitive capitalism, Carlo Vercellone (cited in Terranova 2013, 47), put it: 'The importance of ... material labor decreases in favor of a new paradigm of work, simultaneously more intellectual, immaterial and relational.'

To this we need to reply with two points, both of which are Spinozist at their core. First, as laid out above, this theory concerns real brains and their materiality (whether or not the cortex and socialism are really on the same path). Indeed, denials of this reality—that we possess brains and that materialists *might be able to care* about what Vygotsky, Baldwin, Deleuze and Warren Neidich call 'cultured brains' or 'Bolshevik cortexes'—are typical of the hermeneutico-humanist-Marxist: recall Sartre's cold, blind 'causal chains' that enclose the free human essence, or *Tiqqun*'s denunciation of the mechanisms of control vehicle by cybernetics and artificial intelligence. I've argued for the contrary elsewhere, inspired by Vygotsky, Virno et al (see Wolfe 2010, Gallagher, in press, 2013, and Pasquinelli 2014). But here I would add a second feature, which is my second point: the inclusion of affects and the production of subjectivity.[14]

------

[14] Maurizio Lazzarato interprets in a more anti-cognitivist way than Guattari did, for unclear reasons given his own subtle and well-articulated criticisms of the older dialectical-materialist, Hegelian-Marxist, party-dictatorship model.

**4.**

Calls for a politics of affects have been heard from a variety of quarters, often influenced by Spinoza or at least Spinoza as reconstructed and joyfully revived since the late 1960s, by figures such as Gilles Deleuze, Alexandre Matheron, Pierre Macherey and Antonio Negri.[15]

On the more naturalistic side, such invocations of a return to the primacy of affect, or affects, have sought support in so-called 'affective neuroscience' (e.g. Damasio 2003),[16] which in its most technical sense, associated with Joseph LeDoux (see LeDoux 1998) and Antonio Damasio (more controversially), is the idea that emotions such as fear 'are not necessarily mediated through a cognitive appraisal (that is, a mental representation) of the fearful stimulus, which would necessitate an engagement of the prefrontal cortex (one of the sites centrally implicated in cognitive functioning)' (Papoulias & Callard 2010, 40). For LeDoux, the temporality of affectivity is of a scale such that it cannot be perceived by our senses. For Damasio and LeDoux, then, emotions constitute a pre-reflective realm of affectivity that pre-exists our folk understanding of 'self,' in which a Spinozist automatic background could be imagined; consider that 'the affect is impersonal and is distinct from every individual State of things:

........................................................................................................

[15] In English, a later but extremely useful work is Gatens and Lloyd (1999). Thinkers who continue this trend, in some cases as direct students of some of the above, include Laurent Bove and Pascal Séverac.

[16] For an interesting discussion and overview see Ravven (2003). For an example of political-affective neuroscience in practice (different from the critical neuroscience model, as it is more explicitly political in dealing with race, oppression, poverty and exclusion), see Protevi (2009). Protevi surveys some notions of 'political affect' further in "Political Emotion"(2014). An analysis which actually addresses the *meaning* of 'affect' is Papoulias and Callard (2010)

it is none the less singular, and can enter into singular combinations and conjunctions with other affects' (Deleuze 1986, 98-9).

Closer to home we have the recent efforts of thinkers such as Yves Citton and Fréderic Lordon (2008) to articulate a new Spinozist trend or mood in the social sciences (Citton & Lordon 2008). But what is this politics of affects and why should it matter? Spinoza defines an affect as a 'confused idea by means of which the mind asserts a force by which its body, or a part of its body, exists' (*Ethics* III, general definition of the affects at the end of Book III, in Spinoza 1992). When thinkers today invoke Spinoza on the affects they are often trying to either (a) avoid a kind of rationalism in politics and/or (b) broaden the scope of resistance and struggle.

On the one hand, a politics of affects is a way of avoiding a kind of rationalism, in which everyone has to contribute just so much, and be entitled to so much. Such rationalism may be of the discursive space of rational agents, or indeed of the State shoe factory from which one is entitled to one pair a year. 'Considered from a Spinozist standpoint, political life has less to do with Kantian-Habermasian communicative rationality than with phenomena of composition and the propagation of affects' (Citton & Lordon 2008, 33).[17] Of course, if we stress the emotions instead as somehow primary or essential in politics, the sensible democrat will cry 'Fascism!' (recall the Carl Schmitt debates of the past few decades:

---

[17] Lordon's work is not yet translated into English, although "Willing Slaves of Capital: Spinoza and Marx on Desire" is forthcoming from Verso in 2014. For a useful short presentation, see Jason Read's comments at http://www.unemployednegativity.com/2010/ 12/everyone-is-kettled-lordon-on-marx-and.html [last accessed February 2014].

the moment when the president of the École Normale Supérieure in Paris called the followers of Negri 'left-wing Schmittians'?[18]

But the goal is not to unleash micro-fascisms everywhere, and impose emotions such as fear as paramount; as John Protevi puts it, 'Joy in entrained collective action is by no means a simple normative standard' (Protevi 2014, 335). Rather, we should think of a politics of affects as akin to a Guattarian 'production of subjectivity.' If I am the director of a prison and, instead of imposing solitary confinement or the hosing-down of troublesome individuals, I create a partnership with a community theatre in my city so that groups of prisoners can put on plays, I am facilitating the creation of (joyful, affirmative) affective networks. As such, 'the production of affects, subjectivities, and forms of life present an enormous potential for autonomous circuits of valorization, and perhaps for liberation' (Hardt 1999, 100). This is part of what Guattari meant by the *"ritournellisation du monde sensible"*: not so much the Kantian 'making up a world,' but a pre-individual and relational activity, that can be the way a child fixates on a part of building in the housing projects and thus no longer sees the ugliness, or the way this child might hum a familiar tune (*ritournelle*) when lost in the forest, thus creating a more familiar environment. It may also refer to the invention of new affective territories by the artist, or the militant.

---

[18] (There was some truth to this, if only in a faintly Hegelian sense in which the exaggeration is 'the true.') Yann Moulier Boutang describes the intellectual and political context for the accusation of 'left-wing Schmittianism' (and tries to articulate a model for a 'revolutionary usage of reactionary thought') at http://multitudes.samizdat.net/Y-a-t-il-un-usage-de-gauche-de-la [last accessed February 2014]. For a more precise analysis, see Jean-Claude Monod (2005, 2006). See also Yoshihiko Ichida's very suggestive essay, "Subject to subject: Are we all Schmittians in politics?" (2005).

On the other hand, affect is also an operative term in the notion of 'affective labor,' used by Negri, Lazzarato, Hardt and others to describe, as Jason Read summarizes,

> a particular subset of the larger field of "immaterial labor"; it describes labor that produces emotional states, care, wellness, desire, etc.: it is labor that produces subjectivity, in terms of its most basic conditions of existence through the work of care, and in terms of the feeling and sense of self. Moreover, the history of feminist writing on "care work," reminds us that such work, especially as it performed in day care centers and nursing homes, is devalued because it is seen as natural attribute of being female, as something given rather than learned. Affective labor plunges us into the unstable border between reproduction and production, subjectivity and the conditions that produce it.[19]

If we recall the Spinozist definition of affect as a 'confused idea by means of which the mind asserts a force by which its body, or a part of its body, exists' we can see that the conception of mental life, and how it relates both to 'the' body and to 'bodies' overall, is definitely non-individualist (in the Cartesian sense and beyond), whether or not it is explicitly materialist. Crucial here is Proposition 57 of Book III of the *Ethics*: 'Affects are related to Desire, Joy or Sadness; desire is the essence of a being, and joy or sadness is its way of expressing that essence; they are passions by which our power of acting—our effort to persevere in our being—is either increased or decreased.'

........................................................................................

[19] http://unemployednegativity.blogspot.com/2011/05/affective-composition-of-labor.html [last accessed February 2014] (thanks to John Protevi for sending me to this blog). See also, Silvia Federici (2011).

Negri takes this conception of the affects and emphasizes that an affect is a power of acting, both singular and universal —singular because of its 'vitalistic' overtones (the unmeasurable, the constitutive…) and universal because they are inherently *relational*, in the sense that they relate us to one another (Negri 1997; Wolfe 2011).

This insight we find extended in the work of Negri, Citton-Lordon, Lazzarato, and Ulus Baker: sociology is not value-free (*wertfrei*), since all social actors are both interrelated (whether as brains, imitative machines, sympathetic agents or in the name of a 'relational ontology') and are actively engaged in the *construction of a world*, a world of struggle, power and desire.[20] That by the very fact that we have desires, we are engaged in such construction—in 'ontological constitution'—is exactly the crucial insight missed in the old, stale debate between Habermas and Foucault, in which the former (and his epigones) declared that the latter was guilty of 'crypto-normativity,' or the more common accusation that Foucault's world is one in which resistance is futile (Fraser 1981, 279; see also Rajchman 1988 for a useful overview and retort). In fact, the politics of affects allows for my desires and my body to be part of the fabric of the real and its *revendications*. That affects are inherently relational and that they necessarily involve my embodiments and my desires in relation to the real goes some way towards blunting both Rancière's and Diefenbach's challenges. Specifically, it represents an objection to the challenge that these theories are caught in a self-feeding loop of immateriality, or that they are 'angelic' or 'Romantic' in their vision of a self-actualization of potentiality towards infinite perfection.

----

[20] Ulus Baker was a Turkish radical intellectual whose work on the sociology of culture and cinema explicitly seeks to extend the project of a 'sociology of affects.' In a different version of this essay I seek to contextualize his work in a Spinozist and Negrist context. I thank Harun Abuşoğlu for introducing me to Ulus's work and encouraging me to write on it.

The politics of affects (i) extends the scope of resistance and its actors, by allowing for a dimension of subjectivity and of creation, (ii) allows for a more *embodied* sense of what it is to have a mind, desires and to relate to others (indeed, the language of 'affect' and 'affective' in cultural studies and elsewhere in the humanities is almost synonymous with 'embodiment' and 'embodied'), and by extension (iii) interacts fruitfully with a 'relational' ontology (Morfino 2006; Read 2014). But inasmuch as the claim that thought is affective—and that emotions pertain to the body—is an insight shared both by Spinozism and contemporary affective neuroscience, the politics of affects also opens onto a naturalistic horizon. Recall, this is what is contested by those I termed hermeneutico-humanists. These can be Marxists or not: witness Ricoeur and Habermas, or David Hawkes (2011) in literary studies, with his screeds against what he calls materialism.

**5.**

Prima facie, attempts to give a natural (usually evolutionary) grounding for ethical and political life deserve the suspicious reactions they get (from sociobiology in the old days to evolutionary psychology both then and now). But something quite different occurs in the politics of affect. *Geist* now means the brain, something that was intimated by Deleuze and Guattari (1994, 209) in "What is Philosophy?" when they suggested that the future of the *Geisteswissenschaften*—for them, all disciplines dealing with 'the mental,' from philosophy to art and science—lay in the folds of an uncertain, chaotic, 'nonobjectifiable brain' (see also Murphie 2010). Warren Neidich (2003) has articulated an extremely original model for relating 'cultural plasticity' and 'brain plasticity' in his theoretical work and artistic practice. Basically, if the brain is already social and the organism is a 'developmental system' inseparable from its environment, knee-jerk anti-naturalism is an unnecessary attitude to have towards the politics of affect. It is as if ideology critique always ends up having bad naturalism chase away the better kinds (Citton & Lordon 2008, 11).

The production of subjectivity, the politics of multitude and affect need not rest on a 'humanist' appeal to a transcendental or otherwise anti-natural self, just as it need (indeed, *should*) not rest on dialectical materialism (Lazzarato 2005, 2006).

In that sense, while the goal of liberating affects in a 'production of subjectivity' may run counter to certain impulses of control, management or property in 'neurocapitalism,'[21] (although sadly we can be at once master and slave, including as 'neuroworkers': both immaterial laborers and cognitariat) it has no need or reason to oppose a 'free' self (or brain) to a manipulated creature (of the Rand Corporation, the CIA or MIT's MediaLab). As such, the fear of naturalism is misplaced. Indeed, even the notion of an environment which stands in a dynamic relation to the individual—who is thereby not an 'atom' or a Randian 'superman,' as the Marxist tradition insists (as in Marx's famous definition in the Sixth Thesis on Feuerbach that 'Human essence in its reality is the sum of social relations' (Marx and Engels 1978, 122))—can also be found in biology, for example in the famous ethological theorizing of Jakob von Uexküll (2010), who described in detail how each organism is embedded in its own *Umwelt*.[22] This kind of biology coheres with the overall rejection of 'individualism' we find in the politics of affects; for every affect is relational.

---

[21] I refer back to films such as Ari Folman's *The Congress*.

[22] See the very useful discussion of Uexküll's ideas also in light of contemporary discussions of the embodied, embedded mind by Olivier Surel (Surel 2014). A related concept in more recent biology is niche construction, i.e., the process whereby organisms modify their environment (termite mounds and beaver dams being classic examples), which may result in 'a change in the selective pressures of such organisms, which in turn may affect how natural selection operates in this population' (Lachapelle et al. 2006, 319). It is worth noting that I don't think Uexküll's politics were ours.

In sum, the social brain concept and the politics of affect taken together articulate a social, relational ontology *without* anti-naturalism. Philosophically, this is novel in rejecting the *Natur-* vs. *Geisteswissenschaften* distinction and thus any hermeneutics, while remaining wholeheartedly political. The brain and affect concepts allow for both (neo-)Marxist and naturalistic emphases, such as Deacon's 'co-evolution' of language and brain, and they remove the cognitive capitalism concept from its 'immaterialist' tendency. Cultured-brain neuroaesthetics and pluridisciplinary work on neural plasticity show that the brain is its own symbolic machine. It is worth repeating that this should not be confused with neuroaesthetics *sensu* Semir Zeki (1999), where the term literally means a 'neurology of aesthetics' in the most crude explanatory sense possible, leading to talk of laws of aesthetic experience, and other strange hybrids.[23] To paraphrase Danto, if someone in a West German police station in 1975 with slightly blurry vision is looking at some 'Wanted' posters which feature some prominent members of the RAF, for the neuroaesthetician *façon* Zeki (but not Neidich), she might be having the same experience as a non-contextualised viewer of Richter's 'October 1977' series.

Earlier, I suggested that this materialism of the social, of cultured brains and affects took away some of the sting of objections such as Katja Diefenbach's, since this was neither naïve immanentism (her chosen target) nor crude naturalism (not her target). Yet, recurrently from the beginning (cognitive capitalism as Janus-faced) through the incessantly mirrored figures of emancipation and control or commodification, noopolitics and neurocapital, 'cerebralization and cretinization,' we have run up against a problem.

---

[23] A clear, reasonable warning on these issues (which has the significant advantage of being naturalistic, rather than a defense of the mystique of art) is Malafouris (2013).

This, however, is not some logical or conceptual flaw (of the sort that Rancière thinks he can almost diagnose), but a problem perhaps inherent in appeals to the real itself rather than to old-fashioned normativity. It is the problem that occurs when 'an essentially dynamic, self-organizing biology/nature is presented as the guarantor for an emancipatory and creative politics' (Papoulias & Callard 2010, 49), although this is not a problem for Spinozism.

Granted, it is hard to be optimistic when the brain, network, emotion, desire are all potential 'double binds,' all can be disruptive or commodified, and 'all that is solid melts into air,' especially since it is no longer just the labor of our body which is exploited, but our cognitive capacities. Indeed, as I revise this essay, I see a disturbing piece of news—disturbing also in that it further distorts our sense of the real and the virtual (recall my allusion to *'The Congress,' 'Level Five'* and *'Demonlover'* at the outset): a game designer has quit her job after death threats were made against her and her family, pursuant to her 'designs' in the game displeasing fans (she had revealed that she didn't like violence).[24] I like the sobering way Lazzarato (2008, 174) puts it: art and culture are 'neither more nor less integrated' into the society of control and security than any other activity, and they have 'the same potential and ambiguities as any other activity'. This is what I referred to above as the 'two-faced' nature of cognitive capitalism; but this formulation has neither the cynicism of the 'Rand Corporation theorist,' nor the naïveté of the 'Art School Marxist'.

---

[24] See http://metro.co.uk/2013/08/16/bioware-writer-quits-after-death-threats-to-family-3925970/ [last accessed February 2014].

So there is little to be gained by investing either a substance (brain, frontal cortex, organism) or a potentiality (including that of 'ritournellisation' or 'existentialisation,' in Guattari's processual terms) with an absolute 'saving power.' This, however, does not change the way in which a Spinozist politics of brain and affects is an improvement over those 'planifications' which lay out a blueprint for action, with a hierarchy of actors assigned to their unmoving roles, à la DIAMAT and the dictatorship of the proletariat. Faced with ascetic, idealistic models it can always, in contrast, appeal to the 'indestructibility' of affects. In the words of an earlier materialist, *Le pour et le contre* (1765), III, in Diderot 1986, 9. 'There is no pleasure felt that is illusory (*chimérique*).'

Châtelet, Gilles, 1999. *Vivre et penser comme des porcs. De l'incitation à l'envie et à l'ennui dans les démocraties-marchés,* Paris: Exils (reprint Folio-Gallimard).

Choudhury, Suparna, Nagel, Saskia Kathi and Slaby, Jan, 2009. "Critical Neuroscience: Linking Neuroscience and Society through Critical Practice," in *Biosocieties* 4:1.

Citton, Yves and Lordon, Frédéric Lordon (eds.), 2008. *Spinoza et les Sciences Sociales. De la Puissance de la Multitude à l'Économie des Affects*, Paris: Editions Amsterdam, collection 'Caute !'

Damasio, Antonio, 2003. *Looking for Spinoza: Joy, Sorrow, and the Feeling Brain*, New York: Harcourt.

Deacon, Terrence W., 2003. "Multilevel selection in a complex adaptive system: the problem of language origins," in David Depew & Bruce Weber (eds.), *Evolution and Learning: The Baldwin Effect Reconsidered*, Cambridge: MIT Press.

Deleuze, Gilles, 1986. *Cinema 1: The Movement-Image*, trans. H. Tomlinson and B. Habberjam, Minneapolis: University of Minnesota Press.

Deleuze, Gilles, 1995. "On *The Time-Image*," in *Negotiations 1972-1990*, trans. M. Joughin, New York: Columbia University Press.

Deleuze, Gilles and Félix Guattari, 1994. *What Is Philosophy?* New York: Columbia University Press.

Diderot, Denis, 1986 [1975]. « Le pour et le contre », III, in H. Dieckmann, J. Proust, J. Varloot (eds.), *Œuvres complètes*, vol. 15, Paris: Hermann.

Diefenbach, Katja, 2011. "Im/potential Politics: Political Ontologies in Negri, Agamben and Deleuze," in Vanessa Brito (ed.), *Becoming-major, Becoming-minor*, Maastricht: Jan van Eyck Academie, pp. 211-229.

Donald, Merlin, 2001. *A Mind so Rare*, New York: Norton.

Easterling, Keller, 2007. *Enduring Innocence: Global Architecture and Its Political Masquerades*, Cambridge: MIT Press.

Federici, Silvia, 2011. "On Affective Labor," in Michael Peters, Ergin Bulut (eds.), *Cognitive Capitalism, Education and Digital Labor*, Frankfurt: Peter Lang, pp. 57-74.

Fraser, Nancy, 1981. "Michel Foucault on Modern Power: Empirical Insights and Normative Confusion," in *Praxis International* 1.

Gallagher, Sean (2013, in press). "The socially extended mind," *Cognitive Systems Research*. Available online: http://dx.doi.org/10.1016/j.cogsys.2013.03.008 [last accessed February 2014].

Gatens, Moira and Lloyd, Genevieve, 1999. *Collective Imaginings: Spinoza Past and Present*, London: Routledge.

Guattari, Félixm, 1992. *Chaosmose*. Paris: Galilée.

Guattari, Félix, 2011. "On contemporary art" (1992 interview), in Eric Alliez, Andrew Goffey (eds.), *The Guattari Effect*, London: Continuum.

Hancock, John, 1739. *Arguments to prove the Being of God with Objections against it Answered* in Anon., *A Defence of Natural and Revealed Religion: Sermons Preached at the Lecture Founded by Robert Boyle*, 3 vols., London.

Hardt, Michael, 1999. "Affective Labor," in *Boundary 2* 26(2). Available online (without notes): http://www.generation-online.org/p/fp_affective-labour.htm [last accessed February 2014].

Hartmann, Martin, 2012. "Against First Nature: Critical Theory and Neuroscience," in Suparna Choudhury & Jan Slaby (eds.), *Critical Neuroscience: A Handbook of the Social and Cultural Contexts of Neuroscience*, Chichester: Wiley-Blackwell.

Hawkes, David, 2011. "Against Materialism in Literary Theory," *Early Modern Culture* 9. Available online: http://emc.eserver.org/Hawkes.pdf [last accessed February 2014].

Hutchins, Edwin, 1995. *Cognition in the Wild*, Cambridge: MIT Press.

Ichida, Yoshihiko, 2005. "Subject to Subject: Are We All Schmittians in Politics?," in *Borderlands* 4:2. Available online: http://www.borderlands.net.au/vol4no2_2005/ichida_subject.htm [last accessed February 2014].

Lachapelle, Jean, Faucher, Luc and Poirier, Pierre (eds), 2006. "Cultural Evolution, the Baldwin Effect, And Social Norms," in N. Gontier et al., eds., *Evolutionary Epistemology, Language and Culture*, Dordrecht: Springer, 313-334.

Latour, Bruno, 1996. "Cogito Ergo Sumus! Or Psychology Swept Inside Out by the Fresh Air of the Upper Deck," in *Mind, Culture, and Activity* 3(1), pp. 54-63.

Lazzarato, Maurizio, 2005. "Multiplicité, Totalité et Politique," in *Multitudes* 23 (2005), pp. 101-113. Available online: http://www.generation-online.org/p/fplazzarato3.htm ; trans. J. Muldoon, "Multiplicity, Totality and Politics," *Parrhesia* 9 (2010), pp. 23-30.

Lazzarato, Maurizio, 2006. "Life and the Living in the Societies of Control," in Martin Fuglsang and Bent Meier Sørensen (eds.), *Deleuze and the Social*, Edinburgh: Edinburgh University Press, pp. 171-190.

Lazzarato, Maurizio, 2008. "The Aesthetic Paradigm," in Simon O'-Sullivan and Stephen Zepke (eds.), *Deleuze, Guattari, and the Production of the New*, London: Continuum.

LeDoux, Joseph. 1998. *The Emotional Brain: The Mysterious Underpinnings of Emotional Life*. New York: Simon & Schuster.

Luria, Aleksandr Romanovich, 1978 [1966]. "Vygotsky And the Problem of Functional Localization," in M. Cole, ed., *Selected Writings of A.R. Luria*. New York: M.E. Sharpe Inc.

Malafouris, Lambros, 2013. "Mindful Art," comment on Nicolas J. Bullot, Rolf Reber, "The Artful Mind Meets Art History: Toward a Psycho-Historical Framework for the Science of Art Appreciation," in *Behavioral and Brain Sciences* 36, pp. 123-180 (comment at pp. 151-152).

Marx, Karl and Engels, Friedrich, 1978. *The German Ideology*. London: Lawrence and Wishart.

Monod, Jean-Claude, 2005. "La Radicalité Constituante (Negri, Balibar, Agamben) ou Peut-on Lire Schmitt de Droite à Gauche?," in *Mouvements* 37(1), pp. 80-88 (followed by a discussion with Toni Negri).

Monod, Jean-Claude, 2006. *Penser l'Ennemi, Affronter l'Exception. Réflexions Critiques sur l'Actualité de Carl Schmitt*, Paris: La Découverte.

More, Henry, 1978 [1653]. "An Antidote Against Atheism," in *A Collection of Several Philosophical Writings*, reprinted New York: Garland (1662).

Morfino, Vittorio, 2006. "Spinoza: An Ontology of Relation?" in *Graduate Faculty Philosophy Journal* 27(1), pp. 103-127.

Murphie, Andrew, 2010. "Deleuze, Guattari and Neuroscience," in Peter Gaffney (ed.), *The Force of the Virtual. Deleuze, Science, and Philosophy*, Minneapolis: University of Minnesota Press, pp. 277-300.

Negri, Antonio, 1991. *The Savage Anomaly. The Power of Spinoza's Metaphysics and Politics*, trans. Michael Hardt. Minneapolis: University of Minnesota Press.

Negri, Antonio (Fall, 1995)[1992]. "On *A Thousand Plateaus*," trans. Charles T. Wolfe, *Graduate Faculty Philosophy Journal* 18:1, pp. 93-109 (translation of "Sur *Mille Plateaux*," *Chimères* 17 (1992), pp. 71-93). Available online: http://antonionegriinenglish.files.wordpress.com/2010/ 09/4002-on_gilles_deleuze_and1.pdf [last accessed February 2014].

Negri, Antonio, 1997. "Travail et Affect," *Futur Antérieur* 39-40, pp. 45-56. Available online http://multitudes.samizdat.net/Travail-et-affect [last accessed February 2014].

Neidich, Warren, 2003. *Blow-Up. Photography, Cinema And the Brain*, New York: Distributed Art Publishers.

Papineau, David, 2005. "Social Learning And the Baldwin Effect," in António Zilhão (ed.), *Evolution, Rationality, and Cognition: A Cognitive Science for the Twenty-First Century*. New York: Routledge, 2005, pp. 40-60. Draft available online: http://www.kcl.ac.uk/ip/davidpapineau/ Staff/Papineau/OnlinePapers/SocLearnBald.htm [last accessed February 2014].

Papoulias, Constantina and Felicity Callard, 2010. "Biology's Gift: Interrogating the Turn to Affect," in *Body & Society* 16(1), pp. 29-56.

Pasquinelli, Matteo, 2014. "The Power of Abstraction and Its Antagonism: On Some Problems Common to Contemporary Neuroscience and the Theory of Cognitive Capitalism" (ms.).

Protevi, John, 2009. *Political Affect: Connecting the Social and the Somatic*, Minneapolis: University of Minnesota Press.

Protevi, John, 2014. "Political Emotion," in Christian von Scheve and Mikko Salmela (eds.), *Collective Emotions*, Oxford: Oxford University Press, pp. 326-336.

Quartz, Steven, 1999. "The Constructivist Brain," *Trends in Cognitive Sciences* 3(222), pp. 48-57.

Quartz, Steven and Terrence Sejnowski, 1997. "The Neural Basis of Cognitive Development: A Constructivist Manifesto," *Behavioural and Brain Sciences* 20, pp. 537-596.

Rajchman, John, 1988. "Habermas' Complaint," in *New German Critique* 45, pp. 163-191.

Rancière, Jacques, 2011. "On the Actuality of Communism," in Gal Kirn (ed.), *Post–Fordism and its Discontents*, Maastricht: Jan van Eyck Academie.

Ravven, Heidi Morrison, 2003. "Spinozistic Approaches to Evolutionary Naturalism: Spinoza's Anticipation of Contemporary Affective Neuroscience," in *Politics and the Life Sciences* 22:1, pp. 70-74.

Read, Jason, 2014. *Relations of Production: the Ontology and Politics of Transindividuality*, Leiden: Brill, Historical Materialism Series.

de Ronsil, Arnaud, 1768. *Les Hermaphrodites, Mémoires de Chirurgie*, London: Nourse and Paris: Dessain.

Schmitz, Sigrid, 2014. "Feminist Approaches to Neurocultures," in Charles T. Wolfe (ed.), *Brain Theory: Essays in Critical Neurophilosophy*, London: Palgrave MacMillan, pp. 195-216.

Skarda, Christine and Walter J. Freeman, 1987. "How Brains Make Chaos in Order to Make Sense of the World," in *Behavioral and Brain Sciences* 10(2), pp. 161-195.

Slaby, Jan and Shaun Gallagher, 2014. "Critical Neuroscience and Socially Extended minds." Available online: http://janslaby.com/downloads/gallslaby13critneuro_draftweb.pdf [last accessed February 2014].

Spinoza, Baruch, 1992. *Ethics* (1676), in *Ethics / Treatise on the Emendation of the Intellect / Selected Letters*, trans. Samuel Shirley, Indianapolis: Hackett.

Surel, Olivier, 2014. "Jakob von Uexküll: Une Ontologie des Milieux," in *Critique* 803.

Sutton, John, 1998. *Philosophy and Memory Traces*, Cambridge: Cambridge University Press.

Terranova, Tiziana, 2013. "Ordinary Psychopathologies of Cognitive Capitalism," in Arne de Boever and Warren Neidich (eds.), *The Psychopathologies of Cognitive Capitalism, Part One*, Berlin: Archive Books, 2013, pp. 45-68.

Thompson, Evan, 2007. *Mind in Life: Biology, Phenomenology, And the Sciences of Mind*, Cambridge: Harvard University Press.

von Uexküll, Jakob, 2010. *A Foray Into The Worlds Of Animals And Humans*, trans. Joseph D. O'Neil, Minneapolis: University of Minnesota Press, a translation of *Umwelt und Innenwelt der Tiere* (1934).

van der Veer, René and Valsiner, Jaan, 1991. *Understanding Vygotsky. A Quest for Synthesis*, London: Blackwell.

Vidal, Fernando, 2009. "Brainhood, Anthropological Figure of Modernity," in *History of the Human Sciences* 22(1), pp. 5-36.

Virno, Paolo, 2003. "The Multitude and the Principle of Individuation," in *Graduate Faculty Philosophy Journal* 24 (2), pp. 133-145. French original available online: http://multitudes.samizdat.net/article.php3?id_article=65 [last accessed February 2014].

Vygotsky, Lev S., 1929. *Pedologija Podrotska*, vol. 1, Moscow.

Vygotsky, Lev S., 1997 [1965]. "Psychology and the Localization of Mental Functions," trans. R. van der Veer, in R.S. Rieber & J. Wollock (eds.), *Collected Works of L.S. Vygotsky*, vol. 3: *Problems of Theory and Method in Psychology*, New York: Plenum Press.

Weber, Bruce H., and Depew, David J. (eds.), 2003. *Evolution and Learning: The Baldwin Effect Reconsidered*. Cambridge: MIT Press.

Wolfe, Charles, 2007. "De-ontologizing the Brain: From the Fictional Self to the Social Brain," *CTheory* 30:1. Available online: http://www.ctheory.net/ articles.aspx?id=572 [last accessed February 2014].

Wolfe, Charles, 2008. "L'anomalie du vivant. Réflexions sur le Pouvoir Messianique du Monstre," in *Multitudes* 33, pp. 53-62, reprinted in Vincent Romagny (ed.), 2013. *Sources*, Marseille: Rond-Point and Dijon: Les presses du réel.

Wolfe, Charles, 2010. "From Spinoza to the Socialist Cortex: Steps Toward the Social Brain," in Deborah Hauptmann and Warren Neidich (eds.), *Cognitive Architecture. From Bio-Politics To Noo-Politics*, Rotterdam: 010 Publishers, Delft School of Design Series, pp. 184-206. Available online (short version): http://www.maccs.mq.edu.au/news/conferences/2009/ASCS2009/wolfe.html [last accessed February 2014].

Wolfe, Charles (2011). "Antonio Negri's Ontology of Empire and Multitude," in *Ideas in History* 4:1-2, pp.109-135.

Zeki, Semir, 1999. *Inner vision: An exploration of art and the brain*, Oxford: Oxford University Press.

# The Power of Abstraction and Its Antagonism: On Some Problems Common to Contemporary Neuroscience and the Theory of Cognitive Capitalism.

> Life cleaves to matter, elaborating and contracting matter, bringing to life the virtualities within the material in unknown directions. Life emerges as a becoming-concept, a becoming-thought or—as a consciousness, a becoming-brain. (Grosz 2012)

> We accept far too easily that there exists a fundamental conflict between knowledge and life, such that their reciprocal aversion can lead only to the destruction of life by knowledge or to the derision of knowledge by life. [...] Now, the conflict is not between thought and life in man, but between man and the world in the human consciousness of life. [...] It is not true that knowledge destroys life. (Canguilhem 1965)

The philosophical debate of the last years, at least at the boundaries of French and Italian political theory, has been marked by a conceptual oscillation that has alternately emphasised immaterial labor or affective labor, knowledge economy or desire economy, the cognitive or the biopolitical. No research or political agenda have been immune from such a hypnotic spiral, which can be traced back to a millenary low-intensity hostility between the Western concepts of body and mind. After a period focusing on the knowledge economy and immaterial labor, for instance, at the end of the '90s, the *affective turn* of the humanities forced political theory to give a specific attention to *affective labor*.

On this conceptual journey, theorists rediscovered the reproductive and care labor that feminism attempted to politicise
already in the '70s. In the same period, biotechnologies and
the notion of *bios* occupied centre stage in debates around new
forms of power. A common critique emerged that took the
paradigm of cognitive labor to be overlooking the biological
and genetic materiality of the body, and more importantly its
libidinal and affective dimensions. Lazzarato (2006) proposed
interestingly the idea of *noopolitics* as an extension of the
definition of biopolitics to cover also the flesh of the collective imaginary and mind technologies. It must be underlined, however, that the sphere of affective production was
originally considered within the sphere of immaterial production and never opposed to it (Hardt & Negri 2000, 293).
How can these two spheres once again be put in relation to
each other?

     This essay intervenes in the oscillation between these
two poles and advocates a monistic paradigm, where the
opposition between body and mind, or *bios* and *abstraction*,
may hopefully vanish—as in the works of Spinoza, Marx,
Bergson, Merleau-Ponty, Canguilhem, Foucault and also
Deleuze and Guattari. Yet this time the French lineage is not
followed and the genealogy of the notion of biopolitics is traced
via the German tradition of *Lebensphilosophie,* where 'the
living' was rarely detached from a dimension of cognition and
abstraction. In particular, the German-Jewish neurologist Kurt
Goldstein and his ideas of *abstract behaviour* and *normative
power* of the organism are located at the root of Foucault's
intuition of biopower. In this reconstruction the cognitive
paradigm is turned inside-out: it is in order to understand the
body that we start once again from the brain, it is at very core
of the *bios* (and the whole matter) that *abstraction* is found
at work. The cognitive does not emerge *after* the evolution
of a naked life (and maybe just to become its very enemy),
but it innervates the living matter since its constitution
(as we are reminded in the opening quotation by Grosz).

Eventually in this essay, the brain is taken to be as the first model and terrain of biopower. Going deeper in this genealogy, the *power of abstraction* will be disclosed at the original core that inspired the paradigm of biopower. It is not an exaggeration to affirm that neuroplasticity (as understood by Goldstein) was the original inspiration of the notion of biopower. Exhuming the forgotten 'neurological roots' of the notion of biopolitics helps to clarify the affective vs. cognitive opposition and to describe differently the so-called psychopathologies of cognitive capitalism.

This essay is divided in five sections. The first three sections focus the notion of abstraction in relation to neurology, political economy and ontology—that is, the notions of *abstract behaviour* in Goldstein, *abstract labor* in Marx, and *abstract machine* in Deleuze and Guattari. Abstraction is here understood as an immanent power that makes and undoes connections, that territorializes and deterritorializes, that projects bodies and identities beyond themselves, onto the surrounding environment and towards the infinite cosmos. The power of abstraction is intended also as the power of differentiation with respect to neural matter, the power to produce further bifurcation of information and perception flows, as described by a long tradition spanning from the *Gestaltpsychologie* to Merleau-Ponty. The fourth section shows how the recent discovery of *mirror neurons* in neurology has further implications for political philosophy. It also explores Virno's discussion of mirror neurons within the tradition of Italian *operaismo*, and finally how the notion of abstraction can illuminate them in a different way. By way of conclusion, against a certain fatalistic tone, I propose to reverse the approach to the problem of the psychopathologies of cognitive capitalism by moving away from the *neuropedagogy* advocated by Metzinger.

# 1. Goldstein and the power of abstraction of the organism

There is a nodal point in the history of the relation between French and German philosophy when the notions of *life* and *abstraction* are found still bound together. This is, for instance, a crucial issue in Foucault's analysis of the relation between modern forms of power and modern systems of knowledge, but a more interesting conceptual nucleus is found in the inspiration of Foucault's biopolitics. The idea of biopower emerges in his course *The Abnormal* (15 January 1975) where it is described as *biopolitical normativity*. The innovative idea of the course was that power is no longer investigated as a discipline of the body (*the negative power of repression*) but via the invention of new Norms (*the positive power of normalisation*). The normalization of post-Napoleonic French society is the creative act of power that invents new norms in the fields of industry, administration, education and public health. The Norm and the Normal are the key-words of this institutional consolidation: it is at this time, for instance, that the École Normale is established. Incidentally, the first definition of *dispositif* is given by Foucault in this course, which refers to the genealogy of normativity. Foucault describes this form of power as a *dispositif* of normalization: 'This general technique of the government of men comprises a typical apparatus [*dispositif*], which is the disciplinary organization I spoke to you about last year. To what end is this apparatus directed? It is, I think, something that we can call "normalization" (Foucault 1975, 49). Foucault's idea of *biopolitical normativity* is inspired by his mentor Canguilhem's (1966) idea of *socio-organic normativity* as discussed in "The Normal and the Pathological," which presents the latter's research on the definition of normality and illness in medicine and life sciences. Curiously, Canguilhem himself built upon the neurologist Kurt Goldstein's idea of *organic normativity*.

Goldstein is not an esoteric figure in the history of thought. The cousin of Ernst Cassirer, he was the head of the neurology department at the Moabit hospital in Berlin when he was arrested by Gestapo and expelled from Germany. His seminal monograph "Der Aufbau des Organismus" [The Structure of the Organism] was dictated in exile in Amsterdam in 1934. Goldstein was also an extremely significant inspiration for Merleau-Ponty, who cited him hundreds of times in "The Structure of Behavior" (1942) and "Phenomenology of Perception" (1945). Foucault himself opens his first book "Maladie mentale et personnalité" (1954) with a considerable critique of Goldstein's definitions of mental illness and organic medicine based on the notions of *abstraction, abnormality* and *milieu*. These three notions return consistently throughout Foucault's career. In a bizarre circular coincidence, the last public and authorised text by Foucault is the new version of the introduction to the English edition of "The Normal and the Pathological." Following again Goldstein's track, Foucault states famously in this introduction: 'life is what is capable of error' (Foucault 1985).

In Goldstein *normative power* is the ability of an organism (specifically the human brain) to invent and modify its own norms, internal and external habits, rules and behaviours in order to better adapt to its surrounding environment, particularly in cases of illness and traumatic incidents, in those conditions that challenge the unity of the organism. Goldstein's originality is conceiving sickness and all that is considered 'psychopathological' and socially 'abnormal' as a manifestation of a positive normative process, which today would be defined as *neuroplasticity*. Thus truly 'sick' is the organism that is not capable of invention and experimentation of new norms, the organism that is paradoxically not able of making mistakes. For Goldstein, psychopathologies express the positive self-actualization power of the organism, but Goldstein defines this positive power as a *power of abstraction*.

The so-called 'psychopathologies' are just the attempt of our body to invent new norms in adverse conditions, to project and protect our body beyond itself. This amounts to an *abstract attitude* that goes beyond everyday *concrete attitude* (Goldstein 1934).

## 2. Marx and the power of abstraction of capitalism

The notion of abstraction has been widely shared and debated within Western philosophy, political economy and cognitive sciences throughout the 19th and 20th century, before being recently eclipsed by the rise of the affective studies and desiring philosophies. How can the model of neurological abstraction be linked again to the notions of abstract labor and cognitive labour found in the contemporary theory of cognitive capitalism (Hardt, Negri, Vercellone, etc.)? It is not the time to repeat here the well-known theses about knowledge, language, information and attention as productive and valorising forces in post-Fordism. Also there is not enough space to go back to Sohn-Rethel (1978) and his in-tuitions on the similarity between the abstraction of money and abstraction of thought or to classic texts in Soviet Psychology such as Ilyenkov's "Dialectics of the Abstract and the Concrete in Marx's Capital" (1960). For the time being, it is sufficient to recall how Marx framed abstraction as both the general movement of capitalism and general movement of the resistance to it. Regarding this power of abstraction in Marx, Hardt and Negri shed some light in the following passage:

> Abstraction is essential to both the functioning of capital and the critique of it. Marx's point of departure in *Capital*, in fact, is his analysis of abstract labor as the determining foundation of the exchange-value of commodities.

Labor in capitalist society, Marx explains, must be abstracted from the concrete labors of the tailor, the plumber, the machinist to be considered as labor in general, without respect to its specific application. This abstract labor once congealed in commodities is the common substance they all share, which allows for their values to bc universally commensurable, and which ultimately allows money to function as a general equivalent. [...] Marx views abstraction, however, with ambivalence. Yes, abstract labor and the system of exchange are mechanisms for extracting surplus value and maintaining capitalist control, but the concept of abstract labor [...] is what makes it possible to think the working class. Without abstract labor there is no working class! (Hardt & Negri 2009, 127)

The abstraction of capitalism is a very material process, as stressed in Sohn-Rethel's notion of *real abstraction*. Furthermore the definition of cognitive capitalism should be framed in this manner. Cognitive capitalism is not simply the domain of knowledge production or computer-based labor but, as Vercellone has explained, a whole new division of labor (that is a new different machinic bifurcation, articulation and organisation of flows of matter, energy and information). The history of capitalism is read by Vercellone (2007) in three stages: formal subsumption (*manufacturing capitalism*), real subsumption (*industrial capitalism*) and general intellect (*cognitive capitalism*). As such, capitalist production appears to follow movements of deterritorialization and reterritorialization: the industrial revolution reterritorializes the division of labor of manufacturing inside the factory, whereas cognitive capitalism deterritorializes the division of labor once more across all society. The logical chain described by Vercellone between antagonism, division of labor, machinery and the general intellect perfectly describes a *general abstract machine*. The evolution of the division of labor is indeed this process of abstraction.

However such a power of abstraction must not be understood merely as an evil external force that belongs only to capitalism, but rather as a common potentiality of the multitude. As Negri and Hardt would have it, without abstraction there is no multitude.


# 3. The ontology of abstraction in Deleuze and Guattari

The problem of abstraction is central for Deleuze and Guattari too, despite emphasis throughout the last few decades on the desiring and affective side of their ontology. In their mission to sketch a materialistic ontology and materialistic logic they transformed and subsumed all the metaphysical and transcendental models of modern philosophy within the immanent notion of the *abstract machine.* Here the term 'machine' indicates the very contingent and productive process of abstraction, the connection of different and even radically different substrates and also the projection and 'assemblage' with the infinite and the void. The Abstract Machine is a universal concept introduced so as to ground a manifold ontology: 'The plane of consistency of Nature is like an immense Abstract Machine, abstract yet real and individual; its pieces are the various assemblages and individuals, each of which groups together an infinity of particles entering into an infinity of more or less interconnected relations' (Deleuze and Guattari 1980, 254).

The abstract machine marked a final rupture with the holistic tradition of abstraction, which had been inherited by German idealism, and inaugurated the abduction of the Outside by the double pincer of the Lobster-God (Deleuze & Guattari 1980, 40). Despite having such a cosmological depth, the notion of abstract machine can also be used to explain the role of abstraction in the mundane paradigms of both biopower and cognitive capitalism: the abstract machine points to a power of abstraction that is able to *ab-stract* from its substrates and to produce the universal equivalent of capital and power (biopolitics).[1] This is also the ability of mind: its ability to make connections, but also to sever them, to negate them or to repeat them to infinity, the ability to produce general assemblages. Indeed, Deleuze and Guattari's notion can be very useful to mediate between political economy and neurology, where the abstract machine could be intended as the ability to escape the limit of the brain and the organism, to expand towards an external memory and include the whole universe as an extension of the mind. It is interesting though how the philosophy of Deleuze and Guattari has been received mainly as a celebration of infinite flows of desire. It is true that Spinoza's infinite substance is the essential ground of this philosophy, but without abstract machines construction of any system would not be possible, hence there would be no *becoming* in their ontology.[2]

........................................................................................................................

[1] 'The abstract machine in itself is destratified, deterritorialized; it has no form of its own (much less substance) and makes no distinction within itself between content and expression, even though outside itself it presides over that distinction and distributes it in strata, domains, and territories. An abstract machine in itself is not physical or corporeal, any more than it is semiotic; it is diagrammatic (it knows nothing of the distinction between the artificial and the natural either).' (Deleuze & Guattari, 1980, 587)

[2] The relation between organism and abstraction, the organic and the abstract, can be located in their aesthetic model. See their response to "Abstraction and Empathy" by Worringer (1908), where primitive art, the first art of humankind, was precisely about the rise of the abstract line.

# 4. Socialist cortex and mirror neurons

The notion of abstraction is not just a resonance between distant authors. There is indeed a common background in the contemporary history of cognitive sciences and political philosophy. Wolfe (2010) has underlined this background in an important essay on the fascinating history of the so-called 'socialist cortex,' which captures the idea of collective brain spanning from Spinoza and Marx to Vygotski and Negri and the whole Italian *operaismo*. Another interesting case of the encounter between cognitive sciences and political philosophy is found in Virno's (2004) commentary on the famous research on mirror neurons. Mirror neurons were discovered by a team from the University of Parma, consisting of Giacomo Rizzolatti, Vittorio Gallese and a number of others. They implanted electrodes in the ventral premotor cortex of the brain of few monkeys and recorded neuron activities while these monkeys were engaged in some specific actions. They discovered that: 'a particular set of neurons, activated during the execution of [...] hand actions, such as grasping, holding or manipulating objects, discharge also when the monkey observes similar hand actions performed by another individual' (Gallese 2001). These neurons were firing both when the monkey was doing the action of *grasping* a banana and when the monkey was *seeing* another monkey grasping a banana: for this reason they were called *mirror* neurons. Other studies have since demonstrated the activity of mirror neurons in human animals (Mukamel et al. 2010), but just the discovery of this simple link in a specific area of the primate brain brings incalculable consequences for cognitive sciences and the philosophy of mind. Virno takes Gallese's description of mirror neurons as the proof of a naturalistic basis of human nature and as the basis of the pre-individual sphere of inter-subjectivity that is supposed to be a given before the constitution of the human identity:

'The relation of a human animal to its own kind is assured by an original 'intersubjectivity' that precedes the very constitution of the individual mind. The "we" exists even before we can speak of a self-conscious "I"' (Virno 2004, 175). In this view there is a common empathy between the individuals of the same species that is rooted before any linguistic faculty. Mirror neurons allow Virno to sketch a theory of political agency based on a collective intersubjectivity that is only afterwards crossed and cut by the ambivalence of language and the violence of negation. Virno poses here the common as a pre-given structure of human nature, as a sort of pre-individual space *à la* Simondon. Thereafter, in an elegant way, Virno critiques this substrate of human nature with the introduction of two other logical steps: first, the power to negate natural empathy and communality with other human beings; and, second, the power to negate this negation, to reconstitute the public sphere in a proper constituent sense. What is interesting for Virno is the fact that mirror neurons do not explain the power of negation, while the most peculiar trait of human thought is precisely the ability to negate.

> Language inoculates negativity into the life of the species. It enables the failure of reciprocal recognition. The linguistic animal is the species capable of *not* recognizing its own kind. [...] Language is the antidote to the poison that language itself pours into the innate sociability of the mind. Aside from the being able to cancel out neural empathy, completely or partially, language can also remove this contradiction. [...] In other words the public sphere is derived form a *negation of negation*. (Virno 2004, 176)

Virno's account appears to be rigorous within the tradition of Analytical Philosophy, but mirror neurons can be contextualised in a different way within the holistic logic that spans from German Idealism and *Gestaltpsychologie* to the more recent theory of 'enaction.' Virno seems to forget that the very power of negation (which I prefer to call 'power of abstraction') can be innervated deep into the structure of perception and sensation. There is no ontological difference between thought and perception, abstraction and negation. As much as a century ago, *Gestaltpsychologie* showed that the visual perception of figures is based on the brain's holistic power to generalise points and abstract lines. More recently Noë (2004, vii) has recalled this position: 'perception and perceptual consciousness depend on capacities for action and capacities for thought; perception is... a kind of thoughtful activity.' The theory of mirror neurons finds itself along the epistemological border where the scientific data of neurophysiology and the holistic logic of neurophenomenology look into each other as through a broken mirror. For sure, a new paradigm will emerge along this fault line.

Indeed, the results of the first experiments on mirror neurons can be explained in a different and more dynamic fashion. Evolutionary scientists agree that mirror neurons are an achievement of evolution: very few animals are capable of imitation and learning by imitation to the same degree as primates. The ability of mirror neurons is something that our organism developed. But how? For a long time, to be sure, primates had neurons that were firing independently when an action was performed and when the same action was seen as performed by somebody else: see for instance those monkeys that take up to four years to imitate an action to source food that was discovered or invented by a member of the same group. Then, one day, a link was established in the brain: two different neurological 'circuits' were connected to the same one. In this way empathy can be described as the power of abstraction in an organism that is able to associate with another one that which beforehand was only considered its own. If Gallese points to a pre-individual commonality, here the commonality is only post-individual— the effort and the projection of our power of abstraction.

Empathy is then possible only thanks to the power of abstraction and not the other way around. While negation can be considered a subset of abstraction, abstraction cannot be considered a subset of negation. In a similar vein to Virno, but arriving via a different philosophical tradition, I advance the idea that *the power of abstraction is the only way to the common.*

# 5. Neuropedagogy vs. psychopathologies

If a renewed notion of abstraction is advanced between the domain of neuroscience and political philosophy, it is also to invert the common understanding of the so-called 'psychopathologies of cognitive capitalism' and to frame them from the point of view of an *empowered* subject rather than from the point of view of an *alienated* one. Cognitive capitalism should be defined as the exploitation of the power of abstraction, intended as the cognitive power of the human organism, as the very living force that can project the human beyond its own identity, build empathy and the common, manipulate objects, machines and information. The main thesis of this text is the following: we develop psychopathologies when we lose our power of abstraction, not when we overuse it.

In Goldstein the failure of the power of abstraction is what produces catastrophic behaviour, in a similar way to how Berardi (2010) and Marazzi (2002) have described the reaction of our body to semio-capitalism and digital mediascape as panic and attention disorder. But in Goldstein psychopathologies are a 'positive' symptom, they are the manifestation (sometimes desperate) of the affirmative force of the organism in its antagonism with the environment. So the point is how to defend or expand the power of abstraction of the mind and not simply to make the body an object of passive care, for instance when Berardi (2010) claims that 'if we want to find the way towards autonomous collective subjectivation we have to generate cognitarian awareness with regard to an erotic, social body of the general intellect. The way to autonomous and collective subjectivation starts here: from the general intellect searching for a body.'

The 'psychopathologies of cognitive capitalism' risks an inadequate conceptualization via which we sever again the mind/body unity and we abdicate to the colonisation of our mind by capitalism, leaving our political attention only to body, libido and affects like unaware slaves. The very basic body, the poorest form of perception, do not exist without the power of abstraction, articulation and differentiation (described also by Merleau-Ponty 1945: 35, 85). In this way the solution is not about reclaiming the body, affection, libido, desire and so on. Rather it is about reclaiming abstraction, the power to differentiate, articulate and bifurcate: in order to *perceive* at a higher degree of detail, and *to perceive our feelings at a higher degree of detail*. Instead of the fatalistic tone that meets the current information overload, I prefer to advocate Metzinger's idea of neuropedagogy. In his book *The Ego Tunnel*, Metzinger has framed the so-called psychopathologies of the digital age with these words:

> The Internet has already become a part of our self-model. We use it for external memory storage, as a cognitive prosthesis, and for emotional autoregulation... Clearly, the integration of hundreds of millions of human brains... into ever new medial environments has already begun to change the structure of conscious experience itself... Today, the advertisement and entertainment industries are attacking the very foundations of our capacity for experience, drawing us into the vast and confusing media jungle... We can see the probable result in the epidemic of attention-deficit disorder in children and young adults, in midlife burnout, in rising levels of anxiety in large parts of the population... New medial environments may create a new form of waking consciousness that resembles weakly subjective states—a mixture of dreaming, dementia, intoxication, and infantilization. (Metzinger 2009: 234)

As a response to this scenario Metzinger advances the idea of neuropedagogy, which revolves around the ideas of introducing classes of meditation at the high schools, preparing the young against the commercial robber of attention and teaching different techniques of empowered consciousness. Of course, for Metzinger these classes should be free of any religious or new age tinge: 'They might be a part of gym classes; the brain too is a part of the body—a part that can be trained and must be tended to with care' (Metzinger 2009: 236). Metzinger reserves a particular attention also to the chemical dimension of neuropedagogy (a part that cannot be expanded upon here) and discusses the popular and recreational uses of substances such as mescaline, ketamine, Ritalin, MDMA and 2CB, pointing to the humorous, but indeed very serious, concept of *cosmetic psychopharmacology*.

Neuropedagogy is only the first step of what Metzinger describes as the project of a new Consciousness Revolution, where his tone becomes more militant. As Metzinger (2009: 238) remarks, 'a true consciousness culture will always be subversive.' This political focus on the technologies of consciousness is not new and its fertile influence has been recorded, for instance in the California of the '60s where psychedelic underground, technological innovation and philosophical research were mutually entangled (see the holistic and hyper-textual milieu of the Whole Earth Catalogue that paved the way for the brain frame of the World Wide Web). In conclusion, Metzinger's neuropedagogy and Consciousness Revolution can be described also as the militant response of contemporary living labor to the regime of cognitive capitalism. There seems to be neither fatalism nor victimismization in this proposal: it is about reclaiming, defending and expanding the power of abstraction that is continuously colonised by capitalism. At the end it is about organising an epistemic acceleration, to become more cognitive than cognitive capitalism, not less.

Berardi, Franco "Bifo" (November 2010). "Cognitarian Subjectivation," in *E-flux journal* 20. Available online: e-flux.com/journal/cognitarian-subjectivation [last accessed February 2014].

Canguilhem, Georges, 1965. *La Connaissance de la vie*. Paris: Vrin, (first edition 1952). Trans. *Knowledge of Life*. New York: Fordham University Press, 2008.

Canguilhem, Georges 1966. *Le Normal et le Pathologique, Augmenté de Nouvelles Réflexions Concernant le Normal et le Pathologique*. Paris: PUF, (first edition 1943). Trans. *The Normal and the Pathological*. Introduction by Michel Foucault. Dordrecht: Reidel, 1978 and New York: Zone Books, 1991.

Deleuze, Gilles and Guattari, Félix 1980. *Mille Plateaux. Capitalisme et Schizophrénie*, vol. 2. Paris: Minuit. Trans: *A Thousand Plateaus: Capitalism and Schizophrenia*, vol. 2. Minneapolis: University of Minnesota Press, 1987.

Ilyenkov, Evald Vassilievich 1982 [1960]. *The Dialectics of the Abstract and the Concrete in Marx's Capital*. Moscow: Progress Publishers.

Foucault, Michel, 1954. *Maladie Mentale et Personnalité*. Paris: PUF. New edition titled: *Maladie mentale et psychologie*. Paris: PUF, 1962. Trans. *Mental Illness and Psychology*. New York: Harper & Row, 1976.

Foucault, Michel, 1975. *Les Anormaux. Cours au Collège de France 1974-1975*. Paris: Seuil, 1999. Trans. *Abnormal: Lectures at the Collège de France 1974-1975*. New York: Picador, 2004.

Foucault, Michel (1985). "La vie: l'expérience et la science," in *Revue de Métaphysique et de Morale* 90/1, 1985 special issue on Georges Canguilhem. New version of the introduction to the first English edition of *Le Normal et le Pathologique* by Canguilhem (1978).

Gallese, Vittorio, 2001. "The Shared Manifold Hypothesis: From Mirror Neurons To Empathy" in *Journal of Consciousness Studies* 8/5–7, 2001. For bibliography on mirror neurons see Gallese's personal webpage *www.unipr.it/arpa/mirror/english/staff/gallese.htm* [last accessed February 2014].

Goldstein, Kurt, 1934. *Der Aufbau des Organismus*. Den Haag: Nijhoff. Trans. *The Organism*. New York: American Book Company, 1939; Zone Books, 1995.

Grosz, Elizabeth (2012). "Deleuze, Ruyer, and Becoming-Brain: The Music of Life's Temporality," in *Parrhesia journal* 12.

Hardt, Michael and Negri, Antonio, 2000. *Empire*. Cambridge: Harvard University Press.

Hardt, Michael and Negri, Antonio, 2009. *Commonwealth*. Cambridge: Harvard University Press.

Lazzarato, Maurizio, 2006. "Life and the Living in the Societies of Control" in Martin Fuglsang and Bent Meier Sorensen (eds.), *Deleuze and the Social*, Edinburgh: Edinburgh University Press.

Marazzi, Christian, 2002. *Capitale e Linguaggio: Dalla New Economy all'Economia di Guerra*. Rome: Derive & Approdi. Trans. *Capital and Language: From the New Economy to the War Economy*. Los Angeles: Semiotext(e), 2008.

Merleau-Ponty, Maurice, 1942. *La Structure du Comportement*, Paris: PUF. Trans. *The Structure of Behavior*. Boston: Beacon Press, 1963.

Merleau-Ponty, Maurice, 1945). *Phénoménologie de la Perception*. Paris: Gallimard. Trans. *Phenomenology of Perception*. London: Routledge, 2002.

Metzinger, Thomas, 2009. *The Ego Tunnel: The Science of the Mind and the Myth of the Self*. New York: Basic Books.

Mukamel, Roy et al. (2010). "Single-Neuron Responses in Humans during Execution and Observation of Actions," in *Current Biology* 20.

Noë, Alva, 2004. *Action in Perception*. Cambridge: MIT Press.

Sohn-Rethel, Alfred, 1978. *Intellectual and Manual Labour: A Critique of Epistemology*. London: Macmillan.

Vercellone, Carlo (2007). "From Formal Subsumption to General Intellect: Elements for a Marxist Reading of the Thesis of Cognitive Capitalism," in *Historical Materialism* 15/1.

Virno, Paolo (2004). "Neuroni Mirror, Negazione Linguistica, Reciproco Riconoscimento," in *Forme di vita* 2/3. Roma: Derive Approdi. English translation: "Mirror Neurons, Linguistic Negation, Reciprocal Recognition," in *Multitude: Between Innovation and Negation*. Los Angeles: Semiotexte, 2008.

Wolfe, Charles, 2010. "From Spinoza to the Socialist Cortex: Steps Toward the Social Brain," in Deborah Hauptman and Warren Neidich (eds.). *Cognitive architecture: From Biopolitics to noopolitics*. Rotterdam: 010 Publishers.

Worringer, Wilhelm (1908). *Abstraktion und Einfühlung*. München: Piper. Trans. *Abstraction and Empathy*. New York: International Universities Press, 1953.

# Towards A*cognitive Architecture: A Cybernetic Note Beyond – or the Self-informing Machinery

## Preface

We are writing in the year 2014. Information increasingly becomes a desire, the necessity in the form of communication. Desire is an extension of the brain while communication seemingly combines heuristic operations in design development, and reaches beyond thermodynamics. More than 65 years ago, Norbert Wiener's "Cybernetics – the Control and Communication in the Animal and the Machine" (Wiener, 1948) is published, the Macy Conferences then titled *Circular Causal and Feedback Mechanisms in Biological and Social Systems* are in their 3rd year and following von Neumann's findings on the *Ergodic Theorem*, the *Cellular Automaton* are on their way.[1] In the meantime *Baby*, the Manchester Small-Scale Experimental Machine and the world's first stored-program computer, tested for the so-called Williams Tube (a lightweight storage device) runs its first program. The *Universal Turing Machine* becomes the continuing driver for computation.[2]

---

[1] The Macy Conferences (1946-1953). Core group members included Bateson, Hutchinson, McColloch, Mead, v. Foerster, von Neumann, Rosenbluth and Wiener amongst others. The terms cybernetics or second order cybernetics is not applied yet, however the theories are. First proposals are made that feedback mechanism are also valid for economic and social systems. A general system theory is being developed interdisciplinary.

[2] The Universal Turing Machine, UTM (1936-37, Allan Turing). A UTM has the ability to read any Turing Machine and input for simulation. In this present philosophy of computation al architecture, Turing's UTM is applicable and can be transferred from virtual to tangible.

Within the context of *The Psychopathologies of Cognitive Capitalism: Part Two*, the subject matter of this paper relates to accessing knowledge and tools for observing and designing an interconnected para-metric world; a cybernetic world characterized by multidimensional behavioral structures informed through using the digital as interface. It provides an extension to the existing emergent construct of *The Psychopathology of Cognitive Capitalism* in general and the interdisciplinary *Cognitive Capitalism Project* in particular. The insight given into cognitive capitalism and design strategies are foundations formed in the 20th century and aims at understanding and formulating of what the pathology of *The Psychopathology of Cognitive Capitalism* may possibly be when looking through the lens of cybernetics beyond. It offers an investigation to the understanding and the form of knowledge through communication, a recursive re-invention and re-understanding of how we think, how we decide and how we actually design and behave. Not just as architects in the design process of a building or a city, but as human beings in the design process of the everyday. A compilation, a collection of thoughts and findings, hovering in a paradigm between architecture, cybernetics, system theory, technology and the state of being; Through Wittgenstein's *Tractatus Logico Philosophicus*, and its subject matter language or syntax, the question of what is reality, may operate as a filtering veil through which this essay may emerge.

The paper discusses cultural architectural theory in conjunction with technical, political and economical possibilities in order to produce tangible manifestations in the context of interdisciplinary cognitive work and authorship. In particular, in the context of open source software, virtual and unknown design teams, whose common ground is based on common interests and knowledge, a spatial-temporal structural coupling, which, at times, can occur in parallel. The field of *cybernetics and architecture* within computational design, researches facts and theories developed in the last half of the 20th century, and their relevance to computational thinking and digital making, shaping the built and unbuilt networked environment in the near and distant future. In contrast to the digital, referring to a particular technology of executing calculations, the computational relates to a way of thinking and making reflecting complexity and non-linearity. It is about process, rather than simply input/output. It is informed by issues such as emergence, algorithms, structure, material behavior, data and society. In most cases using computers as interfaces with calculating machines and CNC (computer numerical control) for digital fabrication 3D-printing, laser-cutting and/or robotic fabrication. Underlying principles are not just reduced to architecture; instead they are methods with broad applications to a variety of disciplines; in this case relevant as an application and proof for cognitive capitalism. The model suggested here pushes the boundaries of the contemporary understanding of architecture and as a result reconstructs reality. through experimenting with the scale of buildings, cities and smaller prototypes, understanding the liminal space between the built environment, materials used, the perception of the user, the regulation through the designer, client, budget, and most importantly decision-making processes, the choice of software during the design process, data used and the cognitive capital to inform all of the above. So the questions are: 'Who is the designer?' and 'Who owns the copyright, or rather the cognitive copyright?' Architecture as *building*, as physical form is the proof of the concept of interplay, and most likely is a result of *thinking* and internalizing *dwelling* that has been outlived by the construct *architecture* as organism, evolving and informing itself through filtering, observation and self-observation: "I am the observed link between myself and observing myself" (von Foerster, 1981).[3]

........................................................................................................

[3] In his essay "Building, Dwelling Thinking" (in "Poetry, Language, Thought," 1951) Martin Heidegger discusses the notion that building is only possible if we are know what dwelling means and relates to the relationship of man, space. It is notable that the essay was written in post-war Germany suffering from a shortage of housing.

Von Foerster's paper is structured in a series of parts, which at times overlap and merge. "Defining the Matter" aims to clarify key terms used, and to establish possible relationships between them. These terms—which derive from biology, computer sciences, architecture or mathematics–so far have neither been defined cross-disciplinarily, nor within architecture. Since, however, they do affect how the forthcoming text is understood, and since in an era of rapid technological and theoretical shifts terms and expressions are revisited constantly to receive numerous varying definitions, there is a necessity to delineate their function. This will provide a theoretical basis for the present text and sets the topic into the framework of philosophy of computation at the same time. The main inquiry focuses on the agenda "It's not alone, it's synthetic—the bits are calculating," and provides the reader with a description of A*cognitivist Architecture in a cyber-biological framework embedding its construct within the mind/body phenomenon immanent in social environments. The narrative *Reyner Banham Loves Los Angeles* bridges computational thinking, the body, perception through our senses and the brain in a material world. This part introduces the concept of *Wechselwirkung* offered by biological cognition and the cognitive Internet, with its unknown amount of *reflectors* in an existing non-linear para-space.[4] Here the *cybernetic note* will be woven into a genealogical string of thoughts. The paper concludes with an exploration for and of an interconnected para-metric world by engaging largely with immaterial, *neurotectural* design strategies and the question of collective authorship, relating back to the synthetic that becomes natural, cognitive and bio-semiotic.

---

[4] Jakob von Uexküll (1864-1944), biologist and philosopher coined the term 'Umwelt.' 'Umwelt' is the environment shaped by animal or human due to *Wechselwirkung*. The difference to 'Umgebung' [surrounding] is, that the surrounding accepts its inhabitants and is not shaped by them. A relation to architecture exists within the notion of place as being a *shaped* space.

# Defining the Matter

Decision-making processes in the human brain are predominantly governed and influenced by heuristics (Gigerenzer and Brighton 2009) individually generated through experience, learning and conversations with the living and non-living environment. Heuristics is a relatively fast method of problem solving employing existing knowledge and wisdom to arrive at acceptable but not perfect solutions. Classical methods in computer sciences have focused on optimal problem solving, employing accurate and precise algorithms with little tolerance for perfect outcomes (in many cases with hardly inacceptable time frames due to complexity). The application of incremental search algorithms was first developed in the early 1950s and approached even economic, logistical and infrastructural issues. Search algorithms are programmed as functions to find the shortest path between two or more locations in a field, graph or cell matrix. Certainly restrictive parameters, obstacles and behavioural rules may influence which form the path may finally take and be part of the way-finding strategy. Today search algorithms are used in almost all fields and to a large extent in search engines. A*, a more flexible search algorithm designed in 1968 at the Stanford Research Institute can be combined with heuristic methods and herewith serves as concept for the notion of A*Cognitivist Architecture. It advocates behavior within architecture—a term to be redefined—that equals an organism, a living system, functioning according to a complex set of rules and dynamics, which are alien to linearity or reliance only. Architecture as social agency, understood in that way adapts and decides in accordance with its environment and the knowledge available as nodal points or locations in a dynamic, constantly reconfiguring network, virtually accessible as space and physically existent in form of servers and motherboards. Pathfinding for A*Cognitivist Architecture tracks down the elements of data and information required for successful problem solving and finds the best possible solution for *survival*, or *the shortest path to success*, without the dependency to arrive at a desired form or shape. It is a third order cybernetic system describing communication between itself and its observer in a dynamic multi-layered environment. Due to interaction and communication between the actors (relationship as in the functions between entities are also considered actors) in different velocities, the observer and the observed are interchangeable and regulate each other (Reichenbach 2003). The phenomenon parallels a self-replicating analogue and digital machinery, with a variety of intersections and communication abilities. Hence all operations take place in a 'Self-Informing' system, which refers to Humberto Maturana and Francisco Varela's concept of 'autopoiesis,' established in 1972 (Maturana 1980). The term *autopoiesis* as coined by Maturana and Varela originally meant self-creation of an autonomous (entropic) organisation out of itself. The fractal nature of this machinery's behaviour projects a slight and constant breeze of Gilles Deleuze's *Difference and Repetition* (Deleuze 1968) and *The Fold* (Deleuze 1992) and refers to both a process of topological and structural morphosis in a Deleuzian sense of desire, but also to the process of a series of parts working together in one system. The difference to the known mechanical machine is that the parts of the machine that change their function and form are soft, malleable and almost liquid, and therefore process, product and goal reform accordingly. "A cybernetic Note beyond – or the self-informing Machinery" occupies stages in interfering interfaces, between coding designers and hackers, the Internet, software, external and internal hardware, and cognitive capital as collective design intelligence nurturing and breeding information. It is an 'Architecture Machine' (Negroponte 1973), where the power of emergence and ability of data storage is congruent with the agents inhabiting it in constant data exchange through communication. Decoding and applying exchanged data, as function, is as relevant as the data itself. The form of communication becomes its own communication.

**inFORM** — To illustrate the point of the 'self-informing Machinery' with its data exchange and complex communication methods I would like to sketch out two architectural strategies of inFORMation and data transfer, namely geometrical ones that are distinctly different to cognitive once, but play a role when explored topologically:
a) Algorithmic – means to apply one or more concrete rules or functions, such as the *Golden Mean* or *Brownian Motion*.
b) Parametric – means to apply one or more parameters on top of an algorithm.
Algorithmic design therefore can be regarded as genotypic and isolated, parametric design as phenotypic, objected to an environment. Either is linear and reduced in their cognitive and biological abilities. Both borrow from nature, such as the geometrical Voronoi pattern on a giraffe skin or the Fibonacci series apparent in sunflowers, waves or hurricanes.[5] An example for parametric behavior in nature could be the choreography of a flock of starlings, moving according to certain internal rules, forming beautiful shapes of clustering and aggregating, according to and affected by external environmental parameters, such as wind, circulation of air and temperature. Algorithms acting as a regulating system in this fashion are genetic algorithms, combining biology and geometry. Both the algorithmic and parametric approaches refer to a technique for form finding through computational means and apply one or more algorithms or a combination including behavioural rules to agents in a system, which have the ability to generate a multi-dimensional network of varying forms. Working parametrically is extremely useful in order to investigate and analyse iterations or forms according to fitness values (aesthetics, structural behaviour, material usage, etc.).

......................................................................................................

[5] The Voronoi pattern is a mathematically based diagram describing a way to divide two-dimensional areas or three-dimensional space. The tessellation is a result of an algorithm employed on previously established points.

The famous analogue computational string model by Frei Otto, the father of structural form finding is exemplary for finding a *minimal path* network through self-organization of natural material and environmental behaviour. It is a set up with dry woollen threads stretching across a circular frame in a regular fashion. Once water is added material behaviour is elicited and the threads start to cling together. They create a Voronoi-like pattern. A natural example for minimal-path finding is the behaviour of slime mold, an organism, which naturally finds the shortest path between all points in a network. Ant colonies are also behave along the lines of *minimal path* networks, except that their behavior responds to pheromone spurs. Structural, minimal surface (not path) form finding can be seen in the 1972 Munich Olympic Stadium, also designed by Frei Otto. It is designed according to the natural behavior of soap film. Probably the first building designed through form-finding is the Sagrada Familia, conceived by Antonio Gaudi in 1882 using a physical chain model (algorithm) and gravity (parameter), and recently completed by Mark Burry (RMIT), who used digital algorithmic computation and fabrication for models and prototypes by the means of computers. That is to say that there is a similar decision-making process at play in the choice of algorithm via a specific design model resulting in a finished materialized product owning topography, surface topology and tactility. Using parameters is a technique, an instrument. Notwithstanding, parametric architecture has been used to describe a new style [parametricism] of architecture, which reflects ornament, geometry and the static of the 20th century, and steers away from a context-based, open-system, cognitive architecture of the 21st century. The crux of *A*cognitivist Architecture*, a product of digitilisation and the Internet, lies in the intensity and amount of cognitive capital necessary for producing collective brainpower that is all but reduced to aesthetics only. It is about understanding the logic of becoming form, breeding forms, and understanding form as a result of communication processes and the ability to decode it within a system, rather than form for forms sake.

A*cognitive Architecture is primarily concerned with extended parametric strategies focusing on paths between nodes of knowledge, cognitive capital, all accessed through digital means. A pool of minds is replacing material capitalism. Therefore the model A*cognitivist Architecture suggests is determining for all disciplines. It is a survival strategy, obeying and extending to what Nicholas Negroponte described, as "The Change from Atoms to Bits is irrevocable and unstoppable" when observing the increasing "instantaneous and inexpensive transfer of electronic data that moves at the speed of light..." (Negroponte 1995, 4).

## It's not Alone, it's Synthetic – the Bits are Calculating

**A CYBER-BIOLOGICAL FRAMEWORK** — Changes in socio-economic formations and the rise and availability of "sophisticated communications equipment (cyberdecks or matrix simulators), […] privileged or differential institutional access and specialized hardware and software expertise," (Tomas 1991, 43) elicited a novel cyber-biological framework for a large number of players. The pitch can be regarded as the non-space of a collective, in constant morphis; it also exists as liminal space, consisting of thresholds between individuals. In both cases it is a non-linear paraspace derived through genealogical cultural evolution, a cyber-space beyond the unambiguousness between inside and outside, action and reaction, digital and computational and last but not least cognitive and economic. "Cognition is a biological phenomenon and can only be understood as such; any epistemological insight into the domain of knowledge requires this understanding." (Maturana 1980, 7). The English psychiatrist and cybernetician Ross Ashby summarized the ubiquitous subject matter and the problem discussed herewith and today in his book *Design for a Brain, chapter The Animal as Machine* when he wrote,

"As the organism and its environment are to be treated as a single system, the dividing line between 'organism' and 'environment' becomes partly conceptual and to that extend arbitrary. Anatomically and physically, of course, there is a unique and obvious distinction between the two parts of the system; but if we view the system functionally, ignoring purely anatomical facts as irrelevant, the division of the system, into 'organism' and 'environment' becomes vague." (Ashby 1954, 39).

Ashby's treatise is an early investigation into the behavior of an animal in relation to stimuli from the immediate environment and neural action. More precisely the interaction between an animals' observation of an irritation, followed by information flow to its nervous system and subsequently physical reaction by the animals' receptors affecting relevant muscles and also cognitive responses. To illustrate the apparent complex biophysical mechanism Ashby presents the example of a sculptor's hand holding a chisel, and he goes even further in explaining that the chisel is "a part of the material which the nervous system is attempting to control." (Ibid., 39). The example describes three aspects: an internal infrastructure for data transfer (between the internal human and the external object), an extension of the body through its brain (chisel and sculptor become one, the marble to be sculpted may be included) and an action specific configuration of bodies in time and space (space, time and bodies become one field of relationships and mathematical functions). In science fiction the scene can be described as one re-formation of the 'homos formatos' (maker) and can easily be visualised as a temporal topographical merging of objects and skins made of different materials in order to fulfil particular operations. The organism and its environment as one functional system are structurally coupled within one and the same paradigm.

**BANHAM** — Leaving the discipline of biology and cognition and diving into the same topic through culture, the very phenomenon of merging becomes a tangible one. "There is no such feeling in the world that compares with taking off on a clean seven foot wave crunching down, feeling the forces of the waves [...] It's just the greatest thing in the world, I don't wanna trade it for anything." (Banham 1972). This scene from the 1972 BBC documentary *Reyner Banham Loves Los Angeles* shows a surfer being at one with his board, his body moving according to the rolling waves and his physic, balancing in this changing space of the Los Angeles ocean spirit. The deeply embedded identification with the sea, surf culture as well as the location LA add to the physical and cognitive reactions of the surfer's body affected by the immediate environmental forces. Reyner Banham underpins the notion of organism established by Ashby through observing culture. The movie celebrates driving through Los Angeles, the only way to travel the city, moderated by the latest technology of a Baedeker tape, hence replacing a physical guide. Banham conveys the idea that Los Angeles' architecture is more than an aggregation of buildings, but a hub of interactions happening in parallel changing the city constantly, one city, one homogeneous organism incarnated through the *car*. "So something like a million Angelinos could say that you would never expect to hear them say: I live within walking distance of my work." (Banham 1972). Los Angeles was, and remains to be, a city in which freedom is the driving force for material and cognitive operations. Freedom describes the culture and cultural cognitive capital of Los Angeles that also melts into the export of "Matt Mason space toys, hot wheels and Barbie dolls to all parts of the free world" (ibid. 1972). *Reyner Banham Loves Los Angeles* portrays the convergence of feeling as knowledge (and its export), the success of freedom and waves and an increasing and reflecting globalisation that triggers the breaking down of cultural and communicative differences.

Communicative differences do not relate to rhetorical linguistic or issues of foreign languages, but semiotics, psychology and values (such as, getting each other to know, beginning to understand each other). Reticulating the cyber-biological framework and the above cultural observations within the architecture of Los Angeles one can claim that neither architecture, nor cognitive capitalism is alone. Instead they synthesize as intertwined entities, as a living thing.

**WECHSELWIRKUNG** — There is another notable aspect extending Ashby's organism/environment notion and the above epitomised narrative, namely the one of *Wechselwirkung* as discovered by the biologist and cognitive scientist Jakob von Uexküll (1864–1944). It describes the so-called *Funktionskreis*, where an organism's ability consists of firstly perceiving (memory-net) and secondly acting (work-net). The direct relationship between those two operations (cognitive and physical) is shown in the *Funktionskreis*. Essentially it is an abstracted concept of experience and learning. Linking two or more memory-nets results in inter-net computational operations extending already existing experience and amplifies learning. Humberto Maturana describes breaking down differences and learning–a result of communication–as understanding the code. "Organisms are adapted to their environments, and it has appeared adequate to say of them that their organisation 'represents the 'environment' in which they live in, and that through evolution they have accumulated information about it, coded in their nervous system." (Maturana 1970).

**THE BITS ARE CALCULATING** — As this paper introduces steps towards a cultural theory that discusses common ground between agent-based behaviour through mechanisms of programming and coding cultures, it strongly relates to a multi-ordered cybernetic model drawing from Gregory Bateson's thoughts on *Difference* and George Spencer Brown's *Laws of Form*, 1969. The following part of the paper aims at *A*cognitivist Architecture* to act as epigenetic extension of Humberto Maturana's *Autopoiesis* towards a living organism and open organization of architecture as a construct of information and material alike, acting through and upon a dynamic, complex system, and therefore also operating as the system that allows for creating and transferring information in form of knowledge or, cognitive capital, if you wish. The system to be depicted owns a fractal characteristic akin to what Gilles Deleuze describes in the *Fold* (Deleuze 1991) on one hand, and in the age of immaterial material, cognitivist capital, and computational means of information [ex]change, an exaggeration of our perception through Jean Baudrillard's *Simulacra and Simulation*, on the other.

As seen in the excursion into algorithmic and parametric architecture in the previous part, a field can be a system, dealing with structural behaviour, where human occupancy is not the driving force for finding a form, but physical forces and behavior acting upon one larger entity or specific algorithms choreographing a crowd of agents of the same class. The application of geometric branching algorithm such as L-system or a search algorithm as in an ant-colony may serve to breed forms, structures and spaces, formerly alien to the discipline of architecture. Algorithms may trigger solutions and generate problems alike. Architecture as a cultural critical discipline and model drives itself into a state that increasingly departs from the traditional static understanding and material practice of architecture with all its constraints. Fields allowing human interaction as part of the structuring strategy are breeding grounds for knowledge that changes the surrounding to environment. *Parc de la Vilette* in Paris designed by Bernard Tschumi and the *Fun Palace* designed by Gordon Pask and Cedric Prize for London (unbuilt) are just two examples. The ellipsoid *IBM Pavilion* designed by Charles and Ray Eames with Studio Saarinen for the Expo

1964/65 in New York takes a slightly different approach
and extends the strategy of breeding knowledge through
introducing computer technology and the modern communication systems that tie as well as glimpse into the future
for a audience of 500. A combination of computer controlled
multiple, simultaneous screen projections and the appearance of actors in-between was presented to the *crowd* that
beforehand was physically and collectively lifted into the
space of a 90-foot high theatre. All visitors were part of
one of the first and largest to date public human/computer
encounters. The IBM pavilion housed a physical commonality, which cannot be regarded as an interacting swarm of
agents, but a performance generating a novel kind of communication between computer technology and the visitor.
The existence of simultaneously running sources of visual
information to be transported to the human brain reminds us
of a modus operandus when using the Internet, except, that
the latter is a field that is not the result of a design strategy
anymore but an integral part of the design process itself.
In contrast to the Internet where individual users create a
virtual commonality with interacting agents, collective intelligence, sharing cognitive capital, the Eames' theatre was
physical in all dimensions. The flesh of architecture in the
21st century is driven by a desire towards the optimal and
grotesque, the ultimate beautification and performative,
the unforeseen and magical, finding its foundations in the
mathematical forms and abstractions manifested by Wiener
or Ashby. The desire leaves the three-dimensional Cartesian
grid behind, and indulges in the incorporation of biological
and cognitive behaviour; the bones and veins are encoded
between the surreal and physical in a virtual asymmetry
of statistical mechanics as operation to foster radical constructivism and Eigenform within a field that we ones
called Cyberspace.

**INTERNET — NON-LINEAR PARA-SPACE — GENEALOGICAL STRING OF THOUGHTS** — Since the late 1980s we have grown extensions of our minds beyond the individual body and brain into a physical environment; transformed into binary language, in overlapping simultaneous worlds, providing input from remote locations and IP addresses, output generated by accumulating information originally produced by grey matter around the globe. For approximately the past 15 years architects have officially started incorporating system thinking into their work and admitting that we are designers of systems and fields rather then sculptors of discrete objects or fields only. Since the advent of fast data highways, open source software and a culture that happily shares knowledge in specialized forums the options to design have increased by a large extent. Uploading and sharing code and scripts is extending our individual possibilities to design into the world, *the Internet*, an unimaginable space inhabited by collective design intelligence. Upon the code's return, it may have not merely adjusted its phenotypic character, but possibly even changed into a different creature with new characteristics, mutated through the filter of "Electronics virtual communities [that] represent flexible, lively and practical adaptations to the real circumstances" (Stone 1991, 111). Especially in the field of architects and designers who develop and use tools based on code, the early 21st century offers a quantum leap in the evolution of the virtual excelling traditional methods of design. Drawing boards have been replaced with light programs using slender code rather than heavy three-dimensional 'fancier' models; office, brain and design abilities are extended to forums for multi peer reviews, design changes and advice. This process eliminated economically compensation, local independency, and software packages that in very many cases are free to run on machines that are generally affordable and increased the amount of cognitive capital.

The question and the theory for architecture is if the architect is becoming a mutator, or the inventor of something that can be called 'Neurotecture?' (Werner 2011)[6]. When using code the process to arrive at a final product is closer to neural activities than mastering ones. "Making the link with Deleuze, we can see the embodied and embedded nervous system as a pre-individual virtual field: [...] a set of differential elements—reciprocally determined functions—in other words, neural function is networked: there is no such thing as the function of 'a' neuron;" (Protevi 2010, 171). Bits are the form of operations happening offshore through collective design intelligence that must not be understood as phenomenon, but as an activity, as a process to FORM, at the same time as a form of communication that crates its own syntax and physiology through an active network of computational work, born within human nodes in human brains transported, translated and directed via real-time Autobahns through immaterial real-estate, the internet.
A distinction between Form as a verb and Form as a noun vanishes and becomes obsolete.

**SYNTHETICAL IS NATURAL** — Advanced architecture using the instruments generously offered in the toolbox of Neurotecture is an architecture that embraces multiple authors and multiple hackers at risk of abusing the very same cognitive capital that they produced. Dissipative dynamic virtual space was almost unthinkable only twenty years ago. Benedikt writes,

........................................................................................................

[6] Neurotecture may not to be misunderstood as neuro-architecture, which is a specific interdisciplinary field between neuro-sciences and architecture, examining how architecture or any other man-made structure affects a human. Instead it describes an evolutionary strand of advanced architectural strategies and methods combining ubiquitous artificial computing and human computing.

"The principle of Commonality in cyberspace recommends *that virtual places be "objective" in a circumscribed way for a defined community of users.* More specifically, the Principle of Commonality requires that all comers to a given domain at a given time in cyberspace are to see/hear largely the same thing-the same place, the same objects, the same people-or at least some subsets of *one* "thing," and that the same direction considered as up." (Benedikt 1991, 180).

Since then a defined group of users, the Commonality, has become its own commodity. *The Psychopathology of Cognitive Capitalism* in this context has been breeding an offshore collective of design intelligence, a direct descendant of "electronic virtual communities," the former *Internet* in the 1980s, which has already been described as "complex and ingenious strategies for survival" (Stone 1991, 111). The modus operandus *collective design intelligence* sprawls throughout all disciplines, faculties and individuals in 'hard' sciences such as mathematics or bioengineering and 'soft' sciences, cultural sciences or comparative literature alike, operating in a structurally coupled manner, and using the information exchange through bits and bytes, in an immaterial world, that we once called Cyberspace. Growing collective design intelligence and user intelligence replace designing fields such as Parc de la Villette. Collective design intelligence must not be understood as phenomenon or operator, but as an activity, as a process to FORM. The new cyberspace, the para-space, is very close to "a consensual hallucination experienced daily by billions of legitimate operators, by children being taught mathematical concepts... A graphic representation of data abstracted from the banks of every computer in the human system. Unthinkable Complexity. Lines of light in the non-space of the mind, clusters and constellations of data. Like city lights, receding..." (Gibson 1984, 51).

This present cybernetic note beyond certainly does not claim that computer programs or the Internet have achieved the ability of acting as devices owning artificial intelligence, as envisaged by Marvin Minsky and his peers half a century ago, in fact artificial intelligence still seems to be far off from being implemented in the research laboratories of Computer Sciences of Robotics institutes. Nevertheless, computer programs and their environments such as the Internet seem to start learning and responding as a result of feeding them with a set of algorithms, complex or simple, arriving at an unforeseen behavior as a form of communication. The cognitive, cerebral, data and bits become code and the isolated structure of a genotype subjected to the environment transforms into a phenotype. The architectural result is one of lushness and deep tissue, following periods of abstinence: abstinence of mathematic, abstinence of clarity, abstinence of pattern, abstinence of heterogeneity and abstinence of passion and indulgence. Architecture as Neurotecture in the cyber-biological framework of an interconnected parametric field is a production-system, the product of itself and an evolution of iterations through constant recursive observation and reinvention. It describes alchemy between real and virtual, not withholding the scientific, but re-entering it like a differentiator. A*cognitivist architecture transforms the concept of configuring space, of forming space to a new materialism, a structure considering context, environment, time, behaviour of and relationships between all agents involved; mutating, genetically engineering and processing data within an Architectural Computer Laboratory. We do witness an almost self-organising interconnected para-metric world on many levels owning a variety of intersections and matrixes. Novel immaterial and known material strategies together with new data born every split second synthesize in the self-informing machinery to become the new natural.

Ashby, Ross, 1954. *The Animal as Machine*. New York: John Wiley & Sons Inc.

Baudrillard, Jean, 1994. *Simulacra and Simulation*. Ann Arbor: University of Michigan Press.

Benedikt, Michael, 1991. "Cyberspace: Some Proposals," in Michael Benedikt (ed.), *Cyberspace First Steps*. Cambridge: MIT Press.

Deleuze, Gilles, 1968. *Difference and Repetition,* trans. Paul R. Patton, New York: Columbia University Press (1994).

Deleuze, Gilles, 1991. *The Fold: Leibniz and the Baroque*. Minneapolis: University of Minnesota Press.

Gibson, William, 1984. *Neuromancer.* New York: Ace Books.

Gigerenzer, G and Brighton, H (January, 2009). "Homo Heuristicus: Why Biased Minds Make Better Inferences," in *Topics in Cognitive Sciences* 1, pp. 107-143.

Maturana, Humberto, 1980, "Autopoiesis and Cognition: The Realization of the Living." Dordrecht: D. Reidel Publishing Company. The essay was originally published as "De Maquinas y Seres Vivos," Editorial Universitaria S.A., 1972.

Stone, Allucquere Rosanne, 1991. "Will The Real Body Please Stand Up," in Michael Benedikt (ed.), *Cyberspace First Steps*. Cambridge: MIT Press.

Negroponte, Nicholas, 1973. *The Architecture Machine*. Cambridge: MIT Press.

Negroponte, Nicholas, 1995. *Being Digital*, London: Hodder and Stoughton, p.4.

Protevi, John, 2010. "Deleuze and Wexler: Thinking Brain, Body and Affect in Social Context," in *Cognitive Architecture. From Biopolitics to Noopolitics. Architecture & Mind in the Age of Communication and Information*. Rotterdam: 010 Publishers.

Reichenbach, Hans, 2003. *The Philosophy of Space and Tim,* trans. Maria Reichenbach and John Freund. New York: Dover Publications.

Tomas, David, 1991. "Old Rituals for New Space," in Michael Benedikt (ed.), *Cyberspace First Steps.* Cambridge: MIT Press.

Werner, Liss (2011). "Codes in the Clouds - Observing New Design Strategies," in Gengnagel, Kilian, et al. (eds.) *Computational Design Modeling, Proceedings of the Design Modeling Symposium Berlin.* Heidelberg: Springer Verlag.

# Neuroecology:
# Notes Toward a Synthesis

Few people, even within design today, are aware of how problems are formulated in our field, how they are constituted, and in relation to what forces and developments they are formed. If design may be described as a form of rationality applied to the organization of objects, environments, and behaviors, it is first and foremost a practice of modulating and compelling routines of experience or, within some modalities, a practice of clearing the way for unforeseen experiences to emerge. But what do we mean by the term *experience*? Much of contemporary research is directed to understanding the mechanics and operation—even the history—of what this term might cover and explain in the material and historical world.

In the worlds of design and art practice I would argue, attention has shifted decisively in recent decades from the signifying modes of communication of objects to illocutionary ones, in which the introduction of forms into the world can be said to result in a 'transformation of states.'[1]

---

[1] The theory of speech acts was initially developed by John Austin in the 1950s as part of a development in language philosophy that considered the 'actual' uses and operations of language, rather than its merely formal ones. Austin distinguished between 'constative' utterances whose primary purpose was descriptive of states of things in the world—utterances that 'stated' something—that could be subject to true/false criteria and 'performative' utterances whose primary effect (and purpose) was to effectuate something, to cause an action or change of state. In his inimitable words: "To say something is *to do* something". Typical examples include speech acts such as "I do." through which one changes one's civil status (among other things). (Austin 1962).

Given this shift of focus, a new emphasis on 'continuum thinking' is emerging, in which, among other signal developments, we find an increasing concern with environments (rather than with objects, be these cities, buildings, facades or chairs).

This mode of thought emerging at the center of design practice and thought can be exemplified in a variety of works, even philosophical ones, of which a single recent example is Peter Sloterdijk's *Sphären*. It is in a context such as ours here today that we can recognize some of the complex paths by which the so-called problem of 'nature' (and I use this term as a shorthand only) has impressed itself, both philosophically and practically, as an imperative to be incorporated into design thinking, or into the systematic accounting of what is in play by our, or any animal's, being in the world.

Far from seeking to invoke Heidegger with the use of this latter expression, I wish rather to propose that we free ourselves from the common assumption that we are *in* the world when, in fact, as a great deal of the science we will here consider implies, we *are* the world itself (Stockhausen 1973).

By invoking the broad and frequently challenged term of 'nature', I leave to one side entirely the platitudinous objections of "cultural constructionists" for whom nature is a product of culture and history without independent ontological, or epistemological, status. By nature I invoke those parts of the world around us that are motivated by their own processes and which under normal circumstances are indifferent to our own. The fact that these undergo modification by us (and vice versa)—in the course of history—in no way mitigates the constancy and reliability of nature as an independent term and object of knowledge across a multiplicity of modes.

I refer to the study of the relations of history (society) and nature very broadly as 'ecology'—and it is in this sense that I make reference to something called 'neuroecology.' For purposes of philosophical rigor I situate the origins of ecological thinking in the work—a century before Haeckel—of Alexander von Humboldt, to his *On the Geography of Plants* (1807). Humboldt's work was the first to place plant species into their surrounding contexts—latitude, altitude, geology, climate, temperature, soil type, etc.—even into their human social environment and their relation to animal species, to account for the specific patterns they express. His phrase 'Alles ist Wechselwirkung,' typically translated in thought as well as in language, as 'Everything is connected,' is more accurately rendered, with due emphasis, as 'All is *interaction.*' (Humboldt 1803).

The phrase is in fact a description of what came, 150 years later, to be known as 'the environment' itself. This still nascent concept can be derived from the work of Johann Goethe, whose study of the morphology of plants proposed an algorithmic blending of—*modular*—processes of unfolding at different scales and at different rates, as a generative mechanism of responsive (living) form. Goethe identified three inputs: a type, a gradient and a cycle, that in any combination would not only produce a unique and specific plant form but would account for the variations of forms within a single plant itself: its petals, leaves, calyx and stem (Goethe 1790). His theory placed the improvisational integration of diverse temporalities—each input represented an impetus that unfolded at a different speed—at the center of natural process.

The model that served centrally in many 20th century formulations of 'environment'—in Deleuze, for example, Sloterdijk, Agamben and Rene Thom, to name but a few—was the concept of 'Umwelt' from theoretical biologist Jakob von Uexkull, in many ways among the most useful ones to serve us today.

An Umwelt represents the practical world or environment that corresponds to the sensory and biological endowment of any given organism. In a famous set of cartoons from his book on animal worlds, *A Stroll Through the Worlds of Animals and Men* (Uexkull 2010) the point is made: the worlds of men, dogs and flies overlap, but they do not correspond. And yet each inhabits not only its particular Umwelt, each organism is fully continuous and consubstantial with it. The patches and aspects of the world that represent assets for the organism—in each case a small portion only of what might be said to be 'out there'—correspond to a sensory system that is both possessed by, and which defines that animal. An animal represents a segment of a circuit that connects triggers in the environment to responsive actions in another part: the organism is a more complex and layered part of the environment itself. I will refer to this as the principle of 'immanentism' according to which the distinction between organism and environment, inside and out, is but one of degree: a greater or lesser compression or dilation of information or, as more common parlance would have it, of life.

Von Uexkull's emphasis on the senses—the compound sensorymotor apparatus—as the constitutive actor that establishes the organism's integration or "fit" into, or indeed *as*, its world, represents a significant antecedent to contemporary neuroecology (and formal neurobiology). The field of modern neurology itself, beginning with C.S. Sherrington's *Integrative Action of the Nervous System* (1920) and Kurt Goldstein's *The Organism* (1934) was built on the central observation of the brain's irrepressible drive to cobble together smooth and integral functional routines from whatever partial materials—internal as well as external—that are in its immediate spatial and temporal vicinity. Even a severely impaired organism (brain) will assemble a seamless and whole universe from whatever its senses deliver to it.

From the point of view of design theory this idea has to be seen as a foundational element within any perspective that includes the material world as a site of interrogation. The model of such understanding, both highly developed and powerful, was not explicitly recognized in the brain sciences until the work of Gerald Edelman. I refer here to the principles of evolutionary theory, particularly to the habit of mind associated with what Ernst Mayr referred to as "population thinking" (Mayr 2001). Formerly an immunological biologist, Edelman had originally proposed a model for how a state of the world—a disease or pathogen—could engender a correlative, responsive (not passive) state in an organism—an antibody or immune reaction—with such confoundingly specific accuracy and speed. His discovery of the molecular structure of antibodies and the mechanisms by which they could vary, and his subsequent theory of how the immune system successfully and reliably *couples with the world* to respond with pinpoint precision despite the infinity of possible disease forms the world could present to it, earned not only a Nobel Prize in medicine, but subsequently served as a now widely-accepted model for how the open and multiplicitous environment in which we live sculpts the brain within what amounts to almost infinitely plastic parameters.

This was not the aspect of brain dynamics to which Edelman was directly referring by his famous invocation of Darwin (Edelman 1987)—this was largely reserved for the competition of neurons for spatial and energetic resources during the proliferation and pruning phases of brain development—but the tacit model in which input (information) from the environment served as form-generating engines for the larger structures and competences that account for the brain's more interesting and important social performance.

Hence, the understanding of the brain as the site of social and political as well as psychedelic innovation, or if not only of innovation, also of regressive subjectivation and coercion, must be placed against a larger backdrop of environmental history. This, for all its strengths and weaknesses, means evolutionary theory. Just as the mathematician Rene Thom (founder of Catastrophe Theory, the first comprehensive attempt to mathematize the class of processes—transitional phenomena—that govern the biological sciences) found it congenial to posit 'embryologies' wherever in Nature, or in the world, it was a matter of form developing along partly deterministic pathways, I see no reason to not invoke the explanatory prestige of epigenetic factors to account for the prehistory of contemporary cognitive regimes.[2]

We have learned to refuse the distinction between body and brain, but we have a way to go till we reflexively think the *unity* of our anatomo-behavioral biology in its full polyphony. Yet it is just the habit of mind most usefully and centrally featured in evolutionary theory, and sufficient reason to espouse and engage it.

## Paleopolitical Framework

The primary pressures exerted on the development of human nervous response—thinking, feeling and perceiving—not different, for significantly long period at least, from the pressures on all other organisms—were those directed to predator and anti-predator activity.

---

[2] The debates continue to rage around the claims of evolutionary psychology, neuro-archaeology, paleo-neurology/-anthropology/-anatomy, and so on with respects to what the targets of early developmental pressures on human cognition were (many focus on cortical plasticity, but many also argue for characteristic hardwired and relatively closed attributes). It is sufficient here to beg any final conclusion by emphasizing simply the diversity of uses of the brain in human history that remain, through one channel or another, essential legacies for present usages.

The subduing and incorporation (literally into our own bodies) of those portions of the environment that could serve us either for nutrition or for secondary economic advantage—clothing, shelter, leisure, or procreative opportunity—can all be considered as quarry and object of predatory activity, and regardless of what form of execution they take, can be subsumed under the category of hunt-and-capture. Similarly, the evasion of capture by other predatory agents, to the extent that early humans and prehuman hominins were competitors for the same resources and habitats on the savannahs with other social carnivores (the cats, hyenids and wild dogs) determined to a large degree the forms of vigilance, attention and the extreme acoustic, visual and even the running competences that endowed us in large part with the qualities we now routinely recognize in ourselves, as human (Lieberman 2011, 2013).

Most people outside the field of biological anthropology are surprised to learn that it has been a working hypothesis since the 1960s work of George Schaller and Gordon Lowther (1969) that the emergence of what came to be the human type was determined far more by relationships—convergent developments—with fellow savannah predator populations—lions, hyenas and dogs—than by the ape line from which we are routinely but misleadingly said to descend. Our forms of attention, our diet, our modes of association such as family groups, band size, social structure and divisions of labor, etc. more greatly resemble those of cooperative hunting and meat-eating species than those of the merely prehensile frugivores we left behind in the trees. In this same respect, research in the 1990s showed extraordinarily sophisticated execution of multipart strategies in the hunting methods of lions, hyenas, dogs and other savannah carnivores (Stander 1992, 445-454). Let it be said before moving on however that the adaptations here did not overwhelmingly point to the human as an effective predator.

On the contrary, much in our makeup pointed to our existence as a brutishly hunted creature, who adapted the necessary forms of neurosis, anxiety and fear, (and whose biology has been comprehensively worked out over 40 years by Melvin Konner) as well as the need, more than anything, for a multiplex new organ that could compensate flexibly and innovatively for our anatomical deficits (lack of claws, adequate carcass-penetrating teeth, etc.); a large, pluripotential and highly tunable brain (Konner 2002).

Evolution is in effect a form of biological tuning, especially when it comes to the brain and its modalities of attention. Some of its capacities are hardwired and innate of course, and some merely the result of environmental pressures on the individual rather than on the species itself. This is a topic of vast and serious debate that centers on the prefrontal cortex and on the avalanche of complicated issues that pertain to how this anatomical machinery is taken up and deployed within any specific neuro-ecological framework. The use of the prefrontal cortex is the materialist stuff of cultural history (which, as we know, is not yet materialist at all).[3]

But how the massive human cortex arrived is itself an important neuro-ecological story. Since animals must either ingest or evade one another in order to survive, they must attune their nervous systems to one another's actions, and in

---

[3] One significant point of light on the horizon is Daniel Smail's plea for a 'new neurohistory' that accounts for the constitutive role that psychotropic processes play in shaping and driving human history. See his *On Deep History and the Brain*, University of California Press, Los Angeles, 2008 and Andrew Shycock and Daniel Lord Smail, *Deep History: The Architecture of Past and Present*, University of California Press, Los Angeles, 2011.

particular to one another's actions on the environment, to *spoor* of all kinds [4]. Living in social groups places further demands on the processing power of a species, insofar as one must also track and retain knowledge of past behaviors, character, etc. in order to detect and limit economic cheating, incest, debts, and so on.

More important is the expansion of the entire brain mass—commonly referred to in evolutionary biology as encephalization, a term that is effectively a synonym for hominization. Humans clearly enjoy their extraordinarily large brains but this does not mitigate the fact that their brains are exquisitely expensive. But not only are brains highly expensive to run, requiring a great deal of high quality food to power them, their high metabolic rate makes them prodigious producers of heat, and so they are also demandingly expensive to keep cool.

Brains are made of exquisitely sensitive tissue, even a four degree rise in its temperature is likely to result in death. One can't have a large brain without a highly sophisticated cooling system. But as the newest accounts of the co-evolution of landscapes and organisms develops today, we are also learning that climate change—specifically the dramatic heating up of the environment between 4 and 5 million years ago—was a prime cause of encephalization and hominization.

---

[4] The English word spoor derives from the Afrikaans (and Dutch) and refers to any mark, trace, disturbance or sign in the environment caused by the presence or passage of an animal. It frequently connotes a linear series that in its aggregate produces a 'track' that is typically followed by a hunter and which lends to the word one of its most common, but narrowest, meanings. Spoor refers not only to tracks that one follows, but to the entire system of legible modifications of a world by the organisms that comprise it. Arguably, an organism is inseparable from its spoor, and its relationships to other organisms consists in large part of the readings and communications generated by them, which is arguably the principal task of any nervous system in nature.

As the environment grew hotter, it also became dryer (at least in Africa where it mattered most in the late Pliocene and early Pleistocene) causing forest habitats to shrink and savannahs and grassy plains to flourish. Apes, as the now partially discarded but still useful story goes, needed to find food out in the open—a dangerous place fraught with seasoned predators— and so required an advantage of some type to protect them. What they got were several interconnected ones. The first set of problems requiring solution was how to move quickly through the dangerous open spaces while carrying one's young. This problem was believed to be solved by upright posture and the freeing of the hands for novel uses. With a new set of ecological potentials for the hands (freed from locomotion) came new cultural possibilities (the central problem of hominin ecology). Freed hands provided an opening—perhaps even a demand—for a new and enlarged brain to program them.[5] But the new environmental heat placed unprecedented stress on the animal to keep cool. A large, sensitive, heat-producing and expensive brain represented a dangerous added burden, unless a highly innovative system of cooling could be found, and it was.  The invention of this novel air conditioning system is widely considered to be the defining feature of, and evolutionary impetus behind, the emergence of the human species.

Because humans have large brains, short faces and small, specialized teeth—all effects of the environment-derived pressures to change diet and by extension to change all modalities of combustion including information-processing ones—we do not possess snouts and therefore lack the hollow nasal chambers

---

[5] The rise of tool manufacturing industry in early hominin societies are widely seen as adjuncts to a broader set of geographical and economic developments that subtended human cultural development. New environments, and new parts and aspects (assets) of existing environments, became exploitable through the continuing elaboration—and then subsumption—of the brain-hand-tool assemblage.

and the veinous adaptations in the head that most other animals use to cool the blood that feeds the brain. (Snouts serve as radiators.) If apes aspired to compete in savannah habitats they were going to require innovative adaptations to manage the heat stress that came with this environment. All other savannah mammals use 'selective cooling' based on the protruding face, the hollow snout and an anatomical formation known as the carotid rete in which blood is pooled in the sinus area or neck for cooling.  Humans cannot do this; their brain is proportionately too large and would require a neck as wide as its thorax. Humans must use general (full body) cooling.

The first adaptation towards this end is said to be the achievement of upright posture, which has been calculated to cut heat load by more than 30% by exposing less of the animal's body surface to the direct rays of the sun; it also moves the brain and organs away from the ground surface where temperatures are significantly higher. The second is the shedding of the fur covering, the development of naked skin and the profuse sweating that permits ultra efficient radiation of heat through evaporation. But for this last adaptation, the animal would require regular access to considerable quantities of water on a highly regular basis; the increase in travel range and the size of hunting and scavenging habitat was an important result both of the entirely novel form of human bipedal locomotion and the cerebral cortex used in calculating interrelationships, navigational and otherwise.[6]

......................................................................................................

[6] Interestingly, apes and baboons apparently never leave their home range, despite the fact that their stereoscopic vision permits them to see very great distances. It would seem that humans are the only primates who can—and do—go where they see. See John Reader, Africa: A Biography of the Continent, Knopf, New York, 1998. Also pertinent is the influential work of Robin Dunbar on cortical capacity and psychogeography, "The Social Brain Hypothesis," in Evolutionary Anthropology, Wiley, 1998, pp. 178-190, and "Coevolution of neocortical size, group size and language in humans. Behav Brain Sci 11:681–735. 1993.

But water resource management is clearly a very different affair in highly encephalized mammals—it is cognitive and not only perceptual—as even I have observed, such as in elephants who track and remember locations far beyond perceptual range.[7]

What we encounter at every turn, is a 'modulus' or network of relationships and especially forms, each changing in collaboration and communication with the others. But there were other more internal and less visible transformations that matter, ones involving feedback phenomena. Among the most important is how the emerging human form—and the human cultural type—managed not only its heat budget but its metabolic budget as well. If the brain is made up of expensive tissue that requires a great deal of extra calories and water to maintain, it is also true that no animal could maintain such a high-maintenance economic life if it did not have a very large brain. But more basic than this, is the way the body itself sought to balance its books. It has been widely noted that the human gut is very short compared with that of other mammals for its relative size (half the predicted length).

---

[7] These capacities and performances by elephant groups have nothing to do with 'migratory' impulses as is the sensationalized case with herding and grazing ungulates such as wildebeeste. Robert Ardrey drew an important distinction in the early 1960s between "open" and "closed" programs (or instincts), much the same way Henri Bergson described the increasing complexity and sophistication of life forms as "the injection of increasing amounts of indeterminacy into matter." Ardrey sought to distinguish between mechanical and automatic responses to the environment that secure certain organisms' success in certain niches, from more general forms of direction and proclivity that are worked out in essentially improvisatory manner on an ongoing basis by an organism as it sustains its processing or 'combusting' of the information and resources in its world. See *The Territorial Imperative: A Personal Inquiry Into the Animal Origins of Property and Nations*. New York: Atheneum, 1976 (1966).

Physiological studies show that the intestines contribute as much or more to an animal's "basal metabolic rate"— the rate at which it combusts energy at rest—than does the brain. Intestines it in sum are also *very expensive tissue*. The massive increase in human brain size, according to the current benchmark theory of Leslie Aiello and Peter Wheeler, was thus balanced by a concurrent decrease in gut size, and this secondary adaptation had definitive repercussions on every aspect of the human world. The first and most basic effect was to require a systematic new approach to eating[8] the absolute requirement for very high-quality nutritious foods that can be ingested in small quantities yet at frequent and regular intervals. This meant highly selective foraging behavior and judicious identification particularly of reproductive organs, the most nutritionally dense parts of the environment: seeds, tubers, nuts, eggs [ibid.]. In addition to this, environmental accounting on yet another level beyond kinship structures, orientation, and predator and prey monitoring was required—the consistent registration and calculation of distance to and from water sources since a distance of more than a day's walk would almost certainly result in death. It also meant procuring protein and fat in the form of meat, an activity requiring considerable adaptations for strategic hunting, which included the need to act in coordinated and cooperative social groups, and even, as some have suggested, to the rise of the family group structure, divisions of economic behaviors along age and gender lines, and to the particularities of the age-old relations between the sexes (ibid.).

---

[8] Nearly all the arguments proposed in this direction are summarized in Richard Wrangham, 2009. *Catching Fire: How Cooking Made us Human*. New York: Basic Books.

The large brain is at once directly and indirectly both a product and an expression of climate and ecology: it emerged as a response to an increasingly hot and dry environment and in tandem with the evolution of a novel and biologically unique cooling system. But once the movement toward encephalization began, a broad set of relatively independent social and proto-political regimes necessarily were triggered, based on the budgetary need to extract from the environment the resources to keep the brain running.

Human life in all its diversity and manifoldness, and the human physical form that enacts and gives style to it—and in this I include our beautiful (intelligent) faces, flat stomachs, dexterous hands, subtle humor—our complex behaviors, and our notable species achievements such as language, technology and culture, are certainly at least in part, ecological responses to the broader and more mundane economics of satisfying the dietary and ethological demands of a large brain (Reader 1998, 90).

## The Cognitive-Environmental Circuit

Human social, political and historical life depends upon, but also integrates and exploits, the consequences of our peculiarly formed and organized brain. I follow here the recent work of Bruce Wexler (Wexler 2006; see also Wexler 2010). Following the last three decades of developments in neuroplastic theory (summarized in the work of Edelman, Huttenlocher and others[9]) we learn that the brain's explosive early developmental

--------------------------------------------------------

[9] See Gerald M. Edelman, *Bright Air, Brilliant Fire: On the Matter of the Mind,* New York: Basic Books, 1992; *Neural Darwinism: The Theory of Neuronal Group Selection.* New York: Basic Books, 1987; Peter Huttenlocher, *Neural Plasticity: The Effects of Environment on the Development of the Cerebral Cortex*, Cambridge: Harvard University Press, Cambridge, 2002; Joseph LeDoux, *Synaptic Self: How our Brains Become Who We Are*, New York: Viking, 2002.

schedule of cell multiplication and construction of connective networks (as many as 100,000 per second during the first 6 months) requires that human young be born as still developing fetuses and undergo the greater part of brain development and expansion outside the womb. (The large braincase of the mature human baby would not be compatible with the hip structure of an efficiently bipedal mother.) Hence the period of newborn dependency in humans is immensely prolonged beyond that of any other animal—perhaps by 3 years at least. But most importantly, the billions of cells and quadrillions of neural connections that must be assembled in the immediate post-natal years, and the cognitive functions that they must develop and support, are entirely physically dependent on sensory stimulation to realize themselves. From the moment the fetus is separated from the shelter of its womb, its main business is to extract input from the environment around it, each bit of which triggers reception scenarios in the cellular matrix that are subsequently concretized, and retained and maintained, more or less for its life.[10] In this way the brain "uses" its surrounding environment and the relations it finds within it, as a kind of model or "homologue" to fashion its own internal and functional structure. This process establishes a deeply fateful "coupling" relationship with the world. There is no metaphor here: Sensory input is not an "immaterial"— it is the environment itself, and it is the "becoming brain."[11] The world is literally ingested through all the senses, and not only through the mouth.

---

[10] The latter is a crude approximation that belies the reality that the brain is a dynamic structure that ceaselessly reorganizes, regenerates, and reforms itself—within parameters that are themselves variable and heterogeneous in both its temporal and spatial dimensions (such as the "critical periods", etc.).

[11] This phrase deliberately invokes the work of Deleuze on, among other things, the Pink Panther, in the early sections of *A Thousand Plateaus: Capitalism and Schizophrenia*, trans. Brian Massumi, Minnesota: University of Minnesota Press, 1987.

Besides the Darwinian term 'homology' that I used a moment ago to describe the blueprinting of neural structure by external event structures in the world, we are compelled to deploy here also Darwin's broader concept of 'fit.' Fit would describe the lifelong adjustment of inner to outer states that is the fate and destiny of the massively encephalized organism. The human cannot help, given the overriding impetus to thrive, but seek a complex relationship of continuous accommodation with the world, such that inner and outer states and the forms that represent them, find a degree of dynamic sympathetic mutuality, that can indeed be, as befits us humans, extraordinarily complex—consider only the one we find in the achievements of musical composition and performance or indeed again, in the recreational use of psychotropic substances, be they alcohol, caffeine, psilocybin or opiates.

To return now to Wexler's hypothesis, we note his overriding insistence on two general periodicities in the human life cycle determined by the scheduling of neural development. There is the early period of massive profusion of internal structures—leading into the late teens and characterized by a 'rearing economy' within the protected home environment, and the period that follows that may be characterized simply as the organism's adult phase. The critical shift that needs to be noted is that during the rearing phase the organism's primary orientation is toward stimulus and sensory input (attractiveness of loud music is one characteristic, arguably scheduled, 'episodic' demand) in order to complete and fully enrich the insatiable demands of a trillion trillion neural connections, but during the adult phase, the focus shifts toward reversing the action of the sculptural knife, so that the shaping now of the external world becomes the main priority, in order to bring about, or simply extend, what I call "the dynamic sympathetic mutuality with reality."[12]

------

[12] It bears underscoring here the centrality of psychotropic aspects of historical unfolding and the relevance of the developing claims of the 'neurohistory' group around the work of Smail.

It is only humans that have such a prolonged phase of neural development and dependency on the environment, only humans integrate the structure of their environment ('secondary repertoire') at the ontogenetic level (a supplement to evolutionary capture at the phylogenetic level or 'primary repertoire') and only humans are then, shall we say, neuro-ecologically compelled to modify their worlds, and produce objects of meaning and affective capacity in order to modify in turn their internal body states (art, culture, etc.). Only humans have political relations written into their biological substrates and only humans are biologically as it were compelled to expend energy on nonproductive activities like art, culture and design. And the impetuses, if we are to believe the arguments, are linked.[13]

For every maturing organism notes, almost without delay, the unavoidable non-match between its internal (rearing) environment and the persistent elements of those of the previous (parental) generation's, and hence seek almost immediately to impose upon it images, shapes, relationships whose effects will better correspond to, and generate, the desired internal states that have become existentially necessary to their intuitions of freedom and well-being. This is a profoundly creative as well as destructive and aggressive act.

---

[13] The famous and endlessly invoked case of the Bower bird as an animal who dedicates a great deal of its energy to the arrangement of its environment for attractive or aesthetic purposes does not belong to this category for the simple reason that its performance is not responsive or connected to its temporal or spatial surroundings in any specific way, it neither deploys, nor does its bower display, any innovation that might be called historical or tranformative. It simply reproduces, as if according to a closed and pre-determined plan a form that provokes a response in a female bower bird as a set, and relatively inflexible engram.

Through this line of reasoning, one discovers at once an interesting naturalization and historicization of the principle of 'creation' not so different from that of Bergson's (whose ideas underwrote a considerable portion of architecture theory and production in the 1990s in relation to the digital revolution). Let it not go unnoticed that what we have here is not only a full blown cultural theory but also, a neurally-mediated, biologically and ecologically determined "homology politics"—*a neuroecological politics*. Might the foundations of class struggle (dialectical materialism) and design practice be discoverable in the brain?

It would be useful and appropriate to leave off here with these admittedly outlandish proposals. But there is a final set of ideas that demands to be tabled before ending. First, the environmental dependency of human neurogenesis has a larger-scale evolutionary efficiency that requires serious accommodation: it overwhelmingly favors, in fact guarantees, not just 'good' or efficient brains but regionally specific and highly diverse ones. We are not all the same, and the differences, distributed spatially and hence implying a whole political neuro-geography of another order, require theoretical attention. Second, the advent of writing in human neuroecology is naturally and arguably the first major development in the cultural enterprise of abstraction, one that models and precedes (by almost 2 millennia) the advent of money and the social partitioning it ushers in. But if writing was first evolved as a tool to record economic transactions it soon evolved its dominant function: to record and externalize both "temporary and more enduring" internal states of the organism, and to make these accessible to others (Wexler 2010) Writing is the model of environmental modification whose purpose is first and foremost to transform. And thirdly: The commonplaces of super-structure/base relationships in the analysis of power relations may have here met a further withering refutation.

Uncontested findings in the neurobiological world show that in human and many other mammals, the essential relationship to environment is skewed not toward economic activity and the procurement of food, but toward the extraction of sensory stimulation in order to modify mood and body states.[14] In other words, and once again, psychotropic activity, not economic, is the biological imperative followed by human populations and organisms, the stuff of which civilization is made and transmitted. If class war can be situated in and for the brain, it is driven by poesis, not accounting. Design in its essence is, and in every one of its instances is compelled to be, 'revolutionary.'

---

[14] See Bruce Wexler, *Brain and Culture* and *Shaping the Environments*. The concern with 'body states' is an immensely important one, developed throughout Smail and derived from Joseph LeDoux and Anthony Damasio.

Austin, John L., 1962. *How to Do Things with Words*. Oxford: Oxford University Press.

Dunbar, Robin (1993). "Coevolution of Neocortical Size, Group Size and Language in Humans," in *Behav Brain Sci* 11, pp. 681-735.

Dunbar, Robin (1998). "The Social Brain Hypothesis," in *Evolutionary Anthropology*, pp. 178-190.
Edelman, Gerald M., 1987. *Neural Darwinism: The Theory of Neuronal Group Selection*. New York: Basic Books.

Edelman, Gerald M., 1992. *Bright Air, Brilliant Fire: On the Matter of the Mind*. New York: Basic Books.

Goethe, Johann Wolfgang von, 1790. *The Metamorphosis of Plants*. Cambridge: MIT Press (2009).

Hauptmann, Barbara, and Neidich, Warren, 2010. *Cognitive Architecture: From Biolpolitics to Noopolitics; Architecture and Mind in the Age of Communication and Information*. Rotterdam: 010 Publishers.

Humboldt, Alexander von, 1803. *Travel Notebooks 1-5, Valley of Mexico*. New York: Knopf (1955).

Huttenlocher, Peter, 2002. *Neural Plasticity: The Effects of Environment on the Development of the Cerebral Cortex*. Cambridge: Harvard University Press.

Konner, Melvin, 2002. *The Tangled Wing: Biological Constraints on the Human Spirit*. New York: Henry Holt.

LeDoux, Joseph, 2002. *Synaptic Self: How our Brains Become Who We Are*. New York: Viking.

Lieberman, Daniel E., 2011. *The Evolution of the Human Head*. Cambridge: Harvard University Press.

Lieberman, Daniel E., 2013. *The Story of the Human Body: Evolution, Health and Disease*. New York: Pantheon.

Mayr, Ernst, 2001. *What Evolution Is*. New York: Basic Books.

Reader, John, 1998. *Africa: A Biography of the Continent*. New York: Knopf.

Schaller, G. B. and Lowther, G. R., (1969). "The Relevance of Carnivore Behavior to the Study of Early Hominids," in *SW J Anthrop*. V.25 (pt.4), pp. 307-41.

Shycock, Andrew and Daniel Lord Smail, 2011. *Deep History: The Architecture of Past and Present*. Los Angeles: University of California Press.

Smail, Daniel, 2008. *On Deep History and the Brain*. Los Angeles: University of California Press.

Stander, P.E., (1992). "Cooperative Hunting in Lions: The Role of the Individual," in *Behavioral Ecology and Sociobiology*, Vol. 29, No. 6, pp. 445-454.

Uexkull, Jakob von, 2010. *A Foray Into the Worlds of Animals and Humans*. Minneapolis: University of Minnesota Press.

Wexler, Bruce, 2006. *Brain and Culture: Neuorobiology, Ideology and Social Change*. Cambridge: MIT Press.

Wrangham, Richard, 2009. *Catching Fire: How Cooking Made us Human*. New York: Basic Books.

# Computational Architecture and the Statisticon

## Introduction

The recent connection of neuro-biopolitical inquiry to post-Operaist ontologies has created new linkages towards a deeper understanding of the causes, mediations, and cures of Cognitive Capitalism and opened a new form analysis to an activist readership. I would like to continue this conversation by moving forward the process I started in *Cogntive Architecture: From Biopolitics to NooPolitics* (Hauptman and Neidich 2010) and *The Psychopathologies of Cognitive Capitalism, Part One* (De Boever and Neidich 2013) to produce a new language with which to understand the political and cultural consequences of digital architectures upon our contemporary brain and minds. I would like to suggest a new opening for critical architecture by suggesting an alternative locus for the repercussions of avant-garde architecture and architectural theory that is the neuroplastic potential of the brain which forms one of the core conditions of what I call neuropower. (Neidich 2009) An approach, I might add, that is non-reductive or cognitivist but culturally biased and ontogenic.

The theory of cognitive architecture that I would like to realize in this paper stands firmly in the camp of those theoretical approaches that are unconcerned whether or not architecture and designed space generate platforms for practice in the neoliberal world of commoditized forms and environments. Rather, instead of creating spaces and buildings that potentiate the efficiencies of neo-liberal market networks, this work rather concerns its critique and as such its destabilization. I want to provoke another space for architectural and design discourse to operate in the age of information and cognitive capitalism by understanding its power to provoke new organs of perception and new possibilities for thought. Fredric Jameson, when explaining his initial experience of the Bonaventure Hotel in downtown Los Angeles, implicitly understood this when he stated,

> I am proposing the notion that we are here in the presence of something like a mutation in built space itself. My implication is that we ourselves, the human subjects who happen into this new space, have not kept pace with that evolution: there has been a mutation in the object unaccompanied as yet by any equivalent mutation in the subject. We do not yet possess the perceptual equipment to match this new hyperspace, as I will call it, in part because our perceptual habits were formed in that older kind of space I have called the space of high modernism… The newer architecture therefore-like other cultural products I have evoked in the proceeding remarks-stands as something like an imperative to grow new organs, to expand our sensorium. (Jameson 1991, 38)

Since 1991, when he wrote these prophetic words, the landscape of understanding of the neural plastic potential of the brain and its entangled relation to cultural plasticity with which it creates a unstable and fluid affiliation has changed considerably and as such our understanding of the above statement with it.

Preliminary Remarks:

Before moving on I must first elaborate on some of the essential ideas concerning architectural responses to the new conditions of cognitive capitalism. Firstly, I will tether computational architecture to the other regimes and practices of cognitive capitalism especially its emphasis upon intensive networks. I want to argue, as Greg Lynn and others have, that architecture is no longer about static material space but also concerns mobile and dynamic fields. Not only, for instance, in our new understanding of structural techtonics and form making as multiple inter-acting vectors. (Lynn 1999) We now have a whole host of apparatuses, like smartphones, navigation devices and composite smart buildings containing assemblages of digitally networked self-monitoring devices leading to datascapes of ubiquitous computing. These devices are the new engram-exogram dispositifs of cognitive capital-ism and their actions are directed away from the laboring body towards cognitive labor and the production of the knowledge laborer or Cognitariat.

The second component of this argument is an understand-ing of how the relations of postmodernism as urban design and architectural practices has helped to amplify consumption. Branding in our age of advanced informa-tion technology will be *and now is* available instantly and globally. (Klingman 2007, 63) From movies, to news channels, to universities, museums and even churches are using the methods of creating brands through linkages with lifestyles, contexts and consumers all with the intention of the fulfillment of desires, real and produced. (Ibid., 64) Important to us as we transition to cognitive capitalism is how this branding has linked up with the added value spurred on by recent advances in Neuroconsumerism.

Ronald Braeutigam writes on this subject, "Montague and all have used fMRI to study neuronal responses associated with preferences for soft drinks. During informed testing, as opposed to blind testing, subjects are more likely to prefer Coke over Pepsi, and this preference is reflected in increased neuronal activation in brain regions assumed to be involved in reward. The observations obtained… shed some light on the neuronal underpinnings of brand effects…" (Braeutigam 2005, 355-360) Could the artificial stimulation of these regions one day lead to artificially induced preferences? With this in mind I want to provoke *another* space for architectural and design discourse to operate in the age of information and cognitive capitalism by understanding its power to present, display and bind together fields of exographic engineered phatic stimuli to provoke new organs of perception in the brain as synchronously elaborated neural architectures that Jameson inferred. First the probability that neurons synchronize their responses both within a particular area and across areas should reflect some of the Gestalt criteria used for perceptual grouping. (Singer 1994, 158) As we will note in what follows this synchronization of responses implicates the way that the brain neural plasticity is sculpted. The biophysics of neurons render them more susceptible to synchronized, excitatory synaptic input then to random input and furthermore synchronized synaptic input is usually more efficient at driving its target cell then if the input is desynchronized. (Koch 2004, 43) Institutional regimes of sovereign power utilize gestalt perceptional relations such as closeness, similarity and contiguity and relationship branding found in marketing techniques to enlist different synchronously attended assemblages, which has implications for what will be remembered.

Finally I would like to introduce the term 'neuropower,' which delineates the new conditions of power in cognitive capitalism. Neuropower concerns the ways and means that capitalism intervenes upon the neuroplasticity of the brain in order to produce the perfect consumer through bottom-up processing, activating the primary cortices of the brain like the occipital or visual cortex and the auditory cortex. "The influence of bottom-up factors may be especially strong online, as consumers engage in fast web surfing and often spend very little time on any given page. Systematically manipulating low level visual features to "guide" viewers' eyes to a webpage's regions of interest is possible by utilizing insights from visual neuroscience." (Plassman et al., 2012, 22) To this form of power is added another direct action upon the frontal cortex, which through top-down processing, affects choice and prognostication (this is something I have discussed in greater detail in my own essay in *The Psychopathologies of Cognitive Capitalism, Part One)*. "Pioneering work by Knutson and colleagues showed that a structure within the ventral striatum (VS), the nucleus accumbens (NAcc), is involved in encoding anticipated rewards of monetary payoffs." (Ibid, Plassman 2012, 23) In cognitive capitalism this top-down processing will subsume bottom-up processing just as tertiary service and information economies have subsumed secondary industrial economies. In my concluding remarks I will attempt to use this form of power to construct a new model of archi-power called the Statisticon. This term describes an ongoing process of subjectivation and subjection that commences with the panopticon, continues through the synopticon and has recently emerged as the Statisticon in which architecture and designed space are entangled in synchronous and diachronous datascapes. I want to alert the reader to the possibility that the Statisticon in its future rendition might not just monitor and predict your consumer choices.

# Neuroplasticity

There are two kinds of cultural neural modulation: the generational and trans-generational models. Both models describe a process of epigenesis in which the environment interacts with a priori genetically inscribed unfolding of the matter of the brain. In the generational model, as the name implies, this process is related to events that are occurring in the life of that subject and the changes occurring in the microarchitectures of the brain's basic units of function, its neurons mostly at the axon-dendrite junctions or synapses a process called selective stabilization as well as its dynamic functional networks. (Changeux 1985) In the trans-generational model, recurrent cultural events like the discovery and implementation of reading and writing occurring consistently over the course of many generations and which, therefore become stable conditions of, for instance, built space, as reflected today in our symbolic and mediated spaces, are reflected in changes in the organs of the brain over time.

## Generational Neural Plasticity

In the generational model the human agent is confronted with highly mobile, evanescent and diverse environment for which it attempts to find consistency. In today's world of accelerated forms and images in flux that task can be daunting. Neural plasticity is that quality that allows the unfolding of the genetically prescribed neuro-ontogenic process in the here and now to be linked up with epigenesis. In the restricted sense of the brain, epigenesis refers to the way that cultural influences, which create relationships between things and objects in the environment, affect the course of development of the genetically determined unfolding of the brain. Neural plasticity delineates the ability of the components of the brain, its neurons, their axons, dendrites, synapses and neural networks referred to as its firmware in addition to its dynamic signatures, oscillatory potentials which allow distant parts of the brain to communicate with each, to be modified by that experience. (Edelman 1989) In Edelmans model the diversity of the brain's constituents, its so called primary repertoire, are pruned as a result of its being coupled with regimes of order, either occurring naturally or designed, nested in the chaos of the world. Dynamic oscillations are most informative when they are the result of a process of the synchronization of stimuli, which cause neural entrainment in which independent systems fall into step and become linked together. Intense and naturally occurring, like those making up an ecosystem surrounding a pond and culturally designed distributions of sensibility, those things that are institutionally produced like brands and those artistically invented so called redistributions, for instance, deconstructive architecture, bind and bundle very different combinations of stimuli together in synchronous packages. These then elicit different assemblages of synchronous neural oscillatory potentials which, as we will see further along, have neuromodulatory capacities.

The point that I am trying to make in the following section is that the brain has the capacity to change in the single lifetime of an individual as well as across multiple generations. Importantly, culture has the capacity to modulate the materiality of the brain with significant consequences. Through the traces they leave upon the cultural artifice as recurrent and ordered forms of architectural, poetic, cinematic, and artistic transcription as well as the chaos they produce to obliterate already known forms, in order to rewrite them, human beings alter their environment that shapes their brains to a degree unprecedented in the natural world. "It is this ability to shape the environment that in turn shapes our brains that has allowed human adaptability and capability to develop at a much faster rate then is possible through alteration of the genetic code itself." (Wexler, 2006, p. 4) After the initial events of early childhood when the neural plastic potential is greatest there occurs a period of decreased mutability. Children can recover from brain injury easier than adults and also have the ability to learn other languages more easily. Neural plastic change can and does occur in the adult brain but their capacity to do so is reduced. The child's capacity for neuromodulation is accompanied by a lack of capacity to alter the environment while the decreased capacity of the parents' brain to change is accompanied by a greater ability to change the environment. According to Bruce Wexler much of the adults activity is devoted to making the environment conform to those newly constructed structures of their own childhood, a process he refers to as internal-external consonance. (Wexler 2006, 5) As the child's brain was shaped by very different circumstances than their adults, their attempt to match the environment to their modified neural structures will produce a very different world image or cinema. Importantly, "When young adults act to change the environment to match their internal structures, they struggle with their parents' generation for control of the public space and to the extent that they succeed they alter the rearing environment of their own children." (Wexler 2006, 6) Let us look deeper into this matter as a way to understand the power of art as a cultural and neurobiological modifier. Does it work in the way proposed here? I would argue that artistic production, as a subset of generalized cultural production, elaborates states of diversity and disorder rather then a set of intergenerational consistent linked and delinked patterns. This statement is counter intuitive to normalized accounts for instance of the avant-garde which uses configurations of the myth of Oedipus as a means to understand one generations antipathy to another. The desire to kill it off and replace another more contingent set of practices. This leads to two corollaries. First the inherent variability and difference that is the function of the brains primary repertoire samples the plutipotential cultural plasticity according to different generational logics entangled and deranged as they are by the social, political, economic, psychic and technological relations that delineate it. This leads to different kinds of epigenetically inscribed patterns of neural modulation. Secondly the linking, as it relates to positivist notions of the history of technologies, comes later in the sculpting of this cultural plasticity by the normative processes of sovereign regimes. As opposed to emancipatory delinked artistic processes art history and market forces, operating as apparatuses of institutional normalizing regimes, operate upon the entropic, and diverse conditions of artistic creativity. Conservative regimes in their attempt to control meaning and difference operate to suppress singularities and lines of flight erupting as a result of trans-generational differences in cultural elaboration. Generous forms of a enlightened and liberal forms of governance embrace the inherent dissimilarities understanding their extended neuromodulator capacities which are essential for expanded repertoires of thought.

## Trans-generational Plasticity

Trans-generational changes in neurobiological architecture are nicely exemplified by the development of writing and arithmetic some 6,000 years ago, with the first use of Sumerian tablets. As every neuroscientist knows, when a patient or subject reads while his brain is being scanned inside an MRI machine specific areas of the brain will light up. For instance, there is evidence that an area called the Visual Word Form Area (VWFA) located at the junction of the occipito-temporal sulcus, in the posterior part of the brain, is highly tuned to acquired script. This is paradoxical since there has not been enough time yet elapsed for such an area to form in such a short time period. (Deheane et al. 2004)

This area is very specialized for word recognition. It does not respond to spoken words, it is best stimulated by real words rather then consonant strings and finally the VWFA computes only invariant representations of visual words. Of interest for us here is that a complementary area of the Inferior Temporal Area of the macaques cerebral cortex does similar things and is ideally suited to learn and respond to letters, graphemes and word shapes. Of course the macaques do not speak although they do communicate. This part of the brain responds to a mosaic of simple shapes that resemble our letters. It is hypothesized that this inferior temporal area in the macaques evolved into the VWFA in humans. "In that hypothesis, it is not the human cortex that has evolved for reading—there was not enough evolutionary time and pressure for such an evolution. Rather, writing systems themselves evolved under the constraint of having to remain learnable and easily recognizable by our primate visual system. I postulate that cultural acquisitions are only possible insofar as they fit within this fringe, by reconverting pre-existing cerebral dispositions for another use… It thus becomes important to consider what may be the evolutionary precursors of reading and arithmetic." (Ibid., 141-142) The implication here is that language forms such as reading itself develops with the proclivities of the brains neural anatomy in mind. Terrence Deacon however feels that there is more to this story and that in a human society *symbolic reference is a selection force* working on the neurological resources most critical in supporting it and writes, "This, then, is a case of selection pressure affecting the evolution of a biological substrate (the brain) and yet which is imposed, not by the physical environment, but ultimately from a purely semiotic realm." (Deacon 2003) Taken together there seems to be two systems at work here. First the predisposition of certain areas of the brain for reading and simultaneously tremendous selective pressure operating on the brains neuralplasticity by its own ontogeny.

But there is one more key to understanding this process that is what is referred to as Baldwinian Evolution. (Deacon, 2003) As we saw previously human brains are highly variable at the micro-anatomical level, ie the morphology and distributions of its neurons, dendrites, synapses and glia, resulting from the different genetic contributions of the mother and father but also the results of events happening during pregnancy like illness or starvation. This variability gives certain members of a population different adaptive capacities for the wide variety of changes that they might encounter in the environment during their lifetime: reading in this case being one. Some members of the population could adapt better and take advantage of what reading provided in a broader cultural context. As Peter Godfrey-Smith states: The population will then have the chance to reproduce mutations that cause organisms to exhibit the new optimal behavioral profile without the need for learning. Selection will favor these mutants, and in time the behaviors which once had to be learned will be innate." (Charles Wolfe in this book. 252) Could architecture,  art and other forms cultural production, like language to which they are linked, provide similar patterns of abstract contingencies which act upon distributions of genes within populations?

# Reformatting Architecture in the age of Cognitive Capitalism

Computational architecture is not an isolated sphere of knowledge but in fact linked to a field of similarly inflected discourses in which digital processes have become essential. As such, architecture is but one expertise that has retooled itself for the contemporary demands of neoliberalism as a global system. In modern western countries the cross-disciplinary adaptation to digital machinic technicity has had other effects on other functional systems such as the ascension of information and knowledge based economies in which mass production and industrialization has been subsumed by a performative and communicative based economy, so called Semiocapitalism which, "takes the mind, language and creativity as its primary tools of production of value" (Berardi 2007). In other words, as labor becomes cognitive the machinery of the mind and brain and their attributes, like memory and attention, are the new focus of the capitalist exploitation. Voluntary and involuntary attention as it produces saliency is important for the formation of memories in the neurobiological substrate of the brain. Internalized attention, or contemplating the minds eye, is important introspection and understanding. The terms communicative capitalism and cognitive capitalism had until recently been somewhat interchangeable. As a result of the outcome of two recent conferences entitled *The Psychopathologies of Cognitive Capitalism Part One* and *Part Two* held in Los Angeles and Berlin respectively the signifying ecology of these terms has shifted. What I would like to call the late stage of cognitive capitalism or its 'cognitive turn' shifts its emphasis away from so called immaterial labor in which labor and performance are entangled and which therefore does not leave a physical trace. Instead there is an appreciation for the material changes that occur in the brain. These material traces and their formation and processing are the new focuses of capitalism.

I would like to argue that the transition from architecture as a form of organization to one of enacted articulation and later to one of intense datafication and importantly prognostication, reenacts an alternative history of architecture and urbanization. One that is defined rather as an ontogeny of the optimization of extended cognition in the context of ever increasing technicity for the enactment of political control. Where architecture becomes a method of first capturing data through human-building interfaces. That this data is used to track and subjugate subjectivity embedded in actor networks not only in the past: the where and when you happen to inhabit. As we will see neuropower is interested not in the subject in the here and now but rather in the future. It normalizes futures by reducing chance and the unexpected. First by sculpting the neural plasticity of the brain especially in young children, a future subject is realized. Secondly by creating algorithms that intervene directly with those structures of the brain found to be important for making future decisions. (ibid., Plassmann 2012) Finally as we see here our choices in real time are collated and correlated creating data search profiles which can be used by corporations to create for us personalized consumer environments. In the age of congnitive capitalism this forms the relationship between cognitive (A)rchitecture and cognitive (a)rchitecture.

Furthermore I would like to suggest that this transition, in fact, follows the transition occurring already in an expanded political-cultural field. I have already argued elsewhere that along with this transition has evolved new forms of *biopower*. The disciplinary society of Michel Foucault based as it was on *Betham's Panopticon* transitioned to the society of control of Gilles Deleuze in which the static, enclosed organized architectural frame was replaced by another more incessant, dynamic and modulatory condition (Neidich 2011, 219-268). As we move towards an advanced technologically inflected, infra-structurally dominated designed space two further permutations in powers methodologies occurred. *Noo-politics* and *Neuropower*. Noo-politics was an outcome of moving into what is called the attention economy where value transitioned to valorization in which the number of eyeballs watching an event, the amount of chatter in gossip and social networks became an indicex of profit. Noo-politics took memory and attention as its new territory for exploitation. (Lazzarato) Neuropower piggybacked upon Noo-politics concern for memory and attention. That is to say attention's effects on long-term memory. (Dudukovic et al. 2009, 953-961) It concerns itself less with the indirect comportment of attention networks in designed and built space and more with the consequences of attention upon the configuration of neural networks and long-term memory.

Architectural adaptations trace the story of a static and enclosed surveillance mechanism of the panopticon where one, the guard, watches many, the prisoners, to a more distributed and open variation of the *Synopticon* in which many watch a few, celebrities, in the age of television from their domestic setting. Whether incarcerated in a cell or a domestic setting, both of these models require a stabile subject. I would like to suggest that in the last thirty years architecture and urbanism has had to adjust to the mobile and topologic conditions of the digital age.
First, as it manifests itself in folded and curvilinear surfaces of form finding computational strategies and later on in the new mobility of the subject in the post-Internet digitalized domain where mobile phones, iPads and now smart glasses have made the subject an active rather than a passive entity. Parametric and digital architectures have produced an updated model that takes these dynamic contingencies into consideration and which have already been remodeled to capture and produce data. These form the rudimentary conditions of the Statisticon. Neuropower is an essential component of this Statisticon.

In cognitive capitalism information and the conditions of general intelligence itself, which is now engineered for the efficient use of the machinery of the brain, is sculpting its static and dynamic architecture. In this regard one cannot help but notice the upcoming technologies of direct monitoring. EEG machines and MRI scanners tethered to brain wave devices, first used to help patients who are locked-in, are now finding their way into computer games. "The Emotiv EPOC headset is being marketed as both a gaming device and as an aid for the disabled. It has 14 EEG electrodes to monitor brain activity, a gyroscope so it knows where you noggin is in space and packs a li-ion battery for 12 hours of use. It is also wireless, and charges via USB. The headset reads brain activity related to facial movements, and uses this to infer your emotional state and intentions. This is then translated in software to control various applications, from games to photo viewers to an on-screen keyboard." (Sorrel 2010) In the world of data mining the negative side effects of total datafication of the built environment will be investigated. We have witnessed how the parlor games and entertainment devices of the 19th century like stereo cards and zootropes have evolved into the sophisticated technologies of cinema and virtual realities. What then of these 'brain assisted gaming devices?'

## The Exogram – Engram Assemblage

The mind can be located within and outside the skin and human cognition is locationally uncommitted; a committed in other words to being uncommitted, distributed and de-centralized. Important for us here and for what is to come is that material engagement takes place along a continuum extending between theories of internalization (inside the brain) and externalization (in the environment). It is that continuum as it becomes 'asymmetric' in contemporary cognitive capitalism, as we move into a world of 'exographic excess' that is important for theories of contemporary built space. But allow me to clarify these terms further.

The exogram-engram system is a distributed networked system that does not respect the boundaries of the material world, the body or the brain. It forms the basis of a developmental approach to distributed cognition in which "from birth the rapidly growing human brain is immersed in a massively distributed cognitive network: culture" (Donald 2008). Importantly as we have moved in the past fifty years from an extensive, analogue and linearly mapped world to one that is intensive, non-linear, and self-organized the nature of engrams and exograms followed suit mutating separately and together. As we saw above through generational and trans-generational plastic changes this change is registered in the brain's material nature.

An engram is a memory record stored in the head. There are at least five dissociable engram or memory systems: 1). Motor skills used in activities such as writing, driving or playing video games. 2). Conditional emotional responses like anxiety created by the sight of a rival or autistic ones defined by detachment. 3). Perceptual learning as it relates to learning categories of things like flowers or faces, but also parametrically curvilinear buildings. 4). Semantic memories that tend to abstract generalizations encoded as language. 5). Episodic memories that relate to the memory of personal experiences in one's life. (Donald 2010, 71-79) Exographic systems have important properties absent in natural memory systems that have implications for human cognition. Examples include totems, masks, knotted cords, built environments, cave paintings, stone circles and burial mounds that operate as astronomical measuring devices, trading tokens, written records, works of poetry, mathematical notations, architectural drawings, libraries and archives, scientific instruments, moving pictures and electronic media and recently smartphones and robots (ibid. 72). Basic to any understanding of engrams, exograms, brain-artefacts inter-faces is the primordial 'theory of parity' according to which if part of the world, e.g. a soft-ware program, "functions as a process which were it to go on in the head, we would have no hesitation in accepting it as part of the cognitive process then that part of the world (for that time) is in fact a cognitive process" (Chalmers and Clark 1998, 7-19). In other words portions of the external world can operate as a kind of memory store, either as a remembrance of an event or a process that exhumes and constitutes it as an assemblage in time. However the idea of parity implies that the exogram and the engram are in some way mimetic in their forms, evolution, state relations, and inherent processing operations. Recently the term parity has given way to a theory of com-plementarity (Malafouris and Renfrow 2010). The term 'complementarity' underscores the lack of exact corre-spondence between an inner cognitive memory repertoire, engram, and its external cognitive relation, exogram. For instance, "the reformatable nature of exograms allows for information to be altered and then re-entered into storage in ways that an engram clearly can not afford" (ibid.). In this regard the idea of 'things in motion' or of cultural memory as they travel through different epochs and social constructs taking on different meanings and uses is interesting for us here. Furthermore, in order to comprehend the subtleties of the relationships engram and exogram, as singular entities or as classes of things, it is essential to consider their idiosyncratic diachronic, biographical and historical aspects (Sutton 2008). Their lack of superimposition, due to a distinctive individual and dyadic character, is related to their inherent developmental asynchronicity and asymmetry. One needs to consider engrams and exograms not as crystallized entities but as intensive, inter-active, folded and plicated membranes. Exograms are poly-valent fields not simply equipotential and as such morphing contextual and contingent cultural tableaux create instabilities in them that produce spiking singularities to emerge. These singularities, when they are strong enough, produce catastrophic changes that require morphogenetic restructuring of the form in its internal tectonics and external morphology. This I would argue is where the methodologies of aesthetic form production, where use value is not a priority, and the processes of purposeful tool production, linked as it is to a specific job and use, diverge. As I am describing it here, artistic and architectural production in their most utopian condition, unfettered by for instance client requirements, as knowledge production embraces the catastrophe and the variable uncertain forms it yields.

The 'becoming-cultured brain' calls for on one hand a sympathetic historical materialism of a dynamic and active brain-artefact interface (BAI), which has enabled human beings to further optimize their environments for a more efficient habitation of their world and on the other realizes that mutual engagement can lead to destabilized results as well (Malafouris 2010). The power of architecture on one hand continues positivist progression endemic to theories of the ontogeny of tool production is countered by its other potential as a creative and destabilizing force. In an architectural context BAI could be defined as a specified and engineered technological mediation be it a material structure, process, congregation of objects, socio-material apparatuses or process, that facilitates the arrangement of a dynamic relationship or tuning between neural and cultural plasticity. Importantly in cognitive capitalism BAIs are a subset of a whole host of arrangements under the heading of Cognitive Ergonomics through which design platforms optimize cognition-tool interfaces to optimize cognitive laboring (Neidich 2002). I question the politics of this univocal concept of BAIs as proposed here through an understanding of the importance of noisy forms at odds with this positivistic ontogeny BAIs and the material engagement approach they are imbedded in must be open as the 'Becoming Cultural Brain' model is to the power of noise, chaos, and entropy. For every exogram and engram contains with it unfulfilled promises and possibilities that emerge at points of instability such in phase changes. It is these instabilities as they morph into singularities that have the potential to disrupt the conditions that create the presentation of the exogram or the engram. That in fact allows them to become the other. For a normalized exogram, at the service of governmentality, is a synchronized assemblage of parts, an ecology of epistemic agents of thought externalized which are complexified in specific relational conformations and proportionalities to each other and to the cognitive processes that are implicitly in use by regimes of subjection. This as we mentioned above is the top-down effect of Neuropower. They are like twins and their desire to maintain the web of relations that constitute their relationship creates a field of checks and balances, which stabilize their co-determinant structure. In the process of subjection the machinery of control becomes incorporated in the subjects thinking process as automatic self-regulation.

## Modification of the cognitive life of the life of things

Two brief explanations should hopefully suffice in illustrating how architecture might deregulate this self-regulation by acting to delink and disassemble the crystallized condition of the collective engram-exogram assemblage. Rem Koolhaas' *Junkspace* offers a radically different idea of understanding the condition of space then the model of Malafouris. 'Junkspace' is the apotheosis of modernization with its rational program based as it is on science and universality.

> Junkspace is its apotheosis, or meltdown…although its
> individual parts are the outcome of brilliant interven-
> tions, hyper technical, lucidly planned by human intelli-
> gence, imagination and infinite computation, their sum
> spells the end of Enlightenment, its resurrection as farce,
> a low grade purgatory… Junkspace is the product of the
> encounter between escalator and air-conditioning, con-
> ceived in an incubator of sheetrock… Junkspace is… a
> colossal security blanket that covers the earth, the sum of
> all decisions not taken, issues not faced, choices not
> made, priorities left undefined, contradictions perpetu-
> ated, compromises embraced, corruption tolerated.
> (Koolhaas 2010, 137)

And what are the apparatuses of Junkspace. What are its engram-exogram assemblages? Is there a positivist treatise on
their design history? According to Koolhaas there is no design but only creative proliferation that will in the end produce an alternative history of things in transition. "Where
once detailing suggested the coming together, possibly forever, of disparate materials, it is now a transient coupling,
waiting to be undone, unscrewed, a temporary embrace that
none of its constituent parts may survive" (ibid. 140).

On the one hand such junkspace is the example par excellence of culture as a generator of diverse populations of
evanescent concretions of objects and forms tethered together
by chance. It is about a Situationist derive through tangled
and unhomely forms that through creative sensori-motor cou-
plings produce tethered singularities and new regularities.
New assemblages of forms are created through different
points of view created in human junkspace interactions. As
such junkspace creates epistemological tools based on another paradigm, which is anti-positivistic. Tools that unleash
the potential are implicit in chaotic and anarchic space.

The second example concerns the role of generational understandings of the uses of social media in the production of paradigm shifts that defined the political crisis known as the Egyptian Arab-Spring. The new uses of social media created a technological divide between digital natives, those born after the introduction of digital technologies and Internet immigrants, those that were born before the introduction of digital technologies. Their differences allowed for a catastrophic field change with important consequences for those who only understood the urban space in the form of a static model defined by its buildings and plazas and those who understood it rather as a fluid and dynamic condition, defined as it was by mobile phones, as a place to roam and congregate. As such the points of powers radiation no longer emanated from public buildings, the Murabak Head Quarters were set ablaze, but rather from mobile hubs and their constantly reconfigured net-landscape. As such these mobile hubs and the resulting exographic interconnectivities formed fields of dynamic modulation in which transient consubstantiation of interactivity created morphing complexified exographic interfaces that were sampled by one population but not the other. This difference produced a crisis in surveillance capabilities of the government that had relied on them to track subjects and therefore a disruption in their information gathering capabilities. As such the digital natives were able to creatively reconstruct the fields of meaning as dynamic manifolds in the urban and architectural designed spaces thereby gaining control of the urban situation. Importantly this disruption of the crystallized and instrumentalized distributions of sensibility and their consubstantiated engramic memory fields came under siege and a state of emergency ensued. Policing forms of normalization that had used certain systems of control and depended upon the engram-exographic system of flows historically set in place and who themselves were constituted by those systems as means to engage in a specified form of understanding were at a neurologic disadvantage.

They were neurobiologically blind for as we saw in the opening remarks by Jameson they had not grown the organs of perception necessary to understand the new hyperspace or in this case the new dynamic fields of communication; their neuroplasticity had been sculpted by a less dynamic and non-topological field of space and time relations. As such a crisis and state of exception of thought occurred and a crisis of governmentality resulted. What is the state of exception and how can this theory be of use to us here? As George Schwab states in his forward to Carl Schmitt's *Political Theology*, "In short, 'the exception" said Schmitt, "is that which can not be subsumed." A state of suspension of government ensues, and a state of exception is produced (Schmitt 2005).

## From Taylorism to Hebbinism

Key to our understanding of labor and neural modulation in cognitive capitalism is the concept of Hebbinism; an epistemological tool to understand the conditions of worker efficiency when the factory of the mind is at stake Hebbinism is replacing Taylorism in practices of cognitive laboring and production. In 1910 Charles Taylor wrote his *Principles of Scientific Management* and laid out the fundamentals through which the mass of rule of thumb methods could be replaced by scientific principles in order to improve the efficiency of the laborer's performance and thus increase profits for their respective company. His various methods, from separating the duties of management from that of the laborer to accentuate the capacities for which they were each best suited, instituting scientific time and performance studies to sufficiently study each task, like shoveling ore, which would then be communicated and taught to the laborer, planning the sequences of performance to obtain the best and most efficient results, the addition of monetary incentives for reaching production goals were tethered to the goals and aims of Fordist work environments. (Taylor 2011)

The term Hebbinism is associated with name of the renowned neuroscientist D.O. Hebb, in a general way to describe the results of those practices and theories discovered by the heterogeneous forms of research mentioned above and applied to the production of a more efficient cognitive laborer or cognitariat. In cognitive capitalism we are all mental laborers working for free. In Hebbian efficiency neurons that fire together wire together, neural network dynamics optimize through the force of repetition, contingency and synchronicity are sculpted (Deacon 1997, 202). Please note here that these are the very same strategies of marketers and consumer neuroscientists alike are using to produce desire. His, now classical, principle was suggested as a possible neurophysiological basis for operant conditioning: "when an axon of cell A is near enough to excite a cell B and repeatedly or persistently takes part in firing it, some growth process or metabolic change takes place in one or both cells such that A's efficiency, as one of the cells firing B, is increased." (Bienenstock et al. 1982, 34-35) This law has been used in ways so as to understand the way the world interacts with the brain in the process of epigenesis. It is tethered to the neural plastic potential of the brain as those synapses that are potentiated by synchronous and repetitive stimulation whether man made or occurring freely in nature will develop increased efficiency and will be selected for while those that are not will degenerate and undergo what is referred to as cell death or apoptosis. "As a consequence, a given afferent message will cause the long-term stabilization of a matching set of synapses from the maximally connected neuronal network, while the others will regress."(Changeux et al. 1993, 376) Ostensibly the consequences of this interaction with the environment over time will produce a finely tuned parsimonious brain.

In Hebbinism the conditions of the perceptual and epistemological field are reconfigured in the brain's image in order to maximize the efficiency and decrease entropy in the cognitariats decision-making processes. I call this process cognitive ergonomics (Neidich, 2002). Essential to the argument at hand is that the cognitariat is produced by a process of Hebbinism linked as it is to the overall process of cognitive ergonomics in order to produce the perfect citizen consumer who not only shops but produces good and meaningful data. "The internet is a machine designed for the efficient and automated collection, transmission, and manipulation of information, and its legions of programmers are intent on finding the " best method"-the perfect algorithm-to carry out every mental movement of what we've come to describe as " knowledge work." (Carr 2008) Software agents are playing an increased role in this development and track through the use of, for instance, cookies our every decision and spew their results right back at us with consuming suggestions and individually tailored Google search pages. Assuming the worst or the best, what affect might this have for the way in which our brains are sculpted? Furthermore I would like to take this argument a step further through a quote from Andy Clark's book *Mindware,* in which search engines might in themselves directly affect the way the immature and plastic brain of the child is sculpted.

> "Imagine that you begin using the web at age 4. Dedicated software agents track and adapt to your emerging interests and random explorations. They then help direct your attention to new ideas, web pages and products. Over the next 70 years you and your software agents are locked in a complex dance of coevolutionary change and learning, each influencing and being influenced by, the other. In such a case, in a very real sense, the software entities look less like part of your problem-solving environment then part of you. The intelligent system that now confronts

the wider world is biological-you-plus-the-software-agents. These external bundles of code are contributing rather like the various subpersonal cognitive functions active in your brain." (Clark 2001, 115)

Thus Hebbinism unlike its predecessor Taylorism operates simultaneously on three fronts. First it elaborates an environment in which the very stimuli and their arrangements are organized for the most efficient use by the cognatariat of the brain's cognitive potentials. Secondly, through the analysis of Big Data results, which mirrors the variability of the brains of its subjects, it constructs profiles used to hone in on future decisions. Thirdly it modulates the workers neural architectures no matter how young.

## Neuropower and the Statisticon

Neuropower plays an important role in the Statisticon. We have already looked into its indirect effects, through the modulation of distributions of sensibility, upon the neural plasticity of the brain. To this first condition I would like to add a second method of subjectivation, resulting from research in consumer neuroscience, upon the powers of decision-making and prognostication located in the brain's frontal lobe (Terranova 2011). Time does not allow a thorough investigation but I go into this in more detail in a forthcoming essay for my book *Resistance is Fertile*, Merve 2014. What I would like to say at the start is that the predictive algorithms such as Bayesean inferences are being used in a variety of fields such as cognitive neuroscience to understand free choice decisions in uncertain circumstances as well as in such fields as engineering, philosophy, robotics, economics and law. This desire to affect uncertainty to increase the efficiency of future decisions is related to neural powers desire to create a normalized future subject.

Essential to the expression of Neuropower over Noopolitics is what is referred to as top-down processing. As opposed to bottom-up processing in which varied stimulations inscribe themselves on what are referred to as the primary cortices of the brain, like visual and auditory cortex, where the initial processing of incoming information is begun, top-down processing refers to how this incoming data is modulated by higher brain centers like frontal lobe. In this way incoming information can be deemed as important or unimportant to the organisms future contingent activity and acted upon to be either intensified or edited out. "Indeed, there is ample evidence that the processing of stimuli is controlled by top–down influences that strongly shape the intrinsic dynamics of thalamocortical networks and constantly create predictions about forthcoming sensory events. We discuss recent experiments indicating that such predictions might be embodied in the temporal structure of both stimulus-evoked and ongoing activity, and that synchronous oscillations are particularly important in this process." (Engel et al 2001, 704) In bottom-up processing primary cortical areas are directly linked to the sensorial distributed field, which in our consumer society is designed to attract constituted desire, and are therefore the site of policing action. In Neuropower the emphasis of power shifts to top-down processing is focused upon especially the frontal cortices responsible for decision making and prognostication (Platt 2008 and 2009). In both cases through what are referred to as reentrant processes specific networks are stimulated repetitively and by highly synchronized activity. "Reentry is defined as the recurrent parallel exchange of neural signals between neuronal groups or maps taking place at many different levels of brain organization: locally within populations of neurons, within a single brain area, and across brain areas.
The importance of reentry as a mechanism of neural integration has been realized." (Tononi 1994, 129) This type of activity has the greatest sculpting effect on the neuroplastic potential of the brain and as such forms of governmentality

have added this effect of top-down processing to their armamentarium. I would like to speculate that re-entry is an intra-cerebral and inter-cerebral mechanism and when seen in the context of extended cognition does not respect the skull as a boundary of its operation. In fact in the context of dynamic process oriented engram-exogram complexes re-entry is the apparatus that binds the two together. In a dynamic and mobile informationalized world the importance of mechanisms of the dynamic neural intergration is ever ascending in importance.

# From the Datascapes
# to the Statisticon

Articulatory architectonics is a necessary prelude to the total quantification and intensive datafication of the designed space and as such is linked to a more advanced condition prognostication. Articulated environments allow one to make assumptions of which paths to follow in order to facilitate future encounters. Neuropower is concerned not with the production of subjectivity in the present but in the creation of a perfect consumer of the future. Articulation has moved from proscribed architectural determinations of set pathways to promote social encounters within space/time to that of proscribed contemplative decision making processes or epistemic trajectories in the minds eye. Computationalized spaces like those suggested by the likes of Kas Oosterhuis at the Hyperbody Group at TU Delft, also have the potential to create a pervasive electronic tracking system. Individuals moving in algorithmic environments searching in the datascapes either with apparatuses like Google glasses, smartphones linked to QR coders or through physically compressing new smart materials that are digitally linked to massive data collecting programs. The idea of an architectural 'program' thus takes on a more sinister guise.

Over time these produce massive singular data profiles that understand possible future movements decisions in particular contexts better then the person themselves. "Imagine a city that is described only by data. A city that wants to be explored only as information. A city that knows no prescribed ideology, no representation, no context. Only huge, pure data. Overall, datascapes can also be described as highly sophisticated 3D data-maps that resemble or allude to urban forms or landscape surfaces and spaces. They extrapolate quantifiable data, turning information into abstract spaces." (Maas 1999) What seems to be a kind of Utopian vision for the future city in 1999 becomes a dystopic nightmare of the future. Tracked movements as mere interference patterns become differential equations that create maps of an individuals or population's movements and trajectories in the city as statistics that can, as we remarked, be re-sold as information. "The prospect of so many new (and new kinds of) sensors cannot help beguile those groups and individuals, ever with us, whose notions of safety-or business models-hinge on near-universal surveillance. Law enforcement and public-safety organizations planet wide can be numbered among them, as well as the ecosystem of vendors, consultants, and other private concerns that depend on them for survival. Beyond these, it would already be hard to number the businesses fairly salivating over all the niches, opportunities, and potential revenue streams opened up by everyware. The project of everyware is nothing less than the colonization of everyday life by information technology." (Greenfield 2006, 26)

The Statisticon is an advanced condition of data mining, some of which is already here and some yet to come, where upon data mining is no longer limited to the Internet and World Wide Web, in which it is used by Google and Facebook to track users and this information is sold to corporations, but is a generalized condition of living labor operating in the designed and built space of cities.

With the advent of smartphones with apps that track corporeal function, credit card swiping that tracks shopping profiles has been added Google glasses that monitor gaze of mobile agents and new kinds of smart buildings that create new information vistas to gaze upon but also create environments of data tracking and hunting.

What does this mean for future of digital architecture? When built space becomes a totally interactive and monitored datascape data collection possibilities will abound and idea of crowd sourcing will have new meaning. The perfect consumer is no longer someone who is the perfect shopper, whose mind now is self-regulated and constantly on the lookout for discounts and shopping events. The perfect consumer of the future will be a cognitive laborer whose contemplation and the decision making processes produce actions and thoughts that produce data as well. In the end, will designed software agents, which are connected to datascapes that produce simulated realities and environments tailored to our data profiles? As such will collective assemblages of engram-exogram complexes be folded into these datascapes in which brain-mind-environment becomes a single interactive condition of data production-storage-retrieval-analysis?

Agamben, Gorgio, 2006. *What is an Apparatus?* California: Stanford University Press.

Allen, Stan, 2010. "Field Conditions." in A. Krista Sykes (ed.), *Constructing a New Agenda, Architectural Theory 1993-2009.* New York: Princeton Architectural Press.

Berardi, Franco, 2007. *The Soul at Work, From Alienation to Autonomy.* Los Angeles: Semiotext(e).

Bienenstock, E.L., Cooper, L.N., & Munro, P. W., 1982. "Theory for the Development of Neuronal Selectivity, Orientation Specificity and Binocular Interaction in Visual Cortex." in *The Journal of Neuroscience*, Volume 2, No.1, pp. 34-35.

Braeutigam, Sven, 2005. "Neuroeconomics-From neural systems to economic behavior." in *Brain Research Bulletin*, 67 (2005), pp. 355-360.

Carpo, Mario, 2011. "Digital Style" in *Log* 23 (2011), p. 46.

Carr, Nicolas, 2008. "Is Google Making US Stupid, What the Internet is doing to our brains?" in *The Atlantic Review*, July/August.

Changeux, J.P. and Dehaene, S., 1993. *Neurnal Models of Cognitive Function in Brain Development and Cognition: A Reader*, Ed., Mark H. Johnson. Oxford: Blackwell, Oxford, 1993, p. 376.

Changeux, Jean-Pierre, 1985. *The Neuronal Man.* Princeton: Princeton University Press.

Clark, A. and Chalmers, D., 1998. "The Extended Mind." in *Analysis* 58, pp. 7-19.

Clark, Andy, 2001. *Mindware.* Oxford: Oxford University Press.

Crary, Jonathan, 2013. *24/7: Late Capitalism and the Ends of Sleep.* London: Verso, 2013.

De Boever, Arne and Warren Neidich, eds., 2013. *The Psychopathologies of Cognitive Capitalism, Part One.* Berlin: Archive Books.

Deacon, Terrance, 2003. "Multilevel Selection and Language Evolution" in Bruce H. Weber and David J. Depew (eds.) *Evolution and Learning: The Baldwin Effect Reconsidered.* Cambridge: MIT Press.

Deacon, Terrance, 1997. *The Symbolic Species: The Co-evolution of Language and the Brain.* New York City: Norton.

Dehaene, S., et al (eds.), 2004. *From monkey brain to human brain.* Cambridge: MIT Press.

Delanda, Manual, 2002. *Intensive Science and Virtual Philosophy.* London: Bloomsbury.

Deleuze, Gilles, 1992. "Postscript on the Society of Control" in *October,* Gilles Deleuze, October, Vol.59, Winter, 1992, p. 4.

Donald, Merlin, 2008. "How Culture and the Brain Mechanisms Interact in Decision Making," in Christoph Engel and Wolf Singer (eds.), *Better Than Conscious? Decision Making, the Human Mind, and Implications for Institutions.* Cambridge: MIT Press.

Donald, Merlin, 2010. "The Exographic Revolution: Neuropsychological Sequelae," in L. Malafouris and C. Renfrew (eds.), *The Cognitive Life of Things: Recasting the Boundaries of the Mind.* Cambridge: McDonald Institute Monographs. Available at http://psycwww.wp. queensu.ca/MerlinDonald/Publications/01_Exographic.Rev.2010.pdf [last accessed May 2014].

Edelman, Gerald and Gally, Joseph A., 2001. " Gally , Degeneracy and Complexity in Biological Systems," in *PNAS,* November, 2001, Volume 98, Number No. 24, pp.13763-13768.

Edelman, Gerald, 1989. *The Remembered Present.* New York: Basic Books.

Edelman, Gerald, 2006. *Second Nature.* NewHaven:, Yale University Press, 2006, page 56.

Engel, Andreas, et al., October 2001. "Dynamic Predictions: Oscillations and Predictions in Top-Down Processing." iIn *Nature Reviews Neuroscience,* Volume 2, p 704.

Engel, Christoph and Singer, Wolf Singer, 2008. "Neuronal Correlates of Decision Making" in, Michael Platt et al, *in Better Than Conscious? Decision Making, the Human Mind, and Implications for Institutions.* Cambridge: MIT Press.

Foucault, Michel, 1972. *Power/Knowledge: Selected Interviews and Other Writings, 1972-1977*. ed. C. Gordon. New York: Pantheon Books.
Fuster, Joaquin M.,1995. *Memory and the Cerebral Cortex*. Cambridge: MIT Press.

Greenfield, Adam, 2006. *Everyware: The Dawning Age of Ubiquitous Computing*. Berkley: New Riders Publishing.

Hardt, M., 1994. "Affective Labor." In *Boundary* 2 26:2, pp. 89-100.

Hauptmann, Deborah and Warren Neidich, eds., 2009. *Cognitive Architecture. From Biopolitics to Noopolitics*. Rotterdam: 010 Publishers.

Hays, Michael and Alecia Kennedy, Alecia, 2000. "After All, or the End of 'The End of'." In *Assemblage 41*. Cambridge: MIT Press. http://www.wired.com/2010/03/thought-control-headset-reads-you-mind/ [last accessed May 2014].

Jameson, Fredric, 1991. *Postmodernism or, The Cultural Logic of Late Capitalism*. Durham: Duke University Press.

Thomas Zoega Ramsoy, and Milicia Milosavljevic, *Journal of Consumer Psychology*, Volume 22, Issue 1, January (2012), pp. 18-36.

Kavanau, J.L., 1997. "Memory, Sleep and the evolution of mechanisms of synaptic efficiency maintenance" in *Neuroscience,* no. 79, pp. 44-44.

Kelso, J. A. Scott, 1995. *Dynamic Patterns*. Cambridge: MIT Press.

Ķencis, Toms, 2012. "The Return of Manifestos." Available at http://www.arterritory.com/en/texts/articles/795-the_return_of_art_manifestos/ [last accessed May 2014].

Klingmann, Anna, 2007. *Brandscapes: Architecture in the Experience Economy*. Cambridge: MIT Press

Koch, Christopher, 2004. *The Quest for Consciousness*. Engelwood: Roberts and Company Publishers.

Koolhaas, Rem, 2010. "Junkspace." im A. Krista Sykes, *Constructing a New Agenda, Architectural Theory, 1993-2009*. New York: Princeton Architectural Press.

Lynn, Greg, 1999. *Animate Form*. New York: Princeton Architectural Press.

Malafouris, L. and Renfrow, C. (2010), "The Cognitive Life of Things: Archeology, Material Engagement and the Extended Mind" in L. Malafouris and C. Renfrew (eds.), *The Cognitive Life of Things: Recasting the Boundaries of the Mind*. Cambridge: McDonald Institute of Monographs.

Malafouris, Lambros, 2010. "The brain-artefact interface (BAI): a challenge for archeology and cultural neuroscience." in *Scan*, Volume 5, p 265.

Malafouris, Lambros, 2013. *How Things Shape the Mind*. Cambridge: MIT Press.

Christian Marazzi, Christian, 2008. *Capital and Language: From the New Economy to the War Economy*. Los Angeles: Semiotext(e).

Neidich, Warren, 2002. *Blow-up: Photography, Cinema and the Brain.*, New York: DAP and the University of California.

Neidich, Warren, 2009. "Neuropower." in *Atlantica Magazine of Art and Thought*, pp. 48-49.

Neidich, Warren, 2013. "Neuropower: Is Resistance Fertile?" in Jakon Nilsson and Sven-Olov Wallenstein (eds.), *Foucault, Biopolitics and Governmentality*. Flemingsberg: Södertön University.

Pariser, Eli, 2011. *The Filter Bubble, How the New Personalized Web is Changing What We Read and What We Think*. London: Penguin Books.

Huttenlocher, Peter R., 2002. *Neural Plasticity*. Cambridge: Harvard University Press.

Platt, Michael and Camillo Padoa-Schioppa, 2009. "Neuronal Representations of Value." In Paul W. Glimcher et al., *Neuroeconomics: Decision Making and the Brain*. London: Academic Press.

Ramachandran, V.S., and William Hirstein, 1998. "The perception of phantom limbs. The . D. O. Hebb lecture" in *Brain* no. (1998) 121, p. 7.

Schmitt, Carl, 1992. *Political Theology: Four Chapters on the Concept of Sovereignty*. Trans. George D. Schwab. Chicago: University of Chicago Press (2005).

Schumacher, P., 2012. *The Autopoiesis of Architecture, Part 2.*, New Jersey: Wiley.

Singer, Wolf, 1994. "'Coherence as an Organizing Principle of Cortical Functions" in Olaf Sporns and Giulio Tononi (eds.), *Selectionism and the Brain.* San Diego: Academic Press.

Sorrel, Charlie, 2010. "Thought-Control Headset Reads Your Mind" in *Wired On-line.*, 2010

Sporns, Olaf, 2011. *Networks of the Brain.* Cambridge: MIT Press.

Sutton, J., 2008. "Material Agency, Skills and History: Distributed Cognition and the Archeology of Memory." in C. Knappet and L. Malafouris (eds.), *Material Agency, Towards a Non-Anthropocentric Approach.* New York: Springer.

Tavani, Herman, 2014. "Search Engines and Ethics" in Edward N. Salta, *The Stanford Encyclopedia of Philosophy.* Available online: http://plato.stanford.edu/entries/ethics-search/ [last accessed May 2014].

Tononi, Giulio, 1994. "Reentry and Cortical Integration." in Olaf Sporns and Giulio Tononi (eds.), *Selectionsim in the Brain.* San Diego: Academic Press.

Vygotsky, Lev S., 1978. *Mind in Society.* Cambridge: Harvard University Press.

**INA BLOM** is a Professor at the Institute of Philosophy, Classics, History of Art and Ideas at the University of Oslo. Her fields of research are modernism/avant-garde studies and contemporary art, with a particular focus on media aesthetics and the relationship between art and technology. She is currently head of *The Archive in Motion* – an interdisciplinary research project studying changes in social memory under the impact of new media technologies. Her most recent monograph is *On the Style Site: Art, Sociality and Media Culture* (Sternberg Press, 2007).

**YANN MOULIER BOUTANG** is currently Professor of Economics at UTC. Since 2007 he has taught Humanities, Social Sciences and Digital Culture at the Superior School of Art and Design of Saint Etienne. He is the Director of the quarterly *Multitudes* and he is on the editorial board of journals such as *Traces, Subjectivity, Cosmopolitiques, Vraiment Durable*. He published *Cognitive Capitalism* (Polity Press, 2012) and in 1998 he wrote his PhD on the origin of wage labor and modern Slavery.

**MARIA CHEKHONADSIKH** is a researcher, curator and editor of *Moscow Art Magazine*.

**ARNE DE BOEVER** is Assistant Professor of American Studies at the California Institute of the Arts, where he also directs the MA Aesthetics and Politics program. He has written two books: *States of Exception in the Contemporary Novel* (Continuum, 2012) and *Narrative Care: Biopolitics and the Novel* (Bloomsbury, 2013). He is co-editor of *Gilbert Simondon: Being and Technology* (Edinburgh UP, 2012) and *The Psychopathologies of Cognitive Capitalism* (Archive Books, 2013). He also edits *Parrhesia: A Journal for Critical Philosophy* and the Critical Theory/Philosophy section of the *Los Angeles Review of Books*.

**PASCAL GIELEN** is director of the research center Arts in Society at the Groningen University where he is Professor sociology of art. He leads also the research group and book series "Arts in Society" (Fontys School for the Arts, Tilburg). Gielen has written several books on contemporary art, cultural heritage and cultural politics. In 2009 he edited together with Paul De Bruyne the book *Being an Artist in Post-Fordist Times* and he published *The Murmuring of the Artistic Multitude: Global Art, Memory and Post-Fordism*. In 2011 De Bruyne and Gielen edited *Community Art: The Politics of Trespassing* and in 2012 their book *Teaching Art in the Neoliberal Realm: Realism versus Cynicism* came out. In February 2013 *Institutional Attitudes. Instituting Art in a Flat World* (ed. Gielen) will be released.

**SANFORD KWINTER**, Co-Director, Master in Design Studies Program. Kwinter is Professor of Architectural Theory and Criticism at the Harvard Graduate School of Design. He is a writer and editor who holds a PhD in Comparative Literature from Columbia University. He was cofounder and editor of the journal *ZONE* and Zone Books for 20 years. His books include: *Architectures of Time: Towards a Theory of the Event in Modernist Culture* (MIT Press, 2001), *Far From Equilibrium: Essays on Technology and Design Culture* (Actar, 2008) and *Requiem: For the City at the End of the Millennium* and the forthcoming *Soft Systems* on the life sciences and and their impact on design.

**MAURIZIO LAZZARATO** is an Italian sociologist and philosopher researching areas such as labor ontology, biopolitics, immaterial labor and cognitive capitalism. He is an expert on Gabriel Tarde and cofounder of *Multitudes*, who has been specializing in the analysis of cognitive capitalism, and its discontents, hence his work on the P2P-concept of Multitudes, the coordination format in political and economic resistance, etc. His work is historically situated in the Italian movement of autonomous Marxism.

**KARL LYDÉN** is a writer and critic, and member of the editorial board of Site Magazine. He is the Swedish translator of Michel Foucault's *Il faut défendre la société* (2008) and *Le gouvernement de soi et des autres* (2014), and his writings on art has appeared in Mousse Magazine and kunstkritikk.com. He is an alumni of The Whitney Independent Study Program and The Jan van Eyck Academie.

**WARREN NEIDICH** is a Berlin and Los Angeles based post-conceptual artist and theorist. He is recipient of two The Fulbright Specialist Program Awards first in 2011 and then again in 2013. In 2010 he received the Vilem Flusser Theory Award. His art works have been exhibited internationally at such institutions as The Whitney Museum of American Art, PS1, MOMA, The Walker Art Center, Museum Ludwig, The ICA London and Townhouse Gallery, Cairo. Dr. Neidich is the author of *Blow-up: Photography, Cinema and the Brain* (DAP, 2002) *Cognitive Architecture: From Biopolitics to Noo-Politics* (010 Publishers, 2009) *The Psychopathologies of Cognitive Capitalism: Part One* (Archive Books, 2013). His *Resistance is Fertile* is forthcoming in 2014 published by Merve Verlag, Berlin.

**MATTEO PASQUINELLI** (PhD, London) is a philosopher. He wrote the book *Animal Spirits: A Bestiary of the Commons* (2008) and lectures frequently at the intersection of philosophy, media theory and life sciences. His texts have been translated in many languages and he has contributed to journals and newspapers such as Springerin, Multitudes, Fibreculture, Theory Culture & Society, Leonardo, Lugar Comum, Rethinking Marxism, Open!, Libération, Il manifesto, Der Freitag. Together with Wietske Maas he wrote the Manifesto of Urban Cannibalism. At NGBK Berlin he is co-curating the forthcoming exhibition The Ultimate Capital is the Sun.

**ALEXEI PENZIN** is Reader in Art at the University of Wolverhampton (UK) and Research Fellow at the Institute of Philosophy (Moscow). His major fields of interest are philosophical anthropology, Marxism, Soviet and post-Soviet studies, and the philosophy of art. Penzin has authored numerous articles and is currently completing a book titled *Rex Exsomnis: Sleep and Subjectivity in Capitalist Modernity*. Alexei Penzin is a member of the group "Chto Delat / What is to be done?" (www.chtodelat.org)

**PATRICIA REED** is an artist and writer based in Berlin. Her exhibitions include those at: *Witte de With*, Rotterdam; *Haus der Kulturen der Welt*, Berlin; *Kunsthaus Langenthal*, Switzerland; *Botkyrka Konsthall*, Stockholm; *0047 Projects*, Oslo; *Limerick Art Gallery*, Ireland; *Audain Gallery*, Vancouver; *Program*, Berlin, *Württembergischer Kunstverein*, Stuttgart and *Los Angeles Contemporary Exhibitions*, L.A. As a writer, Reed has contributed articles and essays to numerous publications including: *Fillip, Art Papers, C Magazine, Cognitive Architecture, And The Seasons, A Joy Forever, Critical Spatial Practice, Intangible Economies, The Archive as Productive Space of Conflict* and *#Accelerate*. Lectures include those at Archive Kabinett, Berlin (on Militant Romanticism); Artists Space, New York (on Economies of Common Infinitude); Art Berlin Contemporary (on Ethics of Misunderstanding); Winter School Middle East, Kuwait City (on The Production of Eccentric Space). She plays host to the *Inclinations* speaker-series, at Or Gallery Berlin.

**JOHN ROBERTS** is Professor of Art & Aesthetics at the University of Wolverhampton. He is the author of several books, including *The Art of Interruption: Realism, Photography and the Everyday* (Manchester University Press, 1998); *The Philistine Controversy* (with D. Beech, Verso, 2002); *The Intangibilities of Form: Skill and Deskilling in Art After the Readymade* (Verso, 2007), and *The Necessity of Errors* (Verso, 2011). He has also contributed to a wide range of journals and magazines, including: *Radical Philosophy, New Left Review, Third Text, New Literary History, Oxford Art Journal, Chto Delat, Parallax, Manifesta, Philosophy in Photography, Journal of Modern Craft* and *Journal of Visual Art Practice*. He lives in London.

**LISS C. WERNER** is a licensed German architect based in Berlin, Adjunct Professor a DIA, Hochschule Anhalt Dessau, George N. Pauly Fellow 2012 (Carnegie Mellon University, Pittsburgh), founder of *Tactile Architecture – office für Systemarchitektur*, and the editor of *[En]Coding Architecture – the book*. Werner practiced in the UK, Russia and Germany, lectured, spoke and exhibited internationally at MIT, CalArts, University of Southern California, Texas Tech University, The Bartlett, TU Berlin, Syracuse University, Kunstuniversität Linz, Tongji University, ESARQ Barcelona, Venice Biennale 2012. Her research focuses on cybernetics + architecture investigating in the current discourse of computational architecture towards a relationship focused discipline. Werner chaired *[En]Coding Architecture* at CMU, EXP at Florida International University (Miami), EPFX at SciArc (Los Angeles) and *Architectural Ecologies* (Vienna). Werner holds a Ba(hons), Diploma of Architecture and Master of Architecture from the Bartlett. Further she studied at RMIT, is a Dr. Phil (A.B.D.) researcher at Humboldt-University, Berlin and a member of the American Society of Cybernetics.

**CHARLES T. WOLFE** is a Research Fellow, Department of Philosophy and Moral Sciences and Sarton Centre for History of Science, Ghent University. He works primarily on early modern philosophy and the life sciences—especially medicine, biology and natural history—focusing on themes such as the man-machine, organism, vitalism, materialism, monsters and determinism, and figures including La Mettrie and Diderot, but also Georges Canguilhem. A former co-editor of *Multitudes* and *Chimères*, he has published in journals such as *Early Science and Medicine, Perspectives on Science, Progress in Biophysics and Molecular Biology, Dix-huitième siècle* and *Chimères, CTheory, Flash Art* and *Multitudes*. His edited volumes include: *Monsters and Philosophy* (2005); a special issue of *Science in Context* on *Vitalism without Metaphysics?* (2008); *The Body as Object and Instrument of Knowledge* (with O. Gal, 2010); *The Concept of Organism* (with P. Huneman, *HPLS*, special issue, 2010); *Vitalism and the scientific image, 1800-2010* (with S. Normandin, 2013), and *Brain Theory* (forthcoming 2014). His current project is a monograph on the conceptual foundations of vitalism.

We would like to acknowledge the Institute of Cultural Inquiry, Berlin and the Office of Aesthetic Occupation for their support in the production of the second *Psychopathologies of Cognitive Capitalism* conference held in Berlin (March 7th-9th, 2013).